Burchell's
TRAVELS

Burchell's
TRAVELS

The Life, Art and Journeys of
William John Burchell | 1781–1863

SUSAN BUCHANAN

PENGUIN BOOKS

Published by Penguin Books
an imprint of Penguin Random House South Africa (Pty) Ltd
Reg. No. 1953/000441/07
The Estuaries No. 4, Oxbow Crescent, Century Avenue, Century City, 7441
PO Box 1144, Cape Town, 8000, South Africa

www.penguinbooks.co.za

First published 2015

1 3 5 7 9 10 8 6 5 4 2

Publication © Penguin Random House 2015
Text © Susan Buchanan 2015

PUBLISHER: Marlene Fryer
MANAGING EDITOR: Robert Plummer
EDITOR: Genevieve Adams
PROOFREADER: Bronwen Maynier
COVER DESIGNER: Monique Cleghorn
PAGE DESIGNER: Ryan Africa
TYPESETTER: Monique van den Berg
INDEXER: Sanet le Roux

Set in 10.5 pt on 14.5 pt Minion

Printed and bound by Toppan Leefung Packaging and Printing (Dongguan) co., Ltd, China

ISBN 978 1 77022 755 2 (print)
ISBN 978 1 77022 756 9 (ePub)
ISBN 978 1 77022 757 6 (PDF)

For my husband Richard,
my sons Jonathan and Matthew,
and grandchilden Noah, Willow and Caspian

Contents

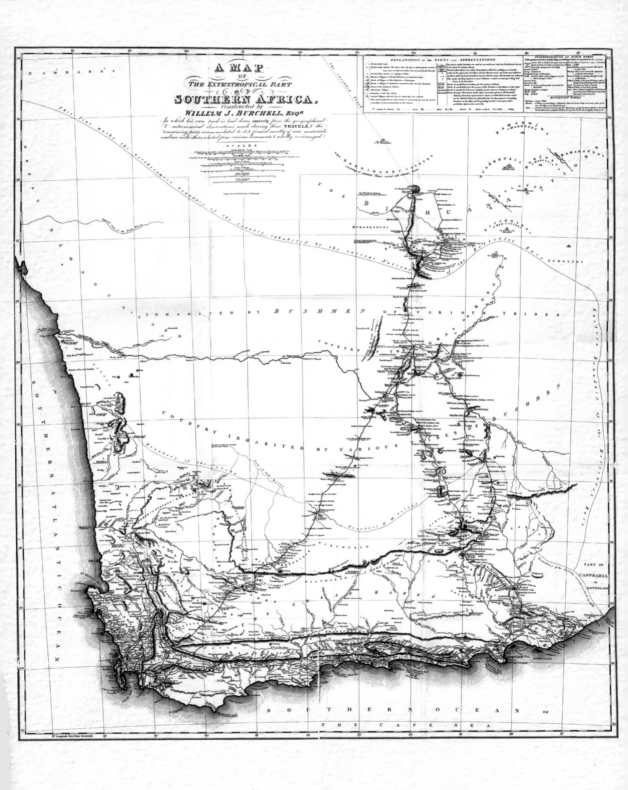

Introduction

'We shall not cease from exploration'[1]

THE EXPLORER, NATURALIST AND ARTIST William John Burchell is probably best known for his travels in South Africa from 1810 to 1815, and for his classic travelogue, *Travels in the Interior of Southern Africa*,[2] published in two quarto volumes in 1822 and 1824. Together they give a full account of his expedition in the interior of the Cape Colony from June 1811 to August 1812, although they do not cover the return trip to Cape Town, which concluded in April 1815. While the journals he kept during his journey are lost, his map, paintings and sketches help to fill in the narrative gaps.

Burchell's *Travels*, in the words of the renowned social anthropologist Isaac Schapera, 'has long been very highly esteemed'.[3] Sidney Mendelssohn, compiler of the *South African Bibliography*, acclaimed the *Travels* as 'the most valuable and accurate work on South Africa published up to the first quarter of the nineteenth century'.[4] The missionary Robert Moffat praised the *Travels* as 'far more correct and interesting than anything of the kind which has been written'.[5] For Mary Elizabeth Barber – the first female naturalist at the Cape in the nineteenth century – it was 'a book of much research and great truthfulness'.[6]

In comparison, Burchell's travels in St Helena (1805–10) and Brazil (1825–30) are less well known; he also travelled extensively in Britain and in Europe from 1815 until his death in 1863. Landscape paintings and sketches of scenery, animals, trees and plants record the localities he explored during these excursions, with dates and the wide range of subjects he was drawn to usually included.

Burchell was a compulsive traveller. His friend, the famous naturalist William Swainson, summed up Burchell's penchant for travelling in a letter to his son (Burchell's godson) in May 1838:

> Dr Burchell went last Autumn to be at the scientific meeting of the foreign naturalists at Gottingin, but when that was over he was seized with a desire to see Italy and off he set for Venice, then he went to Rome, Naples etc. and where he is now, but when he will return nobody knows. He is a very extraordinary lover of

wandering, but not of steady application, so that you can see for the last seven years he has done nothing to show the world what he can do, if he would. Take warning of him.[7]

The comment 'not of steady application' is significant. Burchell, lacking the discipline to complete the publishing of his travels, wrote to his friend Sir William Hooker: '[I] simply was not fitted to run "the publication race".'[8] Indeed, while the journals he kept in the Cape became the two volumes of his *Travels*, his journal in St Helena – which now forms part of the collection of the Oxford University Museum of Natural History – remained unpublished until recently, when Robin Castell, the St Helena historian, transcribed and published it.[9] Burchell published nothing about his expedition to Brazil, hence the relative obscurity of his South American travels.

Burchell's attitude to travelling is explicit in a letter to his father, in which he argued:

I am sure that however much the family and I myself may wish to be passing time in England, yet you all know that too long a residence at Fulham begins at last to look very much like lost time: at least you may say that while absent I am doing <u>something</u>.[10] [Burchell's emphasis]

Travelling improved Burchell's ideas and experiences.[11] He was not a tourist-traveller, but a scientific explorer with strong Romantic sensibilities. The Romantic 'feelings of an enthusiastic lover of scenes of nature' permeate the *St Helena Journal*, *Travels* and Burchell's letters to family and friends. For Ian Colvin, a British historian and journalist, Burchell 'is the equal of the best in this style of writing: not even Ruskin could have improved on many of his passages'.[12] Not one of the pioneer travellers in the Cape – Peter Kolbe, Anders Sparrman, Carl Peter Thunberg, François Levaillant, John Barrow, Francis Masson – match Burchell's glittering literary style.

At the same time, Burchell was an 'archetype' of the scientist of his time. His meticulous and detailed observations of all phenomena around him, from architecture to the sound of a scorpion, are a typical aspect of his empirical approach to science.[13] This ceaseless scientific curiosity led Burchell to amass a vast collection of specimens in South Africa, as he explains in the preface to the *Travels*:

These collections consist of above sixty three thousand objects, inclusive of the duplicates, in every department of science … In addition to these results of the expedition, are about five hundred drawings, the subjects of which are landscapes, portraits, costume, zoology, botany, and a variety of other objects.[14]

He collected a prodigious quantity of material in Brazil: 7 022 plant species (including a few from Madeira, Tenerife and Portugal), 16 000 to 20 000 specimens of insects, and 362 species of birds.[15]

Burchell was also a prolific artist. Ever scientific, he systematically numbered his paintings and sketches. The catalogue of his artworks in Museum Africa in Johannesburg[16] includes numbers he assigned to illustrations in the sketch books he used, and suggests he completed more than 175 artworks in England, before he sailed for St Helena, where he produced at least 239. Burchell completed his South African journey in April 1815, and a pencil sketch of wagons crossing the Cape Flats with Table Mountain in the background, dated 13 April 1815, is numbered 738. In Brazil, he made many drawings and paintings, of which 257 are housed in Museum Africa. Burchell's artistic and scientific achievements are celebrated in that country to this day. According to Jane Pickering, he is acclaimed as one of the 'greatest of the naturalists and artists who arrived in Brazil in the first quarter of the 19th century'.[17]

William Swainson, in a brief biography of Burchell, described him as 'one of the most learned and accomplished travellers of any age or country'.[18] Burchell spoke six languages; was a talented musician who could play the flute, organ, piano and bugle-horn; and was 'learned' in the Enlightenment sense of searching for knowledge. Professor (later Sir) Edward Bagnall Poulton, an eminent evolutionary biologist and Hope Professor of Zoology at Oxford University, delivered a brilliant lecture on Burchell to the British Association for the Advancement of Science in Cape Town in 1905. For Professor Poulton, Burchell was 'by far the most scientific and greatest of the early African explorers'.[19] The lecture integrated Burchell's life, literary talent and journeys, and is drawn on extensively in this book.

Helen Millar McKay was born in Scotland in 1878 and trained as a teacher before marrying and moving to Johannesburg in 1910. Her husband died the following year, and in 1913 she began her South African teaching career. After her retirement in 1933, McKay devoted herself to researching Burchell, and was awarded the degree of Master of Arts *honoris causa* for her work. Her hands-on archival research, which she carried out during World War II, involved visits to Kew Gardens, Oxford University and the Linnean Society of London, where she consulted and transcribed Burchell's manuscripts. At the time of her death in 1952, she was preparing a full-scale biography of Burchell.[20] If only she could have completed it. The publications of both Helen

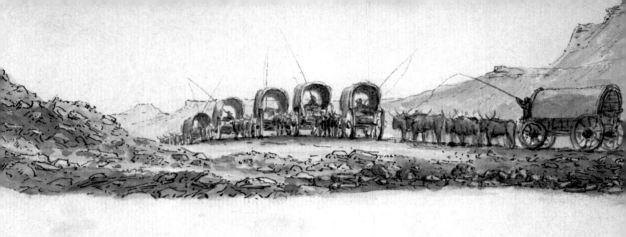

Train of Waggons at Karreebergen Poort, 10 September 1811

McKay and Professor Poulton have been invaluable and inspirational in the writing of this book.

In literary circles, Burchell is possibly best known for his influence on J.M. Coetzee, the internationally acclaimed novelist. Coetzee had been reading and making notes from *Travels* as early as 1962, 'knowing that they would go into some such book as *Dusklands* turned out to be'.[21] In *Youth*, a young John Coetzee, sitting in the great domed Reading Room in the British Museum, 'allows himself the luxury of dipping into books about the South Africa of the old days ... memoirs of visitors to the Cape like Dapper and Kolbe and Sparrman and Barrow and Burchell'. Significantly, he selects Burchell's two heavy volumes to pore over. 'Burchell may not be a master like Flaubert or James, but what Burchell writes really happened ... It dizzies him even to think about it.' This strikes a chord with Burchell's claim that his narrative 'even to the minutest particular, [can be] regarded as a faithful picture of occurrences and observations'.[22] He inspires the young Coetzee to write a book as convincing as *Travels*, 'whose horizon of knowledge will be that of Burchell's time, the 1820s'.[23] The challenge is a purely literary one.

But *Dusklands* is not modelled on *Travels*. Kai Easton suggests Coetzee abandoned Burchell and the 1820s as his initial literary project, and decided instead to replicate 'the conventions of eighteenth-century historiography and fiction'.[24] What is remarkable is that Burchell's *Travels* was able to captivate Coetzee more than the works of Barrow (an enemy of Burchell's), Sparrman (whom Burchell admired as 'he relates many incidents in a very amusing manner'[25]) and Kolbe.

Burchell is famous for his contribution to botany and is commemorated in the scientific name given to the indigenous wild pomegranate, *Burchellia bubalina*. One

The two-horned [black] rhinoceros

of his principal objectives during his 4 500-mile journey in southern Africa was, in his own words, to discover 'a multitude of objects hitherto unknown to science'.[26] He is renowned for his discovery of clivias at the mouth of the Great Fish River; was surprised to discover a lithops after picking up a 'curiously shaped pebble' that proved to be a plant;[27] and described (and misnamed) the Cape chestnut, *Calodendrum capense*.[28]

Zoologists associate Burchell with Burchell's zebra (*Equus quagga burchellii*) and the white, or square-lipped, rhinoceros (formerly *Rhinoceros simus*, now *Ceratotherium simum*).[29] Burchell, however, was more interested in birds than quadrupeds. Ornithologists associate him with five birds: Burchell's coucal (*Centropus burchellii*); Burchell's courser (*Cursorius rufus*); Burchell's starling (*Lamprotornis australis*); Burchell's sandgrouse (*Pterocles burchelli*); and the crimson-breasted gonolek, formerly shrike (*Laniarius atrococcineus*). Other creatures bearing his name include Burchell's sand lizard (*Pedioplanis burchelli*) and an endangered freshwater fish, Burchell's redfin (*Pseudobarbus burchelli*), as well as two butterflies.

Cartographers applaud Burchell's enormous map of the Cape Colony. Published as 'A Map of the Extratropical Part of Southern Africa', it was an influential milestone in the history of mapping in South Africa.[30] Burchell accurately charted his journey, providing meteorological data, distances travelled and very accurate measurements of latitude. The map clearly had an impact on Coetzee. The Coetzee holdings in the library at Texas University include an undated map, modelled on Burchell's, which was drawn by Coetzee and includes Karoo place names.[31] Etienne van Heerden, another internationally acclaimed South African novelist, has a connection with Burchell's map as well. Returning from Graaff-Reinet in April 1812, Burchell and his party overnighted at the farmhouse of Cootje van Heerden,[32] an ancestor of Etienne van Heerden. On his map, Burchell clearly shows Van Heerden's farm and the exact date of his arrival, 28 April 1812. The Doornbosch Farm has been in the Van Heerden family for generations.

Recently, there has been an upsurge of interest in Burchell and his many scientific, artistic and exploratory achievements. Dr Roger Stewart's diverse publications on

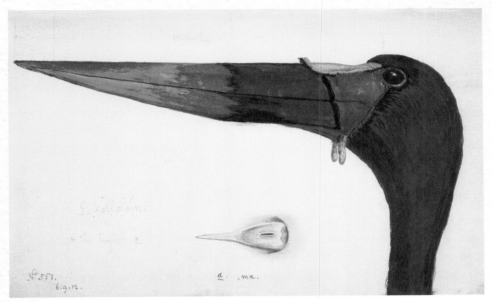

Lekollolani [saddle-billed stork], 6 September 1812

Burchell have certainly popularised his scientific genius, his artworks, and his travels beyond Litakun (known today as Dithakong) and his return trip to Cape Town. This book draws extensively on Stewart's expertise. In September 2014, historical and heritage societies in the southern Cape[33] celebrated the bicentenary of Burchell's encampment in George. A bust and memorial tablet were erected, commemorating Burchell's contribution to advancing the understanding of the natural sciences and other spheres of knowledge in South Africa.

Burchell's artworks are attracting increasing international interest. Maria Cristina Wolff de Carvalho, focusing on his landscapes, reveals the link between science and art in his work:

> The collection, selection, and organization of flora, fauna and ethnographic artefacts; the observation and recording of the vast range of subjects that interested him; and the artistic rendering of natural landscapes and cultural environments were fused into a comprehensive whole. By intuiting a reciprocal relationship between science and art and interspersing written observations with drawings, Burchell eventually created his own poetics, in which environments are presented with utmost concision.

For Wolff de Carvalho, the ultimate goal of Burchell's journeys 'was to traverse unknown regions, compiling an environmental inventory and acquiring a new perspective on human nature'. Burchell sought 'an innate, science-based harmony in each microcosm, which he could then translate into art'.[34]

A productive and versatile artist, Burchell generously gave away many of his creations. His scientific manuscripts and artworks are dispersed among a number of museums and other institutions, including the Royal Botanic Gardens, Kew (which houses a herbarium, as well as related drawings and writings); the Linnean Society of London (correspondence); the Oxford University Museum of Natural History (collections of animal specimens, human artefacts, drawings, maps and writings); and the Instituto Moreira Salles in Rio de Janeiro (eighteen attributed watercolours).[35] Museum Africa in Johannesburg hosts an exhilarating legacy of 558 Burchell items, including many of his drawings and watercolours.

Burchell's botanical art is also of singular interest. Dr John Rourke, an expert on South African botanical history, cites the importance of Burchell's drawings, more scientific than artistic and often recording morphological characteristics of the species he studied.[36] In the field of botany, Burchell was unusual as he was one of the few male botanical artists[37] among – to use Ian Colvin's inimitable words – 'a great galaxy of great travellers and writers' in the golden age of scientific travellers in South Africa prevailing in the latter half of the eighteenth century and the beginning of nineteenth.[38] At this time, botanical art in southern Africa was 'a watershed of pivotal importance'.[39] Women usually emerged as botanical artists and have dominated the field for two centuries. Interestingly, the first South African–born woman to complete an album of Cape flowers and scenes was Anna Maria Truter, the wife of Sir John Barrow, whom Burchell detested.

In the *Travels*, landscape paintings, drawings and portraits are integrated with verbal descriptions. For Burchell, the plates 'may be considered as expressing with fidelity the tints, as well as the outlines, of African scenery'.[40] He values drawings more than verbal descriptions, believing that:

> At all times a sketch is a most faithful and comprehensive memorandum, and describes most things much more fully than the pen can ever do. Whenever time will not admit of using both, there never can be a doubt whether the pencil should be preferred to the pen: it is in fact often the most expeditious mode of making a description.[41]

Art, in Burchell's view, is the best 'means of exhibiting nature, and of conveying information'.[42] For Colvin, 'the accuracy of Burchell's drawings is near to being marvellous' and there is 'a charm above accuracy in his style'. Colvin adds, 'I do not know that justice has ever been done to the genius displayed in Burchell's pictorial handling of his subjects.'[43] Burchell's artworks help to enlarge his biographical window. Helen McKay, editor of *The South African Drawings of William J. Burchell*, comments:

Amaryllis, 13 August 1818

> He wrote no autobiography, but in these sketches he reveals himself as he might not have done by means of the written word or artist's finished picture. What was in his mind was worth transcribing for he ever linked scientific facts about the country with love of beauty: he linked science and art together. In every sketch there is a minimum of ostentation, but permeating each is a tenderness, a love and understanding of South Africa.[44]

Burchell's journeys to St Helena, the Cape and Brazil took place within the 'Age of Wonder',[45] Richard Holmes's term for the years between Captain James Cook's first round-the-world voyage aboard the *Endeavour*, on which he set out in 1768, and Charles Darwin's expedition aboard the *Beagle* in 1831. Lonely and perilous exploratory voyages were, Holmes writes, a 'central and defining metaphor of Romantic science'.[46] Burchell, in common with Romantic explorers such as Mungo Park, sees himself as a solitary Englishman in the wilds of Africa. He habitually contrasts African and European landscapes, cultures and civilisations, and grapples with the differences through internal debate. This sets him apart from earlier travellers who merely recorded their emotional Eurocentric responses, while Burchell frequently tried to find an Afrocentric position. Like the remarkable eighteenth-century scientist, artist and explorer in the Cape, Robert Jacob Gordon, Burchell, using Patrick Cullinan's words for Gordon, 'was a humane and civilized man, a paragon of the Age of Enlightenment'.[47]

The ethos of the Enlightenment, with its multiple and complex focus on reason and sensibility, morality and happiness, justice and benevolence, is overt in Burchell's writings.

Events in Burchell's life are well documented, but *how* he writes about himself remains uncharted and intriguing. Close readings of passages in the *St Helena Journal*, the two volumes of the *Travels* and some extant letters open new areas of personal intimacy. Life-writing and the self-exposure that comes with it reveal the man – the biographical lens illuminating Burchell's thoughts, feelings and speculations. In his own words, he 'beheld everywhere, a harvest of new ideas',[48] and responds to the 'wild beauty and harmonious tints of the landscape'.[49] 'Breathing the air of Africa, and actually walking through it and beholding its living inhabitants', heightens his emotions – his sensations 'gratifying and literally indescribable'.[50] Romantic ideas regularly surface in lyrical prose: the 'magnificence and grandeur of the river *Gariep*' enchant him, the scenery inspiring 'delight and admiration'.[51] Burchell discloses his cast of mind both verbally in poetic images and visually in his art. His sense of wonder, which is so characteristic of the Romantic poets, shapes his lyrical and more scientific prose.

Derek Attridge, professor of English at the University of York, argues that re-reading great literary works 'can continue to offer fresh rewards well beyond a second or third occasion'. For him, 'the inventiveness of a literary work can, in part, be measured by its capacity to be re-read without loss of power'. The same can be said when reading the *Travels* for a second time: it is both enriching and pleasurable, with Burchell's powerful prose offering 'fresh rewards' beyond the first reading.[52]

The astronomer Sir William Herschel had courage, wonder and imagination. Holmes underlines how 'his whole instinct was to explore, to push out, to go beyond the boundaries'.[53] Burchell, likewise, pushes literary, scientific, geographical, physical, social and emotional boundaries. His wide-eyed gaze takes in St Helena and the ever-changing African landscape: inhabitants (colonists, Hottentots, Bushmen, Bachapins, missionaries, slaves); stars, mountains, rivers, plateaus, plants, trees, geology, wagon tracks, wild and domesticated animals; colonial Cape architecture and local kraals; indigenous knowledge; mechanical features of Cape wagons; the personalities of his guides, servants and their families; and local customs and manners. He constantly breaks out of the chronological, journal format. The scattering of amusing anecdotes, serious philosophical reflections, precise scientific detail and perceptive social commentary add lustre to a narrative already enriched by his intellect, humour, and physical and emotional presence.

Burchell was a natural philosopher, believing that religious and scientific knowing were neither separate nor separable categories. When the *Travels* was published, the word 'scientist' did not exist, and the term only came into general use after 1834. The history of the word has a strong Romantic link. Samuel Taylor Coleridge was present at the 1833 meeting of the British Association chaired by the geologist and natural historian William Whewell. Holmes describes the meeting: Coleridge was 'drawn into a passionate discussion of semantics' revolving around the 'question of what exactly someone who works "in the *real sciences*" should be *called*'. Holmes notes there was no general term by which these gentlemen could describe themselves with reference to their pursuits, and sums up the proceedings:

> 'Philosophers' was felt to be too wide and lofty a term, and was very properly forbidden them by Mr. Coleridge, both in his capacity as philologer and metaphysician. 'Savans' was rather assuming and besides too French; but some ingenious gentleman [in fact Whewell himself] proposed that, by analogy with 'artist' they might form 'scientist'.[54]

As a result, 'scientist' came into general use, and practising science became 'profession-alised'.[55] Since Burchell's journeys of exploration predate 1833, the term 'man of science' is used for that time in this book.

In his lively descriptive writings, Burchell uses the social terminology of nineteenth-century Europe, expressing at times Western ideas of race and ethnicity. When citing Burchell, his spelling, syntax, italics, punctuation, local place names, Imperial measure-ments, and expressions such as 'Hottentots', 'Bushmen', 'Bachapins', 'Caffres' and 'Koras' are retained. But in the text, contemporary spellings and modern usages such as 'Khoikhoi' and 'San' have been adopted. However, as Hedley Twidle from the English department at the University of Cape Town reminds us, 'neither "Bushmen" nor "San" are words that can be employed without reservations'. The term Bushmen 'has in recent decades been to some degree reclaimed, acquiring meanings associated with resistance and self-determination'.[56] Burchell, in his encounters with the San, foregrounds some of these positive attributes.

In the chapters that follow, the human qualities of Burchell the man surface in his artworks and excerpts from his writings. His horizons stretch from rural Fulham to St Helena, to South Africa and back to England, to Brazil and back to Fulham and the Continent. For Burchell, exploration never ceases.

1

'A splendid education'

Fulham
1781 to 1805

For the artist Marion Arnold, 'a portrait is a likeness … but a convincing portrait is concerned with more than salient external characteristics: it manifests personality'.[1] There are two portraits of William Burchell aged nineteen: a miniature copy, in colour, done by Miss Bentham, and a chalk drawing by J. Russell R.A. The portraits differ at a glance, with William portrayed with tight curls in the miniature, and sleeker, wavy hair in the chalk drawing. When compared, however, both portraits emphasise his fine features and strikingly intelligent, contemplative gaze. His Romantic and Enlightened personality clearly stands out.

William Burchell, aged 19. Colour miniature by Miss Bentham, 1800

William John Burchell was born in Fulham near London on 23 July 1781. His prosperous father, Matthew Burchell, owned the Fulham Nursery and Botanical Gardens. The nursery was established in the early 1700s in the time of George I, and the Burchell family took ownership of the nine-and-a-half-acre property during the reign of George III.[2] William's family home, Churchfield House, was located in the Fulham Nursery gardens. It remained his home until his death in 1863.

The nursery was on the north bank of the Thames and adjoined the famous gardens of Fulham Palace, the country residence of the bishops of London from the eleventh century until 1975. The palace gardens covered more than thirty acres, and were adjacent to the churchyard of All Saints Church, Fulham, where many bishops and the Burchell family, including William, are buried. The gardens were renowned for containing exotic and hardy plants from all over the world, and visitors streamed in to see the remarkable collection.

The eighteenth century saw an increase of interest in gardening and plants introduced from abroad (particularly those from the Cape), and the Burchell nursery flourished. William grew up in this enriching horticultural milieu, and Helen McKay comments that he was surrounded by the 'most exquisite of exotic flowers' from an early age, and regularly came into contact with prominent botanists who visited the nursery and palace gardens.[3] The discovery, growing, collecting and cataloguing of plants became a lifelong passion.

William Burchell, aged 19. Chalk drawing by J. Russell R.A., 1800

William was the eldest son of Jane (née Cobb) and Matthew Burchell. He had three brothers: George, Charles and James; and six sisters: Jane, Sarah, Anna, Harriet, Mary and Caroline. Two of William's brothers would later emigrate to the Cape, James in 1821 and Charles in 1822. Two of his sisters appear to have married: Harriet to W. Jackson, and Sarah to John Butcher. The Butchers moved to Tasmania, where Sarah collected insect specimens for her brother. Mary was an artist, and fifteen of her sketches – mainly botanical drawings of English plants – are in Museum Africa. She also helped William reproduce some of the vignettes in the *Travels*. The letters William wrote to his family throughout his life confirm affectionate, caring relationships.

Biographical information about William's childhood and his family is scant, but his artworks offer a pictorial record of Fulham and his excursions in Wales and England. Along with his younger brother George, he was educated at the boarding school Raleigh House Academy in Mitcham, Surrey. He made a drawing of the school, titled *Rowley's School, Fulham*, in 1803.

Rowley's School, Fulham, 25 February 1803

McKay provides snippets of William's engaging personality as a schoolboy. When he was about thirteen, he asked his father to stop his pocket money because there was nowhere to spend it. He also suggested his father ask the headmaster to 'allow the boys to take walks' – physical exercise was always a lifelong necessity for William. His formal training in botany began when his Latin teacher was keen to teach him the science. In a letter to his father, William wrote, 'therefore will you send or bring me that book with coloured plates in it, there are two of them: if you have Linnaeus's System of Botany I would much rather have it than the other'. For McKay, this was 'the beginning of his great botanical work'.[4]

Professor Poulton foregrounds William's excellent schooling: 'The variety of his accurate observations in many branches of science, the facility with which he wrote Latin, [Greek] and French, as well as the admirable style of his English prose, prove that he received a splendid education'.[5] Richard Grove, a British environmental historian, expands on the mature Burchell's intellectual achievements: he was 'an imaginative and perceptive thinker and observer'; an 'effective writer whose language and terminology was imbued with contemporary notions of the "sublime" and the "Romantic"'; 'a man of sensitivity comparable with John Clare, and well versed in contemporary literature'; and 'like Wordsworth, Coleridge and Southey [he] used contemporary images and metaphors'.[6] The interplay between factual information, art and the stylistic features pinpointed by Grove shines through in Burchell's *Travels* – a book which, two centuries after its publication, continues to absorb, entertain and instruct modern readers.

Burchell's artistic talent was visible from a young age, his training beginning when he was fifteen years old. He was taught landscape drawing by the distinguished teacher James Merigot, a Frenchman who settled in England to escape the French Revolution. From John Claude Nattes, 'an Irishman of vehement temper and wild enthusiasm' as described by McKay, he received a thorough knowledge of perspective.[7] In an article, 'The Landscape Art of William John Burchell (1781–1863)', Maria Cristina Wolff de Carvalho states that both teachers were 'part of the culture of the picturesque, which considered landscape through rigorous values and principles of geometry and composition'.[8] The lengthy footnote in the *Travels* explaining the technical 'method of *drawing in perspective* on the principle of an imaginary *cylindric medium*'[9] attests to Burchell's technical knowledge of art.

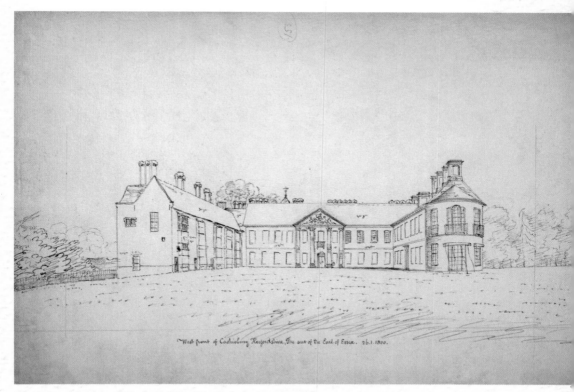

West Front of Cassiobury. The Seat of the Earl of Essex, 26 January 1800

Burchell's copy of Chardin's *The Scullery Maid*,
22 January 1798

Art galleries were relatively rare in the latter half of the eighteenth century, and it was difficult to view works of art in private collections. Burchell was fortunate in that his teachers moved in the circles of art patrons and his father socialised with the Earl of Essex, whose collection was famous.[10] At the age of nineteen, Burchell drew several pictures of the stately home of the earl. His talent, even then, is dazzling.

Among Burchell's youthful paintings are copies of famous artworks. Reproduced here is his copy, dated 22 January 1798, of Jean-Baptiste-Siméon Chardin's *The Scullery Maid* (*L 'Ecureuse*), as well as his copy of Merigot's aquatint, *Bridge of Varus*.[11] Burchell's brown-wash version captures the water agitated with foam, as well as the mountain and trees from the original. The main difference is the omission of the human figures in the foreground. This early work is one of the few pictures signed by Burchell. Altogether, the copies reveal his visual acuity and penchant for painstaking detail.

On 19 April 1798, Burchell made a copy of a landscape by Dutch painter Karel Dujardin. The picture is faint and stained, but of interest are Burchell's handwritten words on the back of the copy:

> Karel du Jardin. —Goats, cows and sheep were his favourite subjects, which he designed with correctness and introduced with judgement: his pencil is delicate and free, his colouring transparent & harmonious, the lustre of the sun at midday he represented with singular effect, brilliancy and truth, his fore-grounds possess considerable force; his distances are tender and beautiful, the light clouds rising from behind distant hills partake of the warmth that is diffused through the whole of his compositions, which are not encumbered with many figures, his drawings are fine and rare. A book of fifty two etchings of cattle are in much esteem, and when found without numbers are exceedingly valuable. He was born at Amsterdam in 1640 and died in 1678. – The beauties of the dutch School.[12]

Burchell's copy of Merigot's *Bridge of Varus*, no date

It is not certain whether Burchell copied this from *The Beauties of the Dutch School*, a book published in 1793, or if they are his own poetic words. If the latter, he comes across as a perceptive art critic.

Burchell did not attend university but went touring after school. His movements can be pieced together from his early artworks, which he systematically dated but did not sign. Between 1797 and 1804, he wandered in the south of England and toured Wales with his sister Mary. The range of subject matter in the artworks is astonishing, providing early evidence of Burchell's encyclopaedic interests. There are drawings of Hyde Park, Brighton (the bathing machine, the theatre, the medicinal baths, a mechanical pump), churches, abbeys, cathedrals, animals, Welsh landscapes (waterfalls, a mill in Glamorganshire, an entrance to a coal mine in Llanelly), and botanical drawings of trees and plants. By sixteen, Burchell was already an accomplished artist, and his sketches give a strong sense of the rural beauty and architecture of his home town. His drawing of the stately *Entrance to the Bishop of London's Palace* shows the clerical elitism of the neighbourhood, with the focus of the drawing on the entrance pillars in a woodland setting. All of Burchell's pictures of Fulham are a visual delight,

Entrance to the Bishop of London's Palace, 12 August 1797

Birch Tree on Putney Upper Common,
26 December 1797

such as a *Birch Tree on Putney Upper Common*; an imposing *House at Fulham*; an interior perspective of the *Bow Parlour, White House*; and *Animal Studies – Horses*.

When Burchell was not touring, he worked intermittently for his father and continued his botanical studies as an apprentice at Kew Gardens under the famous head gardener, William Townsend Aiton. McKay refers to an extract from the records of the Linnean Society of London dated 7 December 1802, in which William Burchell is noted as being 'well versed in the science of Botany' and is recommended 'as likely to become a useful and valuable member'.[13] He was proposed as a fellow of the prestigious Linnean Society, the world's oldest active biological society, and duly elected on 15 February 1803. This was an extraordinary honour for someone so young.

A year later, his father advertised for an assistant or a partner in the Fulham Nursery. He appears to have offered the position to his son, but William, on holiday in Wales, wrote to his father, declining the position:

> The applications which you have received are from persons certainly better fitted to assist you than myself, for you must know that I possess a nature which could it be changed for one more suited to my station, would be happier for my family, and in all probability for myself.

He is adamant that to claim a 'share in those profits to which you only are entitled, and ought fully to enjoy … would be quite repugnant to my feelings'.[14] In this letter, Burchell comes across as independent, forthright, averse to humdrum routine and adventurous. The following year, 1805, his zest for travelling would take him to the distant volcanic island of St Helena.

Before leaving Fulham, Burchell and William Balcombe, a merchant and superintendent of public sales at St Helena under the East India Company,[15] set up a business partnership as merchants in St Helena. They met several times at the Bugle Inn, a pub (now demolished) on the Isle of Wight, and together they drew up an agreement in which they both had equal shares in the business.

House at Fulham, c. 1798

Bow Parlour, White House, 11 January 1798

Animal Studies – Horses, c. 1798

In Fulham, Burchell was also 'enamoured' with Miss Lucia Green, a romance that had been an 'attachment for several years'.[16] His parents opposed an engagement, disapproving of Lucia's family, and causing Burchell great anxiety and suffering. However, he remained steadfast in his devotion to her. When in 1805 he set off for St Helena, he planned for Lucia to join him within three years. There they would be married, as 'I could never live happily in any home without my dear good Lucia'.[17]

On 7 August 1805, Burchell sailed aboard the *Northumberland*. En route, the ship called at Madeira and, being an ardent mountain climber, Burchell scaled, and also drew, the mountains near the town of Funchal.

The *Northumberland*, 12 November 1805

Madeira and Funchal – Two Panoramas, 29 September 1805

Burchell's *On Board the Northumberland: (a) Man with a Telescope and (b) Man with a Sextant* was painted aboard the vessel. The man is undoubtedly Burchell. The imagery – the moving boat, scientific instruments, and the figure's focus fixed on the horizon ahead – capture Burchell's scientific zeal and adventurous spirit. His artworks powerfully add to our understanding of him, highlighting the resonance between the man, his temperament and his art.

On Board the *Northumberland*, 27 and 29 November 1805

2

'The beautiful little Island'[1]

St Helena
December 1805 to October 1810

CHARLES DARWIN, WHO STOPPED AT St Helena thirty years after Burchell, in July 1836, observed that the island 'rises abruptly like a huge black castle from the ocean'.[2] It is 'a curious little world within itself,' Darwin wrote;[3] the 'unique flora excites our curiosity';[4] and the geology is of 'high interest, showing successive changes and complicated disturbances'.[5]

On 13 December 1805, after a four-month voyage, Burchell landed on the remote volcanic island, which measured only sixteen by eight kilometres. At the time of his arrival, St Helena was governed by the English East India Company, and the governor was Robert Patton, who Helen McKay asserts was 'favourably disposed towards the young man'.[6]

Lemon Valley, St Helena, 1808

In November 1806, Burchell started keeping a journal of his day-to-day experiences on the island. The original manuscript (now in the Oxford University Museum of Natural History) has been mysteriously mutilated, perhaps by Burchell himself, and words, sentences and paragraphs are blacked out. Nevertheless, it still exposes the man on a deep personal level.

When Burchell left Fulham, the twenty-four-year-old artist vowed to make drawing and painting what he saw a priority, and 'fancied' the pleasure, amusement and happiness his art would bring 'his dear family'.[7] His pencil sketches, watercolours, and pen and ink drawings capture the natural beauty of St Helena's scenery, with its trees, plants and mountains, harbour and ships, historic buildings, fishermen and animals. Burchell's

Hermit Crab [probably *Pagurus bernhardus*], *c.* 1807

drawings during this time are fascinating, capable of perfectly blending objective science with art. The *Hermit Crab* is a superb example of this talent of Burchell's.

In St Helena, Burchell's relationship with his business partner William Balcombe came under pressure. Balcombe was uncouth and regularly engaged in brawls,[8] and his personality chafed at the honest and incorruptible Burchell, who naturally, to use Robin Castell's words, 'could not tolerate Balcombe's dishonesty and regarded him as an absolute villain'.[9] Their partnership failed and was officially dissolved on 1 January 1808.[10] Disillusioned by the failure of the business, Burchell suffered 'a distressing lowness of spirits'.[11] When he was offered the post of schoolmaster two months after his arrival, and in need of a salary while his business relationship suffered, Burchell readily accepted the position. In November 1806, Governor Robert Patton also appointed Burchell custodian and superintendent of the new botanical garden.[12]

Burchell started teaching in September 1806, but quickly found it 'so disagreeable a duty, a duty indeed for which my nature never designed me, one of the most opposite to my inclinations'.[13] He felt stifled by teaching, viewing it as a 'troublesome confinement to a dull regular duty'.[14] Three years later, in June 1809, he gladly handed over the running of the school:

> What a delightful state I feel in, to be now released from the disagreeable duty I have too long had to perform. I quite disagree with Lock [*sic*] that it is a 'delightful task to rear the tender mind'. I may lay claim to the title of Philosopher in having borne it for so long.[15]

Relieved to be liberated of a career he found so opposed to his nature, Burchell's amusing allusion to the philosopher John Locke highlights his pleasure at no longer having to teach, as well as his knowledge of Enlightenment literature.

Teaching was just one aspect of Burchell's life on St Helena. He was an active member of the community, and worked as a church warden, juror, freemason and the editor of the *St Helena Gazette* at various times during his stay. He was convivial, revelled in mirth and laughter, and relished good food and wine. On one excursion, his picnic lunch comprised 'a small leg of corned mutton, a piece of salt beef, a tongue and a roasted fowl, a bottle of Port wine and a bottle of Hock, cheese &c'.[16] He made use of his musical talents during another occasion when he and two passengers from the HCS *Earl Spencer* 'commenced a concert' and excepting a break for dinner 'played without intermission from 10 in the morning till past 10 at night'.[17]

Botany and gardening always inspired him. Involved in Sir Joseph Banks' endeavour to collect and conserve new species of plants at Kew Gardens, Burchell cared for, packaged and shipped plants from all over the world to the Kew collection. Travellers supplied him with seeds from various colonies, and McKay describes an occasion when he mischievously planted some of them on the island, amusing himself that future botanists might consider them a 'native wild plant' of St Helena.[18] He was the first to successfully grow cotton on the island. A botanical trailblazer, he collected, catalogued and sketched the remarkable plants he found. His *Flora Heleniana*, a small book housed in Kew Gardens, gives detailed Latin descriptions of the plants Burchell identified on the island and, together with his herbarium, has for two centuries provided botanists with a matchless record of St Helena flora.

Always eager to learn as much as possible about his surroundings, Burchell's interests on the island extended way beyond botany. He collected minerals; experimented with chemicals; invented an anemometer, a 'machine' to measure the direction and force of wind;[19] discovered that writing music on coloured paper 'saves the eyesight very much';[20] and produced paints from 'parched soil of various colours'.[21] He was aware of environmentalist issues, observing that the 'wood and verdure' on St Helena were decreasing. Describing the cutting down of trees by soldiers and inhabitants as 'barbarian-like' and 'a wanton waste', the hills that used to have groves of trees growing on them 'now offer to the eye nothing but a cindery barrenness'.[22] He warns:

> the increasing of the price of coals is a most injudicious measure, and will prove of irreparable detriment to the Island, as it will cause a greater consumption of the native fuel. The consequence of which must infallibly be the cutting down of every tree and bush that now give shelter and shade to the pasture.[23]

St Helena was a bustling port of call for ships of all kinds – schooners, store ships, survey ships, brigs, frigates, ships of war, whalers, Indiamen – from the East, Australasia, the Cape of Good Hope, Europe, England and the New World. Burchell sketched many of the fleets and noted the daily arrival and departure of vessels in the harbour at Jamestown Bay. He was particularly struck by a six-foot long Chinese junk that departed the island in September 1807, made 'entirely of ivory and of most exquisite workmanship', to be given as a present to the Prince of Wales.[24]

Politically, the first decade of the nineteenth century was turbulent, and Burchell refers to some historically significant events in his journal. World politics and military news relayed by captains, sailors and passengers interested him, and he habitually went

Ships, 28 November 1805

'down to the Almond Tree to pick up all the news I could hear'.[25] A class-conscious English gentleman, Burchell chose the Almond Tree as 'the customary lounge where the better part of the inhabitants and Officers meet to hear news'.[26]

Men of science, illustrious political figures and accomplished musicians sailed on ships to the island. Travellers from around the world, including those from Tristan da Cunha, Ceylon, Rio de Janeiro, Persia, Sumatra and the Cape of Good Hope, aroused his curiosity. Burchell was in the party that accompanied Martin Heinrich Lichtenstein, a medical doctor and later professor of zoology at Berlin, when he toured the island in 1806. And he dined with Adam Park, brother of the famous explorer Mungo Park.[27] Burchell's complimentary comments for these men demonstrate his high regard for the cerebral stimulation afforded by cultivated visitors.

Burchell's remarks about local inhabitants of the island are more critical. As a man of science, he has strong views about what he perceives as their ignorance:

> I this morning observed the eclipse of the Sun and found that more digits were
> eclipsed than is said in the Ephemeris. During the whole time the sky was free
> from clouds. At this Island the minds of the people are so deeply engaged in their
> worldly affairs, that eclipses and everything of the kind pass unnoticed and

Longwood Lodge, 1807

Anglers, St Helena, 1808

unknown. I believe that scarcely anyone besides myself knew anything of it. I spent the rest of the morning in reading part of Bonnycastle's Astronomy. What great and extended ideas does this science infuse in to one's mind! I felt elevated above the beastly world, and despised everything for its insignificant meanness. Nothing seemed to me worthy of human nature but the love of God.[28]

The 'tempers of its inhabitants, jealousies and mutual mistrust, secret slander and perpetual discord'[29] ruined St Helena for Burchell, but science and religion uplifted him. In his view, there was no disharmony between science and religion.

Burchell was a deeply religious man. For him, as for many other men of science, to study nature was to study the work of the Creator. In Richard Holmes' words, 'science was a gift of God or Providence to mankind, and its purpose was to reveal the *wonders of His design*'.[30] Burchell trusted always in the 'Providence of that Great Being', relying on it to steer him in the right direction.[31] He reveals the depth of his faith in a journal entry dated 16 December 1807: 'Oh God! In this world of wickedness and depravity, protect one who feels there is no reliance but upon Thee.' He expounds his faith in his belief that 'even now as I write I feel something tells me that I pray not in vain'. Reaching a crescendo, he marvels at the omniscience of his Creator:

Oh incomprehensible Power and Goodness! ... Oh Thou Great and Only God! How is my poor weak heart subdued at the contemplation of Thy Glory! How Thou art beyond our understanding! I scarce can presume to address Thee in the midst of Thy Holiness; but Thy Mercy and Kindness give me courage to ask the protection of my Maker, and assure me that Thou will not reject my feeble Hallelujah.[32]

Burchell regularly attended church services on the island. Two in particular, a baptism and a funeral, expose two facets of his personality: light-hearted spontaneity contrasted with serious-minded leadership. The unusual baptismal service he attended on 19 March 1809 is comical for Burchell, who pokes fun at the more ridiculous aspects of an apparently solemn occasion: the second lesson consisted of only two words, 'Flee fornication'; the choir boys sang the baptismal hymn 'worse than ever'; and to 'prevent the appearance of [a] blunder to the congregation', Burchell 'instantly played a short voluntary ... founded on the melody in [Handel's] Messiah, "I know that my Redeemer liveth", and the last ... taken from that fine chorus in the same Oratorio, "For unto us a child is born."'[33]

There is no humour two days later in his account of the funeral of Young, who was killed in a duel. Jones, the parson, refused to 'read the service over him'. But Burchell, moved by the 'groans and lamentations' of the widow, 'declaimed loudly against the cruelty of not taking the body to the Church' and urged the church bureaucrats to 'break open the doors ... and at the same time offered to read the service'. The church was opened and Burchell received the body 'with some melancholy piece of music'.[34] The underlying steel of his personality can be glimpsed here. In Horace's famous words, 'Nothing could shake him from his purpose.'[35] Burchell later reveals the same strength of character in his determination to travel in dangerous zones in the Cape. Although often masked by his Romantic writings, this trait ensured the success of his South African journey, as well as his survival and that of his party.

Another facet of Burchell's personality – physical aggression – surfaces in this tale of McGwyer, a visitor to the island:

a passenger from India, named McGwyer, was on shore, with the intention of shooting any of the Officers of The Antelope ... (he is a noted character, as a quarrelsome man, and bears a villainous name), but at the Tavern happening to meet some Military Officers (from India) [it] was not long before he quarrelled with them and without ceremony pulled out a pistol and fired at one of them; but fortunately the ball passed close by his ear and only hit the ceiling; upon this they

St Helena, 27 May 1808

seized him and kicked him out of the room, and dragged him over to the Main Guard where he was secured. When we heard all this we immediately went down and Davies with us, with an intention of breaking his bones; but we found that he was put in the Main Guard, and secured thus from a good beating … I never saw a man look more like a villain.[36]

In contrast to the humour and compassion he showed in his two church visits, Burchell appears feisty and belligerent at the tavern.

Mistreatment of the powerless always aroused his compassion. Of all the early nineteenth-century British travellers, Kai Easton stresses that Burchell 'must surely come across as one of the most liberal and well-intentioned of his day'.[37] He displayed a great amount of empathy for slaves, believing the word 'slave' sounds 'detestable in the ear of every feeling man'.[38] Witnessing the auctioning of two slaves in St Helena in June 1809 gave Burchell an 'unpleasant sensation at seeing my fellow creatures made a traffic of'.[39] On another occasion, on an outing on Little Stone Top mountain, he discovered a space of a few square feet enclosed by stones piled up like a wall: 'this I am told has been done by the slaves who here secrete themselves after running away from their Masters (indeed I fear they too often have reason for it)'.[40] The hanging of a young slave for stealing a sheep shocked him, although it seemed to be no cause for reflection among the people on the island and 'was talked of without a shudder'. Very observant of children and attentive to their plights, Burchell is therefore appalled when, following the hanging, 'the only notice I could observe being taken of it was the children in the evening playing in the street at being hung'. The indifference of island inhabitants to a fellow being's pain is emphasised in the comment, 'this I think must shew the depravity of morals of these people and how loudly they call for reformation'.[41]

Despite his abhorrence of slavery, Burchell himself employed a slave, a man named May. Their master–servant relationship comes across as mutually considerate, companionable and fun. When Burchell quit the island in 1810, May was in tears: 'he always dreaded going to another Master after I had done with him, as he was sure he should never find such another'. May, in fact, was given leave to hire himself out: from being a slave all his life, he would now be his own master and earn his living by fishing – 'an employment he is fond of'.[42]

Burchell balanced his involvement in the St Helena community with frequent excursions. Communing with nature in remote places and a passion for climbing mountains was characteristic of the famous Romantic poets, Coleridge and William Wordsworth. Burchell, too, had a passion for nature, mountains, rocks and scenery, and was exhilarated by dangerous climbs and magnificent vistas. Two sketches – including *View of Diana's Ridge* – done on the same day and same page in his sketchbook, capture his excitement, enjoyment of a meal, companionship, muscular physique and authoritative body language on the top of the rock-strewn Sugar Loaf Hill.

Romanticism runs through Burchell's lyrical descriptions of his daring excursions. On a fine day in the country, for example,

> butterflies fluttered round every weed and flower, and animated the scene with all those delightful emotions which rural objects and innocent amusement, never, never fail to excite in the tranquil breasts of those who possess minds capable of enjoying the virtuous pleasures which Heaven has so profusely scattered all around us.[43]

On a surveying trip with a friend in November 1806, Burchell remarks on the scenery, which he describes as 'remarkably rude, barren and romantic … no verdure is to be seen, nothing but craggy rocks … just below is a stratum of basaltic rock, the side of which is perpendicular' and had to be descended 'by a rope fixed to an iron cramp in the

View of Diana's Ridge, *c.* 1807

stone above'.[44] In contrast, the view from the top of Sandy Bay Ridge on 10 October 1807 'causes a delightful feeling strangely mixed with sensations of fear and wonder'.[45] The next day, as he ascended Diana's Peak, 'within the paradise of verdure that surround[s]' it, he felt the 'greatest delight that scenes of Nature, clothed in their wildest robe, and pure air, can inspire'.[46]

Burchell, like the Romantic poets, is up-lifted by beauty. He 'gazed with delightful surprise' at the twenty-foot Dicksonia fern with its gigantic leaves, and was struck by the purple and white cabbage trees and large redwoods with handsome white flowers changing to a lively pink hue. He fancies that 'this tree seemed proud of my admiration of its beauty, and I lamented that its flowers should open and fade unadmired or that one

Sketch of Mr Burchell directing Charles, 8 December 1807

The Great Redwood Tree, 27 December 1807

even should drop without having been seen'[47] – a description echoing Thomas Gray's 'Full many a flower is born to blush unseen'.[48]

On these trips, Burchell the artist and mountaineer stepped into the world of investigative science, avidly collecting specimens. He returned from his ventures carrying a 'botanical load' and feeling 'the most peculiar kind of gratification from so novel an excursion'.[49]

But his outings, like those of the suffering Romantic explorers, also caused him physical hardships. Exposure to the sun was hazardous for an Englishman, and Burchell always wore a hat when outdoors. He used a thermometer hanging under his umbrella to help him systematically record temperatures, but this was little protection against 'heat so furious, sultry and scorching'[50] that it gave him severe sunburn. It was only when he travelled to the Cape that he learnt about a sunscreen that worked from the Khoikhoi, who protected themselves from the sun and weather by anointing their bodies with animal fat mixed with powdered sweet-smelling herbs, which they call *Buku* (Bookoo).[51] J.M. Coetzee admires Burchell for his acknowledgement of the traditions of the native peoples he encountered: Burchell, unlike so many early travellers, does not condemn them for 'unsavoury personal habits'.[52]

Burchell's health on St Helena generally concerned him. When he had a consumptive cough, he felt it his duty to 'preserve [his health] for the sake of others'.[53] He was aware of the benefits of exercise, understanding that a sedentary lifestyle was harmful and good health required him to remain active.[54] An elite athlete, his hiking companions usually could not keep up with him or scale the precipitous rock faces as easily as he could.

Weather generally affected his well-being, another typical trait of the Romantic poets. As a consequence, Burchell found his spirits were always raised by 'the cheerfulness of the weather':[55]

The American Aloe on St Helena, 17 February 1807

The day was one of those beautiful St. Helena days, when the sky is nearly clouded over with thin passing clouds which just serve to break the heat of a vertical sun, but which is frequently shining out in full splendour. The wind without being strong as it usually is blew sufficiently to make respiration delightful, and the pureness of which and the exercise of walking, seemed to give the lungs a luxurious treat.'[56]

Heavy rain was another difficulty he faced on the island. When 'the wind roared, the rain streamed and it was pitch dark', Burchell, May and Burchell's friend Cruikshank were forced to shelter in a cottage with no beds. Ever resourceful, Burchell borrowed a flute and amused his companions until 10 p.m. to distract them from the violent weather outside. Although cold and uncomfortable, the three companions 'were merry enough and laughed at our adventure and the oddity of our situation'.[57] While Burchell's endurance was tested time and again, he could call 'fortitude and philosophy' to his aid wherever he was.[58]

The time, however, did not always pass pleasantly for Burchell on the island: 'it will appear to whoever reads [my journal] that my life at St. Helena has been one uninterrupted scene of disappointments'.[59]

Since leaving England for St Helena in 1805, Burchell had been eagerly looking forward to the arrival of his fiancée Lucia Green, whom he planned to marry once she was able to come to the island. The time in which they had been separated had done nothing to dampen Burchell's feelings for Lucia, and only strengthened the love and admiration he had for her before his move.

Unfortunately all correspondence between Lucia and Burchell has been lost. Inferences about their relationship can, however, be made from letters Burchell wrote to his family about her, all of which indicate their relationship had remained loving and constant in the time they were apart (at least on Burchell's side). In a letter he wrote to his father on 23 June 1807, nearly two years after he left England, Burchell affirms that Lucia is an 'invaluable treasure', will be a 'good wife' and has 'the greatest goodness of temper, a kind and humane heart, a mind capable of sound reflection and good judgment, a good education and a love of morality'. Lucia was a 'diamond among pebbles' and someone who 'loves me with the greatest affection'. As a Romantic happily able to surrender to overpowering and consuming emotions, Burchell felt gratitude that he had found someone to whom he could be loyal: 'how can I hope for anyone more perfect,' he asked his father.[60]

After a separation of almost two and a half years, Lucia finally left Fulham for St Helena in early 1808 to be Burchell's wife. But it seems whatever affections she had for William in England suddenly diminished on the voyage to St Helena on the *Walmer Castle*, when she fell in love with the ship's captain, Luke Dodds. As soon as the ship landed on the island on 17 April, Lucia callously jilted William.

Burchell, who had waited for Lucia for so long, and with such devotion, was devastated. He proceeded to shut himself up in his home to avoid seeing or hearing anything about the doings of his erstwhile fiancée and her new lover. In a journal entry dated 12 May 1808, he declares his overwhelming sense of betrayal:

> All this morning my mind was dreadful tortured, for at noon Lucia was irrevocably
> to leave me, and in this most cruel and barbarous manner to terminate my dreams
> of happiness with her. I still could not help hoping that when it came to the last
> trial, she might feel some secret inward horror at her conduct and treatment, to
> one who she had misled by teaching him to rely on her affection and her honour,

and that the baseness of her ingratitude would suddenly flash across her mind and make her relent, and with penitence solicit my forgiveness. But in this reliance of there being one spark of sensibility and virtue in her heart, I was woefully deceived.[61]

For Burchell, who felt so deeply, Lucia's 'heart was so callous to every sentiment of feeling or humanity, that she absolutely quitted St Helena with all the levity and a gaiety of a girl going down a country dance'.[62]

Sometime later, a friend, simply called 'B', told Burchell that Lucia had confided in him about her and Captain Dodds' apprehension that Burchell 'should just at the last moment commit some dreadful act of revenge upon them'. Lucia 'observed to B that Captain D was hastening down to the beach in great agitation, dreading every moment to see me, and meet some desperate act of mine'. However, Burchell's emotions at this time were paralysing and no duel took place: 'they alarmed themselves needlessly, for the most torturing agony and distress was at that time preying upon me and smothered every other sentiment'.[63]

His hopes dashed, Burchell's emotions veer between moderation and extremes of grief when he writes to his parents on 5 May 1808, soon before Lucia was to leave the island with Captain Dodds on 12 May 1808. Burchell reassures them he has overcome his distressing state of mind: 'I have at last by the assistance of Heaven, made use of all my reason and now begin to think I shall surmount all.' He is bitter, though:

> The Walmer Castle with its infamous Captain has not yet sailed. That wretched deluded Girl glories in the blackish ingratitude, and conducts herself in a manner that you would not be able to think possible. She seems lost to shame and every feeling sentiment … and shamelessly passes every moment of her time with that villain whose only design seems that of bringing her to infamy and dishonour. Vengeance will overtake him.

Self-reflective reason, religious faith and hope follow this tirade:

> I who thought myself the most unfortunate of mortals, now, with the greatest gratitude to Heaven for its watchful care of my fate, feel myself a most fortunate young man in having been thus so miraculously snatched from the very brink of an abyss of misery, by the timely discovery of that unhappy girl's indiscretions. An affection like mine is not easily done away, but my only dependence is on God that

he will give me the strength of reason to overcome it and at last to completely eradicate it.

The letter ends with his hope for emotional renewal and the restoration of balance from the peace of nature:

> I am now up in the country for a few days, with the hope that the tranquillity and seclusion of the scene may assist me in restoring peace and ease to my wounded mind. I live to enjoy much true happiness in the bosom of my dear family, whose affection for me is the pleasing prospect that leads me on.[64]

Burchell's despair over Lucia's actions was not easily forgotten, however, and nearly a year later, on 8 March 1809, his grief and anger resurface in a letter to his mother. He is grateful for letters from home that have assisted in consoling him: 'hearing my family speak, has made me almost forget my distress, never have I before been so sensibly convinced of the powerful virtue there is in the affection and esteem of one's family'. The 'dear affectionate letter' from his family has restored his 'drooping spirit', smothered 'disagreeable reflections of the past' and 'half healed deep wounded feelings'. Through this he tries to bounce back: 'I feel my misfortunes become lighter, and begin to hope that it is possible at some future day I shall be able to laugh at all my disappointments.' But his mood changes abruptly, and he finds '[t]he recollections of those diabolical affairs rouses in me so violent a degree of indignation, that I must quit the subject'.[65]

Burchell's experience with Lucia reflects that of another famous explorer, Charles Darwin. Janet Browne, in her brilliant biography of Darwin, writes that he 'was intoxicated by the tumult of feelings that sweep in with first love'.[66] Before he joined the *Beagle*, Darwin was enamoured with Fanny Owen, 'the romantic idol of his heart'; but soon after he left, in 1831, Fanny married a 'dashing aristocrat'. Darwin's response to a situation similar to Burchell's is significant. Darwin was hurt but, unlike Burchell, was quick to recover. Burchell never married, and Professor Poulton surmises that the terrible shock of Lucia's betrayal passed into a lifelong haunting sorrow that deepened with advancing age.[67]

Lucia was not Burchell's only source of grief on St Helena. His happiness on the island had begun to ebb when Governor Robert Patton was unfairly recalled in July 1807,

Jamestown, St Helena, 14 October 1809

and replaced by an acting governor, Colonel Lane, who immediately resolved to undo 'whatever the good and excellent Governor Patton strove to accomplish'. This included altering all of Burchell's plans for the Botanic Garden, as Lane wanted vines planted against the trellis Burchell had made to support the exotic plants he collected and reared.[68] Summoning Burchell to the Botanic Garden, Lane expressed his wishes, but Burchell was fervent in his opposition: 'I refused to agree to his plan of destroying the garden by making it into a vineyard, leaving the plants to shift for themselves between the vines. I parted with him under a threat that he "would not forget me".'[69] Burchell said later that he 'gloried in opposing him'.[70] He prepared a successful petition to have Lane recalled, and Lane was dismissed in disgrace barely a year after replacing Patton.

Lieutenant Colonel Alexander Beatson succeeded Lane as governor on 4 July 1808.[71] But he and Burchell soon clashed as well. Beatson, a keen agriculturalist, was interested in the general agricultural improvement of the island and his economic viewpoint conflicted with Burchell's scientific, botanical one. Burchell's dissatisfaction intensified when the Botanic Garden fell into ruin 'owing to the little notice and support

Psoralea pinnata [gobblygheer], 28 December 1809

which it receives from the present Government'.[72] Communication with Beatson broke down, and by January 1810, Burchell was thinking of leaving St Helena if he did not 'find things going more to my wishes'.[73]

Nearing the end of the month, there had been no progress:

As I am in expectation that the disgust that I feel at my want of encouragement from the Governor here, will soon drive me to resign my situation and go elsewhere, I am giving all my attention to complete the materials for my Flora Heleniana. I have today arranged all my specimens. I feel myself (as it were, involuntarily) preparing for my departure.[74]

On 27 January 1810, Burchell received a letter from Reverend Frederick Hesse in Cape Town with the news that 'Lord Caledon was desirous to know if I would accept the situation of "Botanist to the Cape Colony"'.[75] Governor Beatson continued to exasperate Burchell, and he finally resigned on 16 April 1810. After his confinement on the small island for so long, Burchell was restless and yearned to sail to Rio de Janeiro in the *Camperdown*. However, trouble had arisen between him and the church authorities, who demanded rent for the school house (the reason for this is not given in Burchell's journal). Burchell stood his ground on the issue: 'nothing but compulsion would make me pay a farthing';[76] but in the end he offered to pay fifty pounds instead of the thirty pounds recommended by the council. He was now free to sail to Cape Town.

Before leaving the island, Burchell wrote:

On this day, I took my final view of the interior of the beautiful little Island of St. Helena, an Island which might be made one of the happiest residences for a lover of rural peace and calm retirement, but whose delightful climate is ruffled by no storm, but that of the tempers of its inhabitants, jealousies and mutual mistrust, secret slander and perpetual discord, are here let loose, and murder the tranquil peace and innocent conviviality that ought to be the reigning genii of this delightful spot. But I must leave for ever, those vales, and glens, those romantic hills, where I could have passed some happy years, yet envious Demons have sullied the beauty of the landscape, have blasted the salubrity of the air, by sowing in the hearts of too many there, a ranking discord that makes its rocks a hell indeed.[77]

Burchell quit the island, sailing on board the *Harriet* on 16 October 1810. He was the only passenger, and the accommodation was 'much worse than [he] expected'.[78] His melancholy thoughts quickly fade, however, when he begins to ponder his new under-taking:

Soon afterwards, it became dark, and the Town of St. Helena was seen for the last time. Here, let me pause. First; to reflect on the past, and then to turn my view towards a brighter prospect. I think I can discern it on the distant horizon. I hope. I go.[79]

Burchell, looking towards his hazardous adventure in southern Africa, always 'hopes and goes'.

3

'For the first time on the land of Africa'

Cape Town and vicinity
November 1810 to June 1811

B URCHELL ARRIVED AT THE CAPE towards the beginning of British rule. The British had taken it over from the Dutch East India Company (VOC) in 1795, but they saw their occupation as temporary, and in 1803 they handed the colony to the new Dutch Batavian government.[1] But then the British attacked Cape Town from Bloubergstrand and resumed control of the colony in January 1806. It was finally ceded to Great Britain at the end of the Napoleonic Wars in 1814. When Burchell was there between 1810 and 1815, it was clear that it would remain a British colony.[2]

In common with other British colonies, the Cape was ruled by a civilian governor (from Cape Town), while still being recognised as a Crown Colony.[3] During the transitional period, Burchell observed and documented the linguistic, cultural and social changes to the far from homogenous communities in Cape Town and the colony. He insisted that '[t]o be qualified for judging of the character of these inhabitants, it is not enough to have mingled with the better part of society; the Boors must be heard, the Hottentots must be heard, and the slaves must be heard'.[4]

Two hundred years after it was published, Burchell's *Travels in the Interior of Southern Africa* is still of historical, anthropological and scientific interest. It includes a chapter, 'A sketch of Cape Town and the Colony', written as a technical report without journal entries and focusing on 'local circumstances and customs'.[5] Burchell outlines population demographics, transport facilities, villages and districts, the administrative structures of government, currencies, availability of food and the price of provisions, and climatic conditions. As one of Britain's dominions, the Cape of Good Hope is promoted as 'an important and valuable possession'.[6]

The *Travels* is not a logbook of colonialism, however. Burchell's expedition was undertaken 'solely for the purpose of acquiring knowledge', and he set himself the task of giving 'a faithful picture of occurrences and observations … even to the minutest particular' in both the narrative and artworks. He asserts, perhaps naively, that they were 'commenced with a mind free from prejudice, and in the purest spirit of independence',[7] since he, unlike sponsored travellers such as Levaillant, financed his own expedition. 'The strict form of a journal has been adhered to, as being that which best enables the reader and the author to travel, as it were, the journey over again, and view, in their proper light, the facts in connection, and the impressions made by each event in succession.' To reassure his Victorian readers, he adds that his book, unlike many other travel books, does not 'contain matter offensive to decency', and that 'such indelicacies will never be found in these volumes'.[8]

The 'smooth, continuous narrative'[9] Professor Poulton attributes to the *Travels* is carefully choreographed, the material taken from the detailed notebooks Burchell meticulously kept sitting in his wagon, often late at night during the journey. He avoids interrupting the flow of the text by using footnotes for scientific data, and includes a Zoological and Botanical Index, specifically for scientific readers, at the end of Volume II. His footnotes are so instructive that editors of subsequent editions have not added explanatory notes. A large fold-up map, at the end of Volume I, shows his route. An appendix, 'The Itinerary and Register of the Weather', appears at the end of each volume, tabulating dates, distances, stations, temperatures and weather conditions. Such accurate, reliable measurements were highly valued by Victorian scientists.

Instead of cluttering his narrative with marginal notes, Burchell uses the simple, effective and eye-catching innovation of italicising key words to point out the subject of each paragraph. Navigation in the *Travels* is so simple: every page has a heading and the date; and the General Index (compiled manually by Burchell) encompasses the encyclopaedic content of both volumes, and 'answers the purpose of a glossary for all the foreign words'. Anthropological and sociological observations on the Bachapins, who Burchell visited from July to August 1812, are not part of the journal, but are collated in two chapters after the abrupt ending of the narrative on 3 August 1812 – a strategy that sustains the tension of the story and, at the same time, enables Burchell to convey 'as much general information as may be sufficient for filling up the description of the Bachapins'.[10]

Vernacular words add local sound effects and animate the narrative. Burchell consistently uses indigenous names, placing the English translation in brackets. He is adamant that 'the aboriginal Hottentot names ought, on no account, be altered; they should on the contrary, rather be sought for, and adopted, as being far more appropriate

Within the Lee of Lion's Head, 1810

to Southern Africa, than a multitude of foolish names of modern imposition'.[11] An encounter at a Bushmen kraal in March 1812 shows the dramatic and comic effect of switching languages:

> I was received by the inhabitants with repeated acclamations of *Tway! Tway!* and with every demonstration of their being glad at seeing me: although I do not flatter myself that their joy was entirely personal, as the words *Gooen dakka; Tabakka! Gooen dakka; Tabakka!* plainly betrayed their expectations and the source of their gladness. By this they intended to say 'Good day; give us some tobacco:' wishing thus to render themselves more intelligible by addressing me in Dutch.[12]

The variety of languages scattered throughout the *Travels* mirrors the 'singular mix'[13] of the inhabitants of Cape Town and the colony, which included travellers from Holland, France, Germany, Denmark and Sweden; as well as the local inhabitants, made up of Boers, the San, Khoikhoi, Koras and Bachapins. Here, Burchell found a rich collection of individuals and cultures to stimulate his interests as a man of science.

The *Travels* opens with the storm-damaged *Harriet* approaching the Cape. On board the ship, on 13 November 1810, Burchell and the crew sight land. Table Mountain rises out of the ocean as the vessel glides over 'the blue waters of the deep', and then sails on the 'calm surface of waters of a greener tinge, from which the seals sometimes raised their dripping heads to view us as we passed'. Within half a mile of the shore, 'some

spots appeared of a beautiful purple and others of a yellow colour, occasioned most probably by the abundance of flowers'.[14]

The raging storm contrasts with Burchell's pleasing expectations of what he will see when he reaches land – 'the novelty of the scene, and the interesting objects before me, absorbed the whole of my attention'[15] – and inspires philosophical reflections. Despite the charming scenery spotted from the ship, a landing could not be attempted because of ferocious storms. A violent gale was blowing, and clouds covered Table Mountain: 'Its thin misty skirts no sooner rolled over the edge of the precipice, than they were rarefied into air and vanished.'[16] The moment the ship sailed past the shelter of Lion's Head on 16 November, a furious wind drove the vessel out to sea. For several days, the gale-force south-east wind raged – the 'heavy seas rolled on board with over-whelming force'; 'the peril of the situation increased every moment'; and everyone aboard the *Harriet* feared that 'some unforeseen accident would before morning bury us all in the cold grave of the ocean'.[17] Variable winds and unsettled weather continued for a few more days until 26 November, when the storms abated and the *Harriet* finally entered Table Bay. The anchor cast, Burchell's 'foot stepped for the first time, on the land of Africa'.[18]

Everything wore, to *my* eye at least, a pleasing aspect … whatever I beheld seemed to present itself as a subject for my future investigation … the various shades of human character and manners; the complexion of the mountains and valleys; the ground we tread upon; all open to us gratuitously an inexhaustible source of knowledge and of ideas, and an infinite variety of amusement of the most rational kind.[19]

Burchell, in the footnote to his engraving of the 'jutty', the landing place at Cape Town, excitedly remarks that celebrated characters, eminent navigators and men of science had 'passed along this same platform'.[20] Little did he know that he, like Charles Darwin in June 1836, and Sir John Herschel from 1834 to 1838, would be one of the most distinguished men of science to visit Cape Town in the nineteenth century.

In the depiction in the *Travels* of the approach to the Cape, the narrative perspective varies deftly from danger in perilous storms, to the novelty and grandeur of the scenery, and then to Burchell's animated anticipation of being in a foreign country where he can be 'acquainted with my fellow-creatures living in primeval simplicity', and his delight at 'acquiring new views of human nature'.[21]

This enthusiasm did not wane for Burchell on his 'first African day'[22] in the Cape, and he felt himself gratified with everything. He was hospitably accommodated in the home of Lutheran minister Reverend Frederick Hesse (who had written to Burchell in January 1810 with the job offer of Cape Botanist – a proposal that never came to fruition). Hesse's house is now known as Martin Melck House; it is the only surviving example of an eighteenth-century Cape Dutch townhouse. During his sojourn at the Hesse home, Burchell was enthralled by the scenery and 'the rich and wonderful variety of plants that grew in every spot',[23] and excited about the prospect of rendering this in his own art. Throughout the six months he spent in Cape Town before setting off for Klaarwater (now Griquastad), Burchell was always able to discover new activities and places to absorb his artistic interests.

His illustrations of Cape Town and its vicinity fall into two categories: scenic,

The Jutty [Jetty] at Cape Town

A panorama of Cape Town, 1815: Sheet 4

coloured aquatints and wood-engraving vignettes. As a genre, landscape painting has always been popular, and Burchell's paintings give readers of the *Travels* much pleasure. Keith Dietrich, a South African artist and art professor at Stellenbosch University crystallises the essence of Burchell's distinctive blend of scientific perspicuity, romanticism and art, and his ability to render the technical aspects of what he observed in his artistic creations: 'Burchell's scientific alertness to the world around him, alongside his romantic desire for discovery, for the novel, the unusual and picturesque, led him to find descriptive modes for transcribing empirical data into pictorial data.'[24]

At other times, Burchell uses words to express the impact of things he sees on his journey, their detail amplified by his perspective as an accomplished artist. His description of the view from Kirstenbosch is a perfect example of his verbal virtuosity:

The view from this spot, and, indeed, all the scenery around, is the most picturesque of any I had seen in the vicinity of Cape Town. The beauties here displayed to the eye could scarcely be represented by the most skilful pencil; for this landscape

The Castle Gate at Cape Town

possessed a character that would require the combined talents of a Claude and a Both: but at this hour, the harmonious effect of light and shade, with the enchanting appearance of the foliage in the foreground, and the tone of the middle distances, were altogether far beyond the painter's art. The objects immediately surrounding us, were purely sylvan; a blue extent of distance terminated the landscape both in front and on the right. To the left, the noble Table Mountain rose in all its grandeur … The last beams of the sun, gleaming over the rich, varied, and extensive prospect, laid on the warm finishing lights, in masterly and inimitable touches.[25]

View of Strand-street

J.M. Coetzee considers Burchell to be someone who 'views terrain as a potential subject of painting and whose observation of terrain is in turn educated by his experience of painting … [his] comments … on rendering the tone, light, and chiaroscuro of Kirstenbosch are not empty exclamations but judicious aesthetic observations'.[26]

Vignettes in the *Travels* – *The Jutty*, *The Castle Gate* and *View of Strand-street* – show 'the character of the ordinary buildings of the

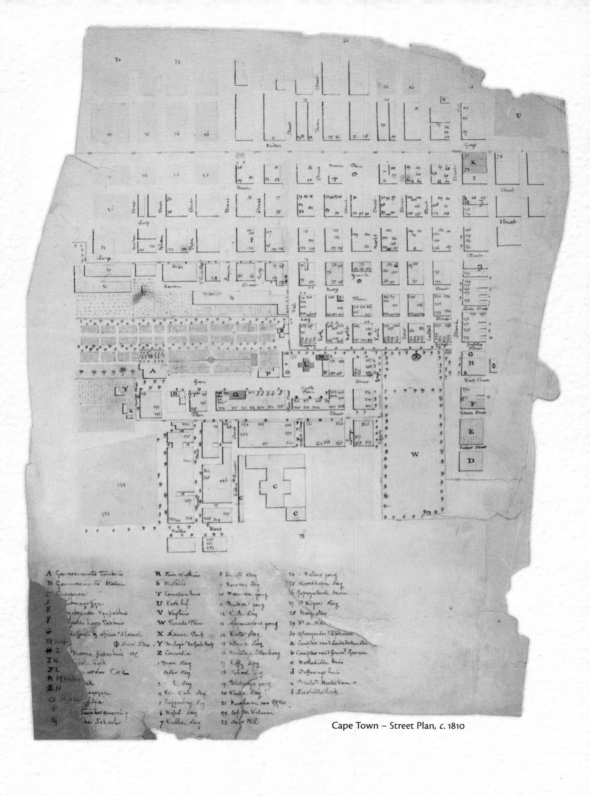

Cape Town – Street Plan, *c.* 1810

A View of Cape Town, Table Bay & Tygerberg, 26 December 1810

town'.[27] The journalistic role of Burchell's vignettes as 'candid visual language' is accentuated by Dietrich:

> These sketches, rather like voyeuristic candid snapshots, are treated as visual diary entries, quickly executed at the moment the scene or image impinges on his retina, and no doubt before the intervention of the imagination. Unlike his portrait sketches, the final engravings of these vignette sketches are not reworked into complicated aquatints, but are directly transcribed into engravings, and, being vignettes within the text, they comply with their intended purpose of journal *impressions.*[28]

The 'elegant style of architecture, regularity, and cleanness of the town'[29] impress Burchell. His *Street Plan* is badly damaged, but the legend, in Dutch, is still legible, and describes sixty-one different structures, including buildings, offices and institutions.[30]

For the anthropologist Tim Ingold, colonialism is 'the imposition of one kind of line on another. It proceeds first by converting the paths along which life is lived into boundaries in which it is contained, and then by joining up these now enclosed communities, each confined to one spot, into vertically integrated assemblies.'[31] This description is a perfect analogy of the colonial street grid in Burchell's painting.

The scenic setting of Cape Town is illustrated in colour in *A View of Cape Town, Table Bay & Tygerberg*, dated 26 December 1810. The surrounding mountains, Table Bay with ships at anchor, flat-roofed houses at the foot of Lion's Head, the Lutheran church and the Dutch church, the Castle, a thatched farmhouse, slaves and an ox wagon feature in the painting. Burchell, in a blue frock coat, is in the foreground surrounded by flowers and low shrubs, drawing under the shade of his umbrella. The painting is explained in a detailed footnote in the *Travels*.[32]

Landscape paintings, which Burchell has not included in his *Travels*, show the undeveloped countryside. Plants, shrubs and the American aloe (*Agave americana*) stand out in the watercolour *At the Foot of Table Mountain*, produced on 15 March 1811. *Liesbeeck River Bridge*, dated 9 March 1811, foregrounds Devil's Peak, the river and the footbridge. The area is of historic interest, as the 'great road into the interior of the colony, branching afterwards northward and eastward'[33] was situated near the lower part of the Liesbeeck River (near today's Koeberg Interchange). Burchell's delight in stunning scenery was complemented by his involvement in social and cultural activities taking place in the vibrant town.

There were a variety of amusements available in the Cape to entertain visitors, and Burchell found himself spoiled for choice in the months leading up to his expedition to Klaarwater. The theatre in Cape Town was 'shut up for want of performers', but there were musical concerts where the ladies were dressed extremely well, in the English fashion, and there 'was none of that talking and chattering which are too often heard at concerts and music parties, and which serve only to distinguish the tasteless lounger from the lover of music, or, perhaps, sometimes, bad performance from good'.[34]

At the Foot of Table Mountain, 15 March 1811

Liesbeeck River Bridge, 9 March 1811

Burchell believed that music 'possesses the power of improving the best feelings of the heart, and of calming, and even annihilating, many of the more turbulent passions of men'.[35] Music, and Burchell's love of it, infiltrates the narrative of the *Travels*.

The government vegetable garden and the menagerie with a lion, lioness and Bengal tiger disappointed Burchell, however.[36] To improve the knowledge of the colonists, he suggested the establishment of 'a well-ordered *botanic garden*' in which plants from more distant parts of the colony could be grown. For the colonists to get an idea of the productions of the country beyond the town and Green Point, he proposed a museum for 'the reception of the rarities of the country'.[37]

On a lighter note, he found red Constantia wines had a very agreeable taste,[38] and horse races – 'a gay scene for the Cape fashionables' – were events where 'Malays and Negroes mingled with whites'. While the races hold Burchell's attention, the 'patient Hottentot views it almost with apathy; and, squatted on the ground, seems to prefer a pipe of tobacco to that which affords such exquisite gratification to his superiors'. Burchell wryly observes that: 'Together with the art of making horses run fast, the science and mystery of betting has found its way to the farthest extremity of Africa; and on Green Point large sums are said to have been won and lost.'[39]

Fashions at the governor's public ball in honour of the queen's birthday catch Burchell's eye. He is up to date with trends in dancing, claiming that: 'Country-dances afforded the chief amusement; neither waltzes nor quadrilles being at that time generally in vogue'.[40] African dancing captivates him throughout his journey: '*Dancing* appears to have been in all ages of the world, and perhaps in all nations, a custom so natural, so pleasing, and even useful … practised as much by the savage as by the civilized.' Dancing culminates in physical excellence, and 'Grace and ease of motion are the extent of its perfection'.[41]

Janet Browne, professor of the history of science at Harvard, identifies botany as the 'big science' of Burchell's day, and 'a rising popular phenomenon'.[42] Cape Town offered the adventurous Burchell an assortment of places in which he could cultivate his botanical interests. On foot, and often 'attended by a good-natured Mozambique slave-boy, named Jak',[43] Burchell explored and collected plants from Lion's Head, Camp's Bay, Green Point, Rondebosch, the Liesbeeck River, Newlands, Constantia and Wynberg. 'The profuse variety which Flora has strewn over this her favoured country, inspired me with the most agreeable sensations, and created new ardour and activity.'[44] To ensure that his collections would be forwarded to England, he appointed agents Messrs Rankin and Scott to take care of the 'different packages that came into their hands'.[45]

On 24 January 1811, Burchell ascended Table Mountain. The day before the planned excursion, however, 'Devil's Mountain'[46] was on fire. Fires were common, some thought to be started by slaves warming themselves. Burchell takes note of the ecological impact of 'a conflagration of this kind, which not only destroys the beauty and verdant clothing of the mountain, but, in time, renders firewood more scarce than ever'.[47] Fortunately, the fire died down, and Burchell was rewarded with 'a rich harvest in botany'.[48] He collected fifty-one species on the ascent and ninety-seven on the summit.

The party climbing the mountain was linguistically diverse. There was Burchell, Mr Hesse from Hanover, Mr Polemann from Denmark (a friend of Mr Hesse and a keen naturalist), the French Mr Renou and the Welsh Mr Jones, as well as the slaves – all of them speaking a 'variety of tongues'. They planned to reach the summit at sunrise on 24 January, so set out in the dark at a quarter past three in the morning. The party was daunted by the 'stupendous precipice' and the exceedingly steep, laborious ascent. When the sun rose 'from behind the distant mountains of Hottentot Holland', Burchell was disappointed: 'I perceived in it nothing remarkable.' But once the streams of light 'illumined, with a reddish tinge, the huge mass of perpendicular rock which towered in majestic grandeur above our heads, and, together with the rude wildness of the scene',[49] the effect on Burchell was glorious. Looking back, the party 'watched the hills and distant mountains to the north and east, slowly making their appearance one behind another, till the extensive and grand range of the Hottentot Holland mountains, stood, with its distant blue craggy summits' came into view. 'These, with

Cape Town and Table Bay from Table Mountain, 24 January 1811

the broad, intervening expanse of level country, were the grandest objects which we noticed during the ascent.'[50]

A great variety of shrubs grew on either side of the path on the mountain despite another devastating fire the year before. A scarlet *Crassula coccinea* peeped 'from between the rocks and herbage'. Burchell collected so many plants that his arms ached from the accumulated load. The party rested at the entrance to the Poort – a fissure dividing the upper edge of the mountain – and by a quarter past seven everyone had summitted safely.[51] 'The view,' Burchell said, 'looking downwards through the Poort, is awful and singularly grand.' Breakfast was prepared with a fire that 'blazed with the fuel of *Cliffortia ruscifolia* [known to mountaineers as 'climber's friend'], *Mimetes Hartogii* [now extinct] and *Aulax pinifolia* [also extinct]; excellent water was found in the cavities of the rocks, and [...] the spirits of our party seemed heightened by the excursion'.[52]

Burchell, as a man of science, accurately describes the geology on top of the mountain:

Although, in a general sense, the top of this mountain may be called flat and level, yet it is much less so than might be supposed, while viewing it only from below. Its surface is, in fact, both hilly and rocky, and consists of a hard sand-stone, which, in the bare and more exposed parts, is very compact and flinty … The whole summit is covered with plants and bushes.[53]

The heights of Table Mountain, Devil's Mountain, Lion's Head and Lion's Rump (Signal Hill) follow this description. Despite the distance from the ground, the view is magnificent: a spectator standing on the precipice overlooking the town 'cannot look down the awful depth directly beneath without feeling some dread, or giddiness'.[54]
On top of the mountain, Burchell is imbued with feelings of imperialism:

In surveying from this high eminence, so great an extent and such a variety of objects, sensations are produced of a very agreeable kind, not at all connected with the idea of picturesque scenery. They seem rather to arise from a feeling of superiority and command, which a great height above all we behold, and an elevation above the inhabited earth, seem to inspire in the spectator, who, at the same time, breathes the freest and purest air.[55]

The weather on the mountain eventually changed: 'the wind increased, and misty clouds flying with rapidity past us, threatened soon to envelop, both us and the whole mountain'. By this time the rugged and sharp rocks 'had literally worn the shoes off [Burchell's] feet' but fortunately the 'French companion' in the party had a second pair of shoes which Burchell could use.[56] The climbing party descended in two and a half hours, and as the slaves were 'well acquainted with every turn of the path', they felt no apprehension of missing their way. By eight o'clock that evening, they were home.[57]

In April 1811, Burchell, accompanied by Mr Polemann, travelled on horseback through parts of the Cape familiar to Polemann. Burchell gives the reason for the trip: 'One of the objects which we had in view, was to purchase a couple of teams of oxen.'[58] With Polemann as a guide, they rode through the Hottentots Holland Mountains to the hot springs at Zwarteberg (Caledon), and from there visited the mission stations at Genadendal, Tulbagh and Winterhoek. Two teams of oxen were purchased in the Koue Bokkeveld.[59] Burchell and Polemann returned to Cape Town on 21 April, via Paarl and Stellenbosch – Burchell illustrating local architecture on his way in vignettes.
During his outing with Polemann, Burchell revealed his fascination with the 'great space within the terrestrial shell'[60] of the globe, and he wondered at the subterranean spaces and forces found in the Earth, and the many mysteries they held. The hot springs

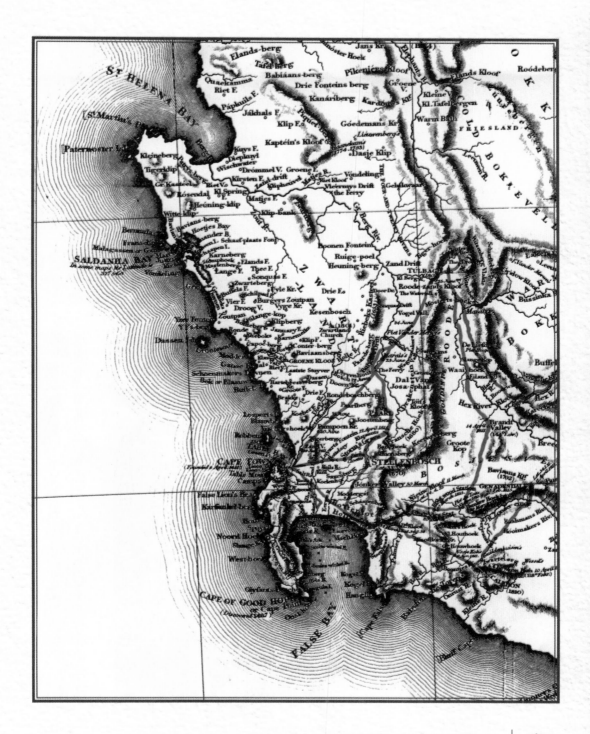

at the Zwarteberg trigger an honest response from Burchell, who is open about his ignorance on their formation:

> I shall not here amuse myself in proposing or supporting any hypothesis on the cause of hot springs; but shall confess myself very much at a loss in attempting to account for the great subterranean operations of Nature, whose dark recesses in the centre of our globe are not less out of the pale of observation, than the wide space beyond the starry system.[61]

Burchell saw a more aggressive demonstration of this hidden power of the Earth when he experienced earthquakes in Cape Town. In a journal entry dated 26 December 1810, he records the anxiety suffered by the town when 'a slight trembling of the earth was felt'.[62] Panic prevailed, but the actual damage to the town was minimal. However, 'the slightest symptom of its recurrence' caused apprehension, which multiplied on 2 June 1811 when there was a second tremor. Burchell was in his room preparing for his departure for Klaarwater when 'a sudden and violent explosion shook the whole house, with a noise as loud as that of a cannon fired close at the door. In three or four seconds after this, another report, still more violent and sharp, like the loudest clap of thunder, shook the building more forcibly than the first; and at the same moment I felt a strange and unusual motion.'[63] All the inhabitants fled from their houses, and this time the damage done by the quake was severe.

For Burchell, the earthquake 'bore so much the character of electricity, that it could not easily be viewed in any other light than as the explosion of electric matter'. More superstitious inhabitants 'coupled the *comet*, which had been seen every night, …

The Bath-house at Zwarteberg

The Church at Genadendal, 12 April 1811

and the earthquake', believing that they signalled the annihilation of the Cape. But the true nature of the earthquake in Burchell's view could be 'understood as the result of laws established by the Divine Power at the creation'.[64] For Burchell, matters of science can be comprehended only by the use of the 'divine gift of reason':

> The wild speculations and unfounded theories of those who go in search of knowledge without this for their guide, will surely, like the misty imagery of a dream dispelled by the morning light, vanish at the first dawn of the light of truth.[65]

Two years before Burchell landed in Cape Town, a disastrous expedition led by Dr Cowan and Captain Donovan from the Cape garrison left for Mozambique in September 1808.[66] The party, consisting of a Dutch colonist, two Englishmen, private soldiers, about fifteen Khoikhoi (two from Klaarwater), and four wagons, reached the Molopo River on 24 December. No further news was ever heard of them, and 'it was generally believed that all must have perished'. In the light of this tragic event, friends in Cape Town tried to dissuade Burchell from going north to Klaarwater. They believed that Burchell, slightly built, and only five feet four inches tall, would falter on such an arduous trip, seeing his 'bodily strength and constitution as unequal to the

The Village of Tulbagh, 18 April 1811

task' of the journey. For Burchell, however, these 'well-meant representations made no impression, and I continued unmoved in my resolution'.[67]

When Burchell arrived in Cape Town, he had 'decided on nothing more than the general outlines of the plan for my future travels'. His intention was to explore the 'less frequented or unknown parts of Africa, for the purpose of becoming acquainted with its inhabitants, and of increasing my own knowledge by the addition of whatever facts I might have the opportunity of observing'.[68] He only delayed his journey until he had 'collected some information respecting the country, and acquired some experience and knowledge of its customs and peculiarities'. Although a fluent speaker of Dutch, he made sure to learn the 'proper pronunciation of the Dutch language, according to the Cape dialect', so that he 'could converse with every class of its inhabitants'.[69]

Teams of oxen to pull the wagons were essential, and Mr Polemann had already selected and purchased two teams in the Bokkeveld with Burchell in April. Procuring men to accompany Burchell was more problematic, since very few Khoikhoi men were legally 'free' to join him, and the disappearance of Dr Cowan's party deterred others from going on any expeditions.[70] Professor Poulton, drawing from a letter Burchell wrote on 15 August 1815 to Lord Charles Somerset (governor of the Cape Colony from 1814 to 1826), observes that, throughout his epic journey, Burchell was perpetually constrained by 'the fears and unwillingness of his men to venture farther'.[71]

In preparation for his trip, Burchell gleaned 'information from every quarter within my reach'.[72] William Anderson, a missionary from Klaarwater, gave him 'much satisfactory information'.[73] He told Burchell about five hundred emigrant 'Caffres', 'a warlike set of men, discontented and irritated at the treatment they had received from all quarters, and at variance with the colonists', had formed a settlement near Klaarwater and could attack them.[74] (In the *Travels*, Burchell uses the term 'Caffres' in two senses: 'To the *Caffre Race* belong the Bichuanas, and the Dammaras, together with the Kosas or Caffres Proper, the Tambookis, and probably all the tribes on the eastern side of the Continent, as far as Delgoa Bay.'[75]) Bushmen were considered dangerous too. For these reasons, Anderson asked that Burchell join his party as far as Klaarwater for their mutual safety. Initially rejecting the proposal because he objected to the delayed departure date, Burchell eventually reconsidered, and immediately commissioned 'the building of my waggon'.[76]

Geometrical drawing of the waggon

The construction of the wagon, designed by Burchell himself, was completed by the end of April 1811. An engraving shows its geometrical elevation; a second engraving displays a transverse section, while the narrative gives the technical 'specs' of the vehicle in minute detail.

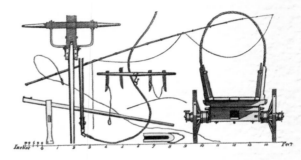

Section of the waggon, with various articles appertaining to it

Burchell explains its unique design: 'The principal and very important advantage of a Cape-built waggon consists in its sides, bottom, and carriage, not being joined together; a construction admirably well adapted for rough and uneven roads, by admitting each part to play freely, so as completely to avoid that straining and cracking to which solid built waggons are subjected, when travelling over irregular ground.'[77]

A coloured painting in the Oxford University Museum of Natural History, completed in 1820 but based on earlier sketches while Burchell was still in the Cape, shows the interior of the wagon where over eighty articles are visible. To assist other travellers, Burchell lists the contents of the wagon in the *Travels* under headings:

> Goods as presents to the chiefs, and for bartering with the natives; Clothing and blankets for my own Hottentots; Arms and ammunition; Carpenter's tools; Waggon-stores; The English colors; Provisions; Fish-hooks and lines; Water-casks; A chest of select medicines; Books: consisting of various works on zoology, mineralogy, natural philosophy, mathematics, medicine, &c.; amounting, all

Inside of my African Waggon, exhibited at the Royal Academy in 1820

together, to more than fifty volumes …; A large assortment of stationary, and
every requisite for drawing in water and body-colours; together with prepared
canvas, and the articles used for painting in oil; Spare deal packing-cases; And
a multitude of other things …[78]

Once the wagon was packed, Burchell's preparations were complete, 'excepting one,
which was not of trifling importance: I was still without the proper complement
of men'.[79]

In March 1811, Burchell had followed up a suggestion that he hire Jan Tamboer,
who was enlisted in the Cape regiment and stationed in Wynberg, as his wagon-driver.
But ten days before the date of departure, Tamboer was in hospital, too ill to undertake
the journey. Fortunately, Philip Willems, also from the garrison, 'instantly accepted
the offered appointment, overjoyed at exchanging a military life for one so much more
congenial' and 'having neither family nor possessions, nor, indeed, any property', he was
ready to start at a moment's notice.[80] Anderson engaged two Klaarwater Khoikhoi –

Magers and Jan Kok – to accompany Burchell as far as Klaarwater.

By the day of departure, however, Burchell was still without the number of men necessary 'for a journey over deserts and through uncivilized nations', and hoped to procure men on his way through the colony.[81] Fortuitously, an acquaintance of Willems', Stoffel Speelman, recently discharged from the Cape regiment, 'expressed the greatest desire to go with us' and 'got himself ready in less than half an hour, with his wife' to set off with the rest of the party. He was an excellent marksman, a 'great traveller, and had visited most parts of the colony.'[82] Speelman's wife, Hannah, accompanied him on the journey. While Burchell feared that she would be an encumbrance (which she was, being lazy and withdrawn), he 'consented to add a lady to our party'.[83] Luck was also on Burchell's side when Gert Roodezand, sent by the Moravian missionaries at Groenekloof, joined them in Tulbagh.

Portrait of Speelman, a Hottentot, 21 September 1814

Finally, at about noon on 18 June 1811, 'everything being ready for starting, Philip mounted his seat, and taking in his hand the great whip, the emblem of his office, made the street echo with one of his loudest claps; at the same moment, with an animated voice, calling out to the oxen, *Loop!* The waggon moved steadily away.'[84] On horseback, Burchell followed to check that the wagon was 'properly secured for the night'.[85] He then turned around and returned to Cape Town, intending only to join his party and the missionaries in Salt River the following day, as he had a 'farewell dinner at the Governor's table' to attend in Cape Town.[86] He experienced his third Cape earthquake on 19 June, on the same day he would depart from his friends in the town. Undeterred, and two hours after the tremor, Burchell, accompanied by two friends, 'took his final departure from Cape Town' and rode to Salt River, where he would meet his party. Exhausted by the preparation for the expedition to Klaarwater, Burchell was finally able to rest for a short while. He threw himself on the mattress in his wagon,

> to repose a while, and recover from the bodily fatigue and exhaustion of spirits, which the exertions of the last two days had occasioned; as well as to relieve some perturbation of mind, arising from the thoughts of having now taken leave of my family, and all my friends, perhaps forever.[87]

4

'Traversing and exploring so interesting a portion of the globe'[1]

Cape Town to Klaarwater
June to October 1811

T HE JOURNEY FROM CAPE TOWN to Klaarwater was action-packed, the changing scenery spectacular. It was here that Burchell first encountered the Khoisan
and 'Koranas' – 'man in an uncivilized state of society'.[2] After the comfort of congenial Cape Town, the thirty-year-old explorer was now in unknown terrain, travelling
with Khoikhoi assistants, the missionaries' caravan, oxen and dogs. Along the way
he encountered hospitable Boer farmers, usually with itinerant tutors 'completing the
education of a boor's family',[3] and he describes these visits with humour. But Burchell's
vision and discoveries extend way beyond the commonplace: the designs of the 'Great
Creating Power'[4] in the arid country constantly shape how he looks at Nature. Adventure, scientific inquiry and poetical sensibility blend seamlessly.

Burchell meticulously measured the distance travelled each day by counting the
number of revolutions made by the 'greater wheel'[5] of the wagon, estimating that it
equalled 791 miles from Cape Town to Klaarwater. Altogether, the party were on the
road for three and a half months.[6] Burchell, always systematic, gives a clear, condensed
route outline, the chapter headings in the *Travels* effectively signposting key locations:

Cape Town to Tulbagh; From Tulbagh, through Hex-river Kloof, to the Karro
Poort; Journey over the Karro; Journey through the Roggeveld to the borders of
the Colony; Journey from the borders of the Cape Colony, through the country
of the Bushmen, to the river Gariep; Journey in the country of the Koras, from
the Gariep to the Asbestos Mountains – Stay at the Kloof village – And arrival at
Klaarwater.[7]

In modern-day terms, Burchell travelled via the Roggeveld plateau, through what is now known as Ceres, Sutherland, Fraserburg, Carnarvon, Prieska and Hay.[8] The route is of environmental interest as well, divided into the distinct ecological zones of the Cape Floral Kingdom (or the fynbos biome), the Succulent Karoo, the drier areas of the Great Karoo, and the desert areas of the Northern Cape.[9] Burchell meticulously catalogued plants, their localities and the dates he found them in all of these biomes.

On the first night of the journey, the caravan halted at a pool of water situated between Tygerberg and False Bay. Here, Burchell slept in the open air for the first time, and the 'novelty of the scene kept my mind continually amused'.[10] For him,

> These fire-light scenes have always a picturesque appearance … My health and strength improved daily by the exercise of travelling; and the novelty and interest of the country, and its productions, increasing as we advanced, inspired me with a high degree of alacrity, and surprisingly raised the spirits. My mind glowed with the sanguine expectation of succeeding in all my plans. I began to lose sight of the Cape of Good Hope, and to turn my view forward, often imagining myself arrived at the termination of my long and laborious journey.[11]

Burchell's sunny confidence is instantly visible. Likewise, he is always curious and alert. Straight away, his eye is on the Khoikhoi: 'all their movements, fixed my attention';[12] and throughout the entire expedition, his focus on his Khoikoi assistants never wavers. His impressions swing between admiration for their patience, navigational skills, indigenous knowledge, telescopic vision and 'their quickness and memory, in everything relating to cattle';[13] and his impatience at their dullness, idleness, want of perseverance and irresponsibility. The more unfavourable characteristics irked Burchell, and had serious consequences for the travelling party, including the loss of cattle and sheep. A specific behavioural trait of the Khoikhoi surfaced five days into the journey, on 23 June, when Burchell's overloaded wagon sank into the wet, sandy ground and the pole broke:

> This affair gave me an opportunity of witnessing the helplessness of Hottentots, and their want of contrivance, in occurrences a little out of the common way. They could not imagine any other mode of extricating the vehicle than by main force; and it was in this foolish attempt that the pole was broken. When they discovered that such means would not answer, they stood looking on with a most provoking apathy, silently smoking their pipes; and even while I was pointing out

how they were to dig the channel, they stood as unmoved as if they had been statues fixed there upon a pedestal.[14]

Three days later, a new pole was purchased from a farmer, and a second, though inferior, wagon to lighten the load was bought in Tulbagh.

Danger and trouble loomed constantly for Burchell's party: crossing flooding rivers was hazardous, and threats of attack from hostile tribes were persistently magnified by Mr Anderson,[15] whose alarming reports caused panic. Characteristically, Burchell wanted to ascertain the truth of the rumours and was determined to continue. Free-booters, marauders and robbers also caused anxiety. One night, Burchell 'felt by the motion of the waggon that someone was endeavouring to get in ... I drew a pistol ... Of what nation these robbers were, or their number, we never could discover.'[16] On another night, fear struck the travelling caravan when several wagon-drivers heard the cry of '*Whoo-ah! Whoo-ah!*'

> We instantly halted, thinking some attack had been made by the Bushmen, or that some formidable wild beast had carried off an ox or one of our people. We ran back to their assistance with some loaded guns in our hand; but our fears were soon relieved, on being told, as we approached, that it was nothing of this kind: and yet, the *accouchement* of one of the Hottentot ladies, was certainly an occurrence that happened very awkwardly just at this time, and in such a spot.[17]

The care and protection of women and children generally concerned Burchell. The Khoikhoi 'female being able to endure the fatigues of so rough a journey' surprised him at first, but he 'learnt at last to consider a *Hottentot woman* as fully equal to the task of following her husband in all his migrations and wanderings, and of bearing all the hardships of a savage life'.[18]

Physical hardships were gruelling. The caravans, as well as those who had to walk, travelled long distances, were exposed to hunger and thirst, wild predatory beasts and adverse weather conditions, and endured rocky, precipitous terrain. A serious accident occurred that 'nearly cost a Hottentot the loss of his life, and me that of an eye'.[19] Speelman was 'busy with the lock of the great rifle-gun', when Burchell, not realising the gun was loaded, snapped the cock and 'the ball, by a providential guidance passed between the people', the flash scorching his eye. Bathing the eye with warm water

Crossing the Berg River, 23 June 1811

alleviated the pain and inflammation, and after 'the painful operation of picking the grains of powder out of my face', he rejoiced that his sight was not damaged. Burchell, notably, does not castigate Speelman, and instead accentuates the fortunate escape.

Contagious diseases, serpent bites and possible attacks from San men with deadly poisoned arrows were also menacing perils. Burchell had contact with leprosy when his medical expertise was sought by a Boer and his family. The daughter had 'all the symptoms of the loathsome leprosy' caused by a vaccination. He left the family with the 'most heartfelt commiseration'.[20] To his dismay, a missionary communicated the fatal prognosis to the patient and distressed the family.

Scenes depicting Burchell's journey to Klaarwater are illustrated in coloured aquatints or in black-and-white vignettes. The drawings and vivid verbal descriptions work together, and the drawings' captions accentuate at times the influence of the European gaze, and the expectations and assumptions Burchell brings with him. Burchell views the 'admirable perfection of *Nature* in a new light, and not less beautiful in the wilds of Africa'. The novelty of the scenery is 'heightened by the interesting consideration of Human Nature under forms perfectly new to me'.[21] Rivers and human settlements attract his artistic eye. The aquatints *Crossing the Berg River*,[22] dated 23 June, and

Cyprinus aeneus [yellow-fish], 2 September 1811

Scene on the River Gariep,[23] produced on 16 September, reveal Burchell's romantic sensibility, the scenery inspiring 'pleasing sensations'.[24] His first and picturesque view of the 'Hottentot's mode of life' is represented in *A Hottentot Kraal, on the banks of the Gariep* on 17 September.[25] The complex vistas portrayed in these carefully crafted scenic paintings differ markedly from the vignettes, which Dietrich observes were 'quickly executed at the moment the scene or image' impinged on Burchell's retina.[26]

Followed sequentially, the vignettes give a quick visual record of the journey. These 'candid snapshots', as Dietrich calls them,[27] depict humans, scenery and natural history

Passing Roodezands Kloof

Arrival at the Karroo Pass, 13 July 1811

specimens. Science was of consuming interest to Victorians, so precise scientific drawings – such as those of a 'Karro-thorn',[28] 'some *cubic pyrites of iron*'[29] and a close-up of one of the 'crags of the Asbestos rock'[30] – are interspersed among the landscape engravings. Burchell painted a 'Yellow-fish', 'a beautiful kind of carp, entirely of a yellow-green with a brazen lustre', which he found in a deep pool in the Zak River.[31]

One vignette, too dark to be reproduced in proper detail, depicts the wagons and travellers around a blazing fire at the start of their trek. All 'were in the height of good humour' and 'they sat up till midnight, talking and smoking'. The sound of Burchell playing his flute captured everyone's attention and increased their satisfaction.[32] Convivial fireside scenes attest to Burchell's goodwill and personal engagement with men, women, children and animals during the expedition.

On 4 July, on a narrow track in the Western Cape, the wagon had to pass one approaching in the opposite direction. The engraving[33] of this scene shows the precipitous Roodezands Kloof, the Little Berg River (near Tulbagh), the mountains with 'their rocky sides thickly clothed with bushes and trees',[34] the travellers, two wagons and oxen. The landscape presents 'a beautiful and romantic picture', but the terror of travelling on the treacherous track through the kloof can be felt when viewing the drawing. More peaceful is a painting dated 13 July, of the wagons, the unyoked oxen, and the party taking 'up our station, under the shelter of two large bushy trees of Karrée-hout, near a small stream of water'[35] in the Karoo, the 'very door of the desert'.[36] Burchell provides geological and linguistic facts of the area: 'the strata of the mountains here, on each side, are inclined in opposite positions, and curiously curved in undulating

Crossing the Karroo

lines. The word *Karró* belongs to the Hottentot language, and signifies *dry*, or *arid*.[37] On 14 July, the party continued travelling through the Bokkeveld-Karoo. An engraving displays the 'immense plain, unbroken by hill or eminence, stretching before us in every direction, as far as the eye could discern'.[38] The party quit the Karoo plains on 19 July.[39]

Two '*Makke Boschjesmans*', or tame Bushmen, from a kraal near the Zak River, rode up to Burchell, mounted on oxen, on 19 July. Burchell's engraving of this scene depicts the energetic riders trotting away.[40] The impact of colonialism on the men is evident: one of them, called Captain, carried the 'ensign of his authority, a staff about four feet long, having a large tabular top of brass, on which were inscribed a few words, showing that he had been elevated to that rank by Governor Caledon'.[41] The captain, accompanied by four others on oxen, returned the next day.

Contemporary prejudices, rife in Burchell's time, are reflected in his opinion of the Bushmen.

A Bushman chief and his companion on ox-back

This race of people had been pictured to me in the most wretched colors; and, having been led to expect only a set of beings without reason or intellect, I was now much pleased at finding that they might be viewed in a more favourable light, and that the first individuals of this nation, whom we fell in with, were men of lively manners and shrewd understandings. They were all of small stature (about five feet) and dressed partly in the colonial, and partly their own costume.[42]

321 : 1.8.1811.

Gerrit Snyman's Farm, 1 August 1811

Despite the entrenched Eurocentric views typical of his time, Burchell was open-minded about the many kinds of people in the Cape, and interested in their cultural and physical attributes. He displays his fascination with the Boers in his painting of the 'miserable abode' of Gerrit Snyman the veldcornet. It is but one example of how the Cape's inhabitants intrigued him.[43]

Hottentots Sitting Round their Fire[44] is the caption for the next scene Burchell illustrates. The journal entry complementing the picture describes the party experiencing freezing-point temperatures, rain, hail and violent winds in August 1811. Burchell's attention is fixed on the resilience of Speelman, Hannah, Philip and Gert:

> The only shelter my men could find, was a few bushes, against which a mat was placed. Here they sat the whole day, their chief employment being smoking,

326 23.8.1811

Hottentots Sitting Round their Fire, 23 August 1811

Caravan of Waggons assembled at Zak River, on the Borders of the Country of the Bushmen, 3 September 1811

talking, keeping up the fire, or attending their pot. Each in his *jas* (great-coat) defied the weather, and sat quite at ease.[45]

Unlike other travellers of the time, Burchell names his assistants. Social anthropologist Isaac Schapera notes Burchell's focus is firmly on 'his fellow creatures as human beings, and not as mere ethnic specimens'.[46] He comments on each individual 'Hottentot':

The brim of *Speelman's* grand hat was now let down, and, during the rain, completely answered the purpose of an umbrella. *Hannah*, wrapped in her kaross, seldom stirred from her seat under the bush; while *Philip*, to show his greater civilization and polish, seated himself on one of the water-casks, leaving *Gert* to take advantage of a small mound of earth near the fire.[47]

So far the engravings mostly show Burchell's two wagons. On the first day of September, this number increased to eighteen at the Zak River, the northern boundary of the Cape Colony, and the appointed rendezvous with the missionaries' caravan. Burchell's commentary supplements the aquatint *Caravan of Waggons assembled at Zak River, on the Borders of the Country of the Bushmen*:

> on a wide open plain, where nothing covered the red arid soil, except here and there a scrubby stunted bush ... It seemed as if a village had suddenly risen up in the desert. Each waggon had its own fire, around which a little party appeared sitting, generally protected from the wind by a screen of mats. The oxen, sheep, and goats grazing close by; the women going to the river or returning with their

Zak River, 4 September 1811

calabashes filled with water; the children running about at play: the men, some
carrying loads of firewood, others coming home from hunting; together with
horses and dogs moving in all directions; constituted a novel and busy scene that
rendered, by contrast, the silent lifeless waste by which we were surrounded, more
forlorn and cheerless.

At this place happened the birth of our Hottentot captain's child; and, for the
sake of the mother, we delayed our departure: but it did not seem that travelling
was afterwards of any inconvenience, either to her or to the infant.[48]

Burchell's portrayal of the gathering at the river is full of detail and an art form in its
own right. Like Lady Anne Barnard who lived in the Cape from 1797 to 1802, Burchell
painted and described scenes. 'The truth of the matter,' wrote the historian Nicolas
Barker, 'is that Lady Anne was an equal artist in words and paints, and the two could
not be separated in her hands or mind.'[49] The same was true of Burchell.

Not included in the *Travels* is Burchell's watercolour *Zak River*. After crossing the river
on 4 September, Burchell, for the first time, quit 'the jurisdiction and protection of

regular laws, and committed myself to the hostility, or the hospitality, of savage tribes'. Sanguine as always, he writes:

> My notions of human nature were not so harsh as to forbid me expecting virtues
> among savages; and I looked forward with pleasure and increasing eagerness to
> that part of my journey which was hereafter to follow.[50]

Life-threatening challenges did indeed lie ahead: a 'huge lion' was encountered;[51] the Gariep River had to be crossed; the threat of invisible, armed and hostile Bushmen attacking them was always prevalent; and water was scarce.

Burchell's 'talent of descriptive representation'[52] dazzles in this landscape portrayal of the caravan in the silent, bare and open desert:

> The train of waggons, steadily following each other at equal distances, drew a
> lengthened perspective line over the wide landscape, that presented the only object
> on which the eye could fix. While the van was advancing over the highest swell, the
> rear was still far out of sight in the hollow. Waggon behind waggon, slowly rose to
> view; and oft at intervals, the loud clapping of the whip, or the jolting of the

A view of the mountains of the Karreebergen

wheel, disturbed the silence of the atmosphere, rolling its sound in a half echo along the surface of the sun-baked earth. Not a green herb enticed the eye; not a bird winged through the air: the creation here, was nought but earth and sky; the azure vault of heaven, expanded into the boundless aerial space, seemed lifted further from the globe.[53]

Sound, imagery and colour are absent in Burchell's engraving[54] of the caravan crossing 'an immense plain, bounded on the right and on the left, by the level-topped mountains of the *Karreebergen*'.[55] The verbal picture and the 'snap shot' vignette expose Burchell's contrasting modes of representation.

Since leaving the Zak River, the caravan 'had not seen a single native; a circumstance occasioned, most probably by their universal distrust of all strange visitors from out of the Colony'.[56] However, a party of eleven San with three women, confident that the travellers were friendly, came to meet them on 8 September. At first Burchell observed 'in their looks great mistrust, and symptoms of much fear', but this gradually wore off, and 'after we had confirmed the assurances of our peaceable intentions, by presents of tobacco and beads, they recovered their natural tone, and chatted and clacked with each other in a very lively manner'.[57]

Predictably, Burchell the ethnographer focuses on physical appearance: 'They were, in stature, all below five feet; and the women still shorter; their skin was of a sallow brown color, much darkened by dirt and grease.' He is open about European prejudice in his comment that 'with all the remains of ancient prejudices, I could not help viewing as interesting' some young men:

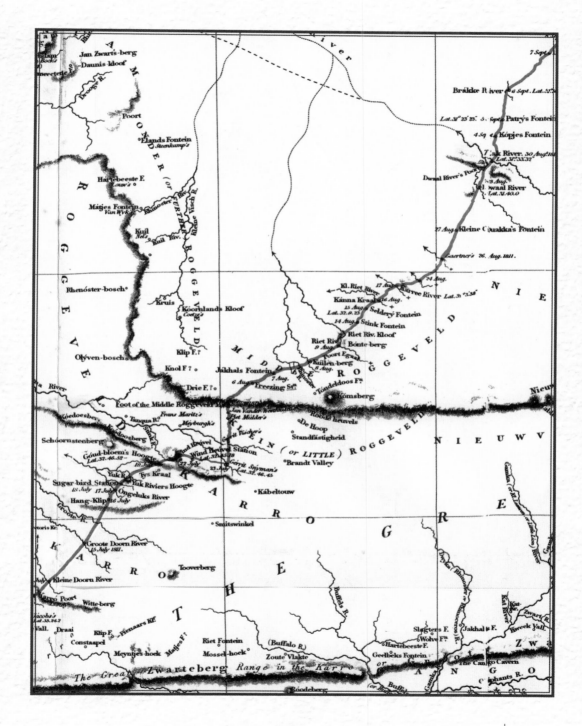

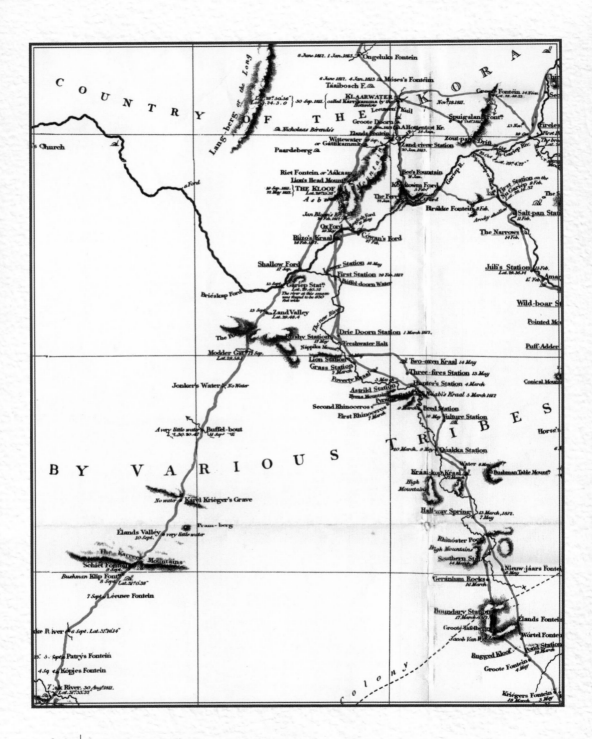

Though small, and delicately made, they appeared firm and hardy; and my attention was forcibly struck by the proportional smallness, and neatness of their hands and feet. This conformation is common (perhaps in Africa, peculiar,) to all the Hottentot race.[58]

A Bushwoman and her child

The young women also attract his attention: 'their countenances had a cast of prettiness, and, I fancied, too, of innocence: their manners were modest, though unreserved'. As a young mother with her infant on her back turned to talk to her companions, Burchell 'drew a sketch of her unperceived'.[59] The impact the visitors had on Burchell is noteworthy: 'I now stood amongst them on their own soil, I never, more than at this moment, longed to possess that command of language, and that talent of descriptive representation, which might enable me to impart all those peculiar sensations with which my first interview with this singular nation, inspired me.'[60]

The next day, he delighted in another encounter with a San party when he descended into a ravine to view a spring, the source of a 'never-failing' supply of water. As he was alone and unarmed, a Khoikhoi advised him to take his gun.[61]

The sound of the voices of two San men and three women, with children on their backs, reverberated in the ravine. Burchell felt 'so much confidence in their good intentions', that he made a sketch of the spot and the San figures.[62] The coloured plate *The Rock Fountain, in the Country of the Bushmen* is based on the sketch. Time slipped away, and the wagons were already in motion when his absence was noticed. He had to 'hasten to overtake the caravan'.[63]

A few days later, on 11 September, the party travelled without water, food or rest for fifty-two and a half miles. Caught in the dark in a thunderstorm, lightning 'dazzled and bewildered them', and even the 'Hottentots themselves became confused, and lost their way'. Burchell, with the help of his compass, pointed his wagon in the correct direction. The Khoikhoi could not conceive how an 'utter stranger' would 'know anything about the way to Klaarwater' and, only after the missionary persuaded them, did they 'suffer themselves to be guided' by Burchell.[64]

Just before twilight, water was discovered, but it came from a 'little dirty hole in

The Rock Fountain, in the Country of the Bushmen, 9 September 1811

the bed of a periodical rivulet' and the oxen and sheep 'trampled it into thick mud'. Unable to assuage their thirst they 'stood around us, incessantly making a mournful piteous noise, as if to reproach us for bringing them into a country where thirst and starvation seemed to await them'.[65] Burchell, displaying such empathy, reveals what J.M. Coetzee terms the 'sympathetic imagination' – a sympathy for animals that allowed him to share at times the being of another.[66] Like Darwin, Burchell has fellow feeling and compassion for humans, animals and insects.

Dangers and difficulties were happily surmounted when the travellers, on 15 September, reached the Gariep River (named the Orange River by Colonel Robert Gordon in 1777)[67] near present-day Prieska. The road to Klaarwater would be 'pleasant and unobstructed', and all could indulge in feelings 'of ease and security'.[68] Burchell's watercolour *Hunting Station near Orange River*, dated 16 September 1811, which is not included in the *Travels*, portrays the sight of human activity that inspired the painting:

'these marks of human labor, appeared to me the more interesting, after traversing so great an extent of country, in which no vestige of art had been seen; for not a trace of the kraals and huts of the Bushmen were observable from our road, as they had been cautiously placed in the most secluded spots, for the purpose of keeping, as much as possible, their situation unknown to all but themselves'.[69]

San figures are in the foreground in the watercolour *Scene on the River Gariep*; a footnote to the painting names the trees: willows, karee trees, acacias, all of these common on the margins of rivers.[70] The scenery elicits literary thoughts: 'The first view … realized those ideas of elegant and classic scenery, which are created in the minds of poets, those alluring fancies of a fairy tale, or the fascinating imagery of a romance.'[71] No other traveller in the Cape can match Burchell's Romantic gusto:

> The waters of the majestic river, flowing in a broad expanse resembling a smooth
> translucent lake, seemed, with their gentle waves, to kiss the shore and bid it
> farewell for ever, as they glided past in their way to the restless ocean; bearing on
> their limpid bosom the image of their wood-clothed banks; while the drooping
> willows leaned over the tide, as if unwilling to lose them; and the long pendent
> branches, dipping their leafy twigs in the stream, seemed fain to follow.[72]

He is 'rapt with the pleasing sensations which the scenery inspired', enjoying it so much that 'here I could have fixed my abode for months: enjoying the delightful shade, and

Hunting Station near Orange River, 16 September 1811

inhaling the refreshing air'.[73] But the river was not fordable from this bank and had to be crossed nine miles higher up.[74] Travails ensued, as the road was very uneven, the wagons threatened to overturn, there were hippopotamus holes, and the oxen had to be restrained from 'turning down with the current'. In the painting, *Shallow Ford, Orange River*, the drama of crossing this formidable barrier complements Burchell's colourful account in the *Travels*:

> As one waggon plunged into the stream, another descended headlong down the steep bank, closely followed by another; and as these moved on, others in their turn advanced from the rear, till the line, stretching entirely across the river, seemed like a bridge of waggons. The train at first took a very oblique direction downwards, till they had reached the middle of the river, and from that point, proceeded directly across to the opposite side. The bottom was found to be full of large pebbles, and the greatest depth no more than two feet and eight inches; but the current was therefore very rapid and strong ... Each waggon took a quarter of an hour to perform the passage, which might be estimated at a little more than a

Scene on the River Gariep, 16 September 1811

Shallow Ford, Orange River, 17 September 1811

quarter of a mile. The oxen were driven through by about a dozen Hottentots; and as many were required to swim the sheep and goats over in safety.[75]

The crossing was accomplished on 17 September without incident, and 'with so much less difficulty than had been expected'.[76]

The travellers now entered a new region 'on the northern side of the Great River': 'the river being impassable to many animals, is a zoological line, marking the southern-most range of some, and the northern-most of others'; it is also a 'botanical limit, in a multitude of instances'.[77] Here, Burchell viewed and painted his 'first genuine *Hottentot kraal*'.[78] In the text, Burchell draws attention to their pastoral lifestyle, before the ravages of colonialism:

These mats, and the form of the hut here represented, more resembling an inverted basket than a building, are the same which have been in use among all the various tribes of Hottentots, from time immemorial; and are, I believe, quite peculiar to this remarkable and distinct race of men. Such huts have their convenience for the Hottentot's mode of life: they may be taken to pieces in an hour, and packed on the back of a couple of oxen, together with all their utensils and young children, and transported with ease and expedition to any part of the country ... Nor is it likely, so long as they continue to lead a pastoral life, and are free to roam wherever they please, that they will voluntarily exchange their tent of mats, for any dwelling of solid and immovable construction.[79]

A Hottentot Kraal, on the banks of the Gariep, 17 September 1811

In contrast, the Khoikhoi Burchell encountered in towns, villages and on the farms of colonists were certainly not 'free to roam wherever they please'.[80] By the end of the eighteenth century they had been forced into the role of subsistence labourers, herding the Boers' cattle rather than their own.[81]

Another colonial legacy, tobacco dependency, is unashamedly exploited by Burchell. In his amusing words:

> We were visited this morning [18 September 1811] by a party of ten Bushmen, who had been obliged to cross the river to us. I neglected no opportunity of making friends with this nation, and had already discovered that in negotiating a treaty of peace and alliance with them, *tobacco* is a most successful plenipotentiary, or rather a *sine-qua-non*.[82]

The party remained with Burchell's for most of the day, although the description of the visit is brief.

The heat was intense on the way to the Asbestos Mountains. After travelling through the night, the party arrived at the Kloof, a village situated in a Romantic setting with mountains on all sides. The settlement was 'under the religious care and instruction of my fellow travellers', the missionaries, and Burchell beheld with pleasure the friendly welcome they all received.[83] The missionaries visited the different dwellings and examined the state of the settlement,

Rocks in the Asbestos Mountains

and in the 'cool of the evening' on 19 September, they took leave of Burchell and 'proceeded on their way to Klaarwater, accompanied only by that part of our caravan, whose homes were at that station: the rest either remaining at the Kloof, or taking a different road, each to his own kraal'.[84]

The villagers harassed Burchell by begging 'strenuously for some article in the waggon; and, when that was refused, asked, unabashed for something else', but in a 'good-natured way [he] withstood almost all their importunities'.[85] He and his party, wishing to rest there for a few days, selected a convenient place for the wagons. They endured the bleak surroundings 'at the mouth of a narrow valley, closed both at the upper end, and on each side, by high rocky mountains' for ten days: 'No grass, nor verdure, covered the stony ground; a few scattered bushes contributed scarcely a tint of green to vary the barren brown color which distinguished all the mountains around.'[86] Burchell made significant geological discoveries in these mountains, identifying asbestos and describing two derivative gemstones: 'a handsome kind of *jasper*, brown, striped with black' and 'a green opal'.[87] An engraving by Burchell of one of the crags of the asbestos rocks[88] illustrates the thin horizontal layers in which asbestos, of a blue colour, is found.

The party departed from the Kloof on 29 September and, at eleven o'clock that night, unyoked at a spring called Gattikamma, where a kraal of Koras were stationed with their cattle.[89] They wanted the strange white man to 'come out of the waggon'. Burchell decided to entertain them with his 'looking-glass': 'they called to each other to come and see; and presently the end of my waggon looked like a heap of faces, all distorted

Kora Hottentots, 10 December 1811

either with surprise or laughter'.[90] Everyone, including Burchell, was light-hearted and mirthful. Instructive ethnographic facts follow:

> The people usually called *Koránas*, are a numerous, and distinct, tribe of Hottentot race. In features they possess the common character, but in stature are larger than the *Bushmen*, and equal to the *Hottentots*, properly so called: by which term I would be understood to mean the aborigines of the Colony. In customs and manners, the *Koránas* are several degrees more civilized than the *Bushmen*, and possess much cattle; but their dress and arms are the same in kind, though better in quality. They are considered rather as peaceable and friendly people: their mode of life is purely pastoral, and, consequently, their places of abode unsettled.[91]

The linguistics of the people also interests him: the Kora language, a 'dialect of the Hottentot', possessed a great number of words peculiar to it, but 'seemed to require a much less frequent use of the clap of the tongue than the Bushmen dialect; but, at the same time, a little more than that of the Cape Hottentots'.[92]

Burchell continues his scientific discourse, this time on the structure of their communities: 'this nation is found dispersed widely over the country on the northern side of the Gariep', with many of their moveable villages found along the river banks. He remarks that 'it is difficult to define the *boundaries* of the country inhabited by these wandering African nations', and comments that 'with respect to *territory*, they have none of those ideas which a European would attach to the word'. He provides an African perspective:

> The soil appears never to be considered as property, nor is it hardly ever thought worth claiming or disputing the possession of: the water and pasturage of it, is all that is rated of any value; and when these are exhausted, the soil is abandoned as useless. Wherever they find a spring unoccupied, there they feel themselves at liberty to plant their huts; and, on their removal, others, if they chuse, come and fix their quarters. This last observation, though holding good in many cases with respect to different tribes, is applicable more strictly to different kraals, or families, of the same tribe.[93]

Like the Korana, both the Khoikhoi and the San had no conception of private property. Once settlers laid claim to land, water and grazing, the nomadic pastoral lifestyles of these people ended. The Khoikhoi began to work for European settlers, but not the nomadic San hunter-gatherers, who had no tradition of contractual, client labour.[94]

Burchell left the kraal the next day with a 'favourable impression of the friendly character of the whole tribe'. He was amazed 'that their crowding round me, was from pure curiosity … strongly proved by their never once begging, even for tobacco. This last circumstance appeared to me the more remarkable, as I had been told that I should find begging an universal practice'.[95]

The distance of twenty-two miles from the Kora kraal to Klaarwater was covered in seven and a half hours. The road was rocky and the wagons rattled over the stones. Burchell's party reached Klaarwater on 30 September 'at that hour of the night, or rather morning, when all its inhabitants were fast asleep'; the 'loud and ceaseless barking' of the watchful dogs eventually announcing their safe arrival. The missionary Mr Anderson came out to welcome them, and as soon as the oxen were unyoked, the party 'preferred sleep to supper; and the men, wrapping their karosses closely round them, laid themselves down under the waggons for the night'.[96]

Burchell and his party planned to remain in Klaarwater for three months – 'a pleasing sensation seemed, with all of us, to attend the idea of being about to terminate a long journey'.[97] Dangerous challenges had been overcome, and 'it was at the small price of a few bodily comforts, that the gratification of traversing and exploring so interesting a portion of the globe, was obtained'.[98] Burchell, finding 'himself eight hundred miles in the interior of Africa', reflects on travelling: 'to an individual so situated, reflections and comparisons constitute the salt, without which travelling would be insipid, and little better than fatigue and drudgery'.[99]

5

'Some peculiar feelings and a strange interest in everything'[1]

Klaarwater and an excursion to the Ky-Gariep
October to November 1811

WILLIAM BURCHELL IMAGINED KLAARWATER AS 'a picturesque spot surrounded by trees and gardens, with a river running through a neat village, where a tall church stood, a distant beacon to mark that Christianity had advanced thus far into the wilds of Africa'. However,

> the first glance now convinced me how false may often times be the notions which men form of what they have not seen. The trees of my imagination vanished leaving nothing in reality but a few which the missionaries themselves had planted; the church sunk to a barn-like building of reeds and mud; the village was merely a row of half a dozen reed cottages; the river was but a rill; and the situation an open, bare, and exposed place, without any appearance of a garden, excepting that of the missionaries.[2]

The engraving of the reed-and-mud church shocks the reader expecting a European-style building such as the church in Genadendal. His watercolour, *A View of Klaarwater, looking towards the North-East*,[3] illuminates various aspects of the village: the kraals for oxen and sheep fenced in with large branches of trees; the position of Burchell's wagons; and various groups of Khoikhoi, some basking in the sun, others smoking or conversing, 'some stretched out upon sheepskins spread on the ground', and four men working on sheepskins.

Burchell, typically, maps the village facts: about twenty-five Khoikhoi houses surround the church, while others are scattered within fifty miles in various directions. The population in 1809 was 'seven hundred and eighty-four souls'. Koras and Bushmen also

The church at Klaarwater

live in the vicinity, but are not part of the community. They 'cannot be considered as belonging to the establishment, since they show no desire to receive the least instruction from the missionaries, nor do they attend their meetings, but continue to remove from place to place, a wild and independent people'. Burchell's report covers the ancestry of the 'tribe of Hottentots',[4] including the numbers of oxen, cows and calves they own;[5] vegetables grown; an unfinished building[6] (proof, according to Burchell, of the laziness of the Khoikhoi); weather;[7] and medical facts. An ophthalmic condition, smallpox, convulsions, jaundice and 'the most dangerous malady', a cancerous ulcer, are itemised.[8]

Although disappointed at Klaarwater's appearance,[9] Burchell looked on the labours of the missionaries with 'double interest'.[10] Agricultural images convey his hopes for the future of the mission: 'Yet, notwithstanding its discouraging appearance, this colony of Hottentots, and its different outposts, is a field in which the seeds of civilization and religion may be sown with a probability of success.'[11] During his stay, Burchell made portrait sketches of the missionaries – Lambert Jansz from Holland; Cornelius Kramer, who was the first South African to volunteer as a missionary among the indigenous inland tribes;[12] and William Anderson from London. Burchell's feelings on the first night he dined with the missionaries expose his European consciousness and his delight in everything novel:

> the circumstance of our being the only white people in this part of the world, and
> all seated round the same table, together with the idea of our being in the heart of

A View of Klaarwater, looking towards the North-East, 5 June 1812

a wilderness, and surrounded only by savage nations, created in me some peculiar feelings, and a strange interest in everything that was passing, and in all that I saw about me.[13]

On arrival in Klaarwater, Burchell's first priority was to attend to the thin, weak oxen he had travelled with from Cape Town. Meticulous records were to be kept, and specimens preserved and carefully packed. Science had a downside. For Burchell, the tasks were 'very far from being an interesting or agreeable occupation in the midst of pursuits of science'; but they were 'a duty of the first importance, and one which consumed a large and valuable portion of my time'.[14] The wagons needed maintenance as well, and Burchell had to contend with the problems of his employees. Speelman's hut burnt down on 20 October – 'the whole conflagration was occasioned by his dear spouse's tobacco-pipe'.[15]

Even more serious, on 21 November Gert Roodezand's gun 'burst' as he fired it to drive away crows from eating the stock of dried meat he was protecting. His hand was literally blown to pieces.[16] The Khoisan believed in the powers of '*Boekoe-azyn*' (Buchu

vinegar), and Burchell confidently used it to clean the wound. Dr Roger Stewart, chronicling Burchell's medical challenges during his travels, highlights this ability of Burchell to integrate the use of indigenous herbal medicines with his own knowledge of European medicines.[17] He successfully treated the wound, and within six weeks 'the wound was covered over with a new skin, and the thumb and finger were reunited'. When the matter was over, Burchell said, 'I saw reason for rejoicing that I possessed neither instruments nor the skill of a surgeon; for, otherwise, my poor Hottentot would have been all the remainder of his life with a useless stump, instead of half a hand.'[18] Particulars on the management of the wound are given in detail in the *Travels* for the benefit of other travellers.[19]

On Sundays in Klaarwater, Burchell attended church services. However, the 'ordinary routine of the business of the mission' failed to impress him. After four months of observing the missionaries and their 'converts' in action, he censures misleading accounts sent to Europe by missionary societies. He is aware of the difficulties of civilising 'wild men', but instead of converting them 'to new opinions in religion and morality', he thinks they should be instructed 'in such arts as have for them an evident utility'.[20] An Enlightened man of reason, Burchell is realistic about the practical needs of the colony's indigenous inhabitants, believing much could be gained from educating them in European arts and skills:

> If there really do exist so much goodwill … towards all the untutored savages of the globe … why, therefore, has it not shown itself in some endeavour directed exclusively to the object of instructing them in those arts and practices, from which we derive those superior comforts which, in a worldly point of view, distinguish us from them? Why have no missionaries been sent to them with this as their first great object? … I mean, that as mere men, and having to deal with mere men, there is no absurdity in trying how far worldly means are likely to produce those good effects on our fellow-creatures, which we are so desirous of witnessing.[21]

Lambert Jansz – Portrait Sketch,
3 December 1811

Burchell, in his contacts with 'mere men' encountered in his travels, certainly uses 'worldly means' – food, tobacco, friendship, music – to promote goodwill. Benevolence and goodwill were highly esteemed in the Enlightenment, and Burchell's hospitality and humanitarian actions are very much part of this ethos.

During his stay in Klaarwater, Burchell went on a twenty-six day excursion to the Ky-Gariep River. Joining him were his own party, as well as Klaarwater men, women and children, Jansz the missionary, and a few horses, sheep, goats and dogs. On 24 October 1811, ten loaded wagons left Klaarwater for the river.

For Burchell, the object of the excursion was scientific: he wanted to explore the 'upper part of the course of

Cornelius Kramer – Portrait Sketch,
6 December 1811

the *Gariep*, and two or three large branches which were said to join it higher up'.[22] McKay designates Burchell the 'first white man to visit the confluence of the Riet and Vaal Rivers, and also that of the Vaal and the Orange'.[23] With 'indisputable reasoning', Burchell hypothesised that floods and inundations of the Gariep River were occasioned by water coming from the 'highest part of the southernmost quarter of Africa'. Using scientific language, he states:

> There is, it must be acknowledged, some presumption in thus pronouncing the nature of a country never yet visited by any traveller; but as we are living in the age of hypotheses in geography and natural philosophy, the presumption will appear the less remarkable; nor indeed do I much care whether this hypothesis be hereafter proved or disproved, if it do but excite the curiosity of some properly qualified traveller to explore that region.[24]

William Anderson – Portrait Sketch, 1 December 1811

Stimulating the scientific wonder of other travellers and the readers of the *Travels* is Burchell's principal concern. From a natural history perspective, the excursion was exhilarating: plants, trees, animals, birds, fish, insects and worms new to him were discovered and identified, and his collection of specimens multiplied. He also had rare opportunities to investigate 'man in an uncivilized state of society' by interacting with the Khoikhoi, the San and the Koras at various points in the journey.

The hippo hunt was a highlight. The hunters, their families and dogs all looked forward to enjoying 'a plenteous feast of Hippopotamus-fat' when it was over.[25] Two watercolours, *Landing the Hippopotamus* and *Cutting up the Hippopotamus*, not included in the *Travels*, depict the busy party 'surrounded by the sweetest

Gert Roodezand [after the gun damaged his right hand] – Portrait, 17 August 1812

Landing the Hippopotamus, Vaal River, 30 October 1811

Cutting up the Hippopotamus, Vaal River, 30 October 1811

scenery that landscape can produce'.[26] 'Every man was now turned butcher'; it was sometime before Burchell could get them to 'cut off the head, that I might draw it'.[27] His picture of the hippo head 'is a most faithful and comprehensive memorandum'[28] supplemented by anatomical details in the text.

The safari increased Burchell's knowledge of the San people. He saw the 'Kysi-pits' – the holes the San dug to entrap animals. Contact with San men, women and children who joined the Klaarwater 'sea-cow eaters'

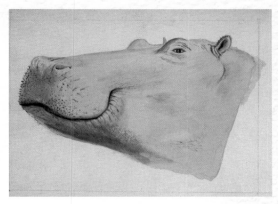

Head of the Hippopotamus or River-horse

was harmonious: 'our hunting seemed to have spread a joy over their kraal, and they viewed us not as intruders among them, but as friends of a most useful kind'.[29] Burchell was clearly at ease in their company:

> Our Bushmen friends, wrapped in their karosses, lay down also, within a few yards of us, and took their rest; a proof of the really friendly terms we were upon. For it was not possible to have given a stronger assurance of our confidence in each other's good intentions, than that of lying thus exposed and unprotected, in each other's power, perfectly unsuspicious of treachery, and fearless of harm.[30]

Burchell believed he had a 'more friendly reception' on his trip than other European travellers, and attributed his safety to the 'kind treatment' he received from local inhabitants. He was alert to the manners and customs of the local people, and observed that 'all the offal, bones, and head, fell by custom to the Bushmen's share. No sooner was the carcase cut open, than they fell to work upon the entrails; occasionally wiping the grease from their fingers on to their arms, legs, and thighs; they were, besides, plentifully bespattered with the blood and filth, each rejoicing at the portion he had obtained.' Also present 'among these happy, dirty creatures' was the 'prettiest young *Bush-girl* I had yet seen'. But to his European eye, he saw her airs and dress as revealing her 'vanity, and too evident consciousness of her superiority'; this 'rendered her less pleasing'.[31]

About the girl's female companions, he says:

> the season of beauty had long passed by, and, if that season with other nations may justly be called shortlived, it may among Bushwomen, with more than equal

justice, be termed momentary. In five or six years after their arrival at womanhood, the fresh plumpness of youth has already given way to the wrinkles of age; and unless we viewed them with the eye of commiseration and philanthropy, we should be inclined to pronounce them the most disgusting of human beings.[32]

Author Elana Bregin points out that the writings of early travellers in the Cape frequently depicted Bushmen as a 'degraded and subhuman species'.[33] Burchell reiterates this perception, but for him the 'quick fading, and decay of the bloom and appearance of youth' is caused by hardship which comes from 'an uncertain and irregular supply of food, exposure to every inclemency of weather, and a want of cleanliness which increases with years'.[34]

The 'beautiful *symmetrical form*' of a San guide with 'a gait the most easy and free' impresses him:

> All the limbs, unshackled by clothing, moved with a grace never perhaps seen in Europe. The contemplation of his well-proportioned, although small and delicate figure; his upright, manly port; his firm and bold step; and the consciousness of liberty, which beamed in his countenance; afforded an indescribable pleasure; and I envied the Bushmen the uncontrolled freedom of their lives ...[35]

Thoughts of the advantages enjoyed by superior, civilised European society instantly surface. Burchell saw no way in which the freedom the San enjoyed could be unified with European ideals: '*civilization* and this species of *liberty*' cannot go 'hand in hand'. But,

> the Wisdom of Providence scatters its blessings over the globe, with, perhaps, an even hand; yet, if not, that secret influence of Nature, which teaches every nation to view their native soil and customs as superior to all around them, perfectly regulates the balance of worldly enjoyments.[36]

Burchell's 'train of reflections'[37] – from the movement of the San guide, to European civilisation, to the wisdom of Providence and Nature – give a sense of his extraordinary agility between different zones of thought and observation. He displays a remarkable ability to draw knowledge from the objects of study encountered on his journey. Through this, he goes beyond the generic boundaries of travel writing.

For Burchell, dogs are a unique species. He believes they 'feel a desire to be useful to man'[38] and spontaneously attach themselves to humans. His discourse on dogs during the hippo hunt is unique. The dogs,

> who had been slyly watching all our movements … must, in some sagacious manner, have caught a notion of the carnivorous nature of the expedition; otherwise, so wretchedly thin and emaciated as they were, they never could have felt the animation and strength to produce those rapid vibrations of tail, and to caper round us with such delight, as they exhibited at first setting off.[39]

Burchell singles out three of his companion dogs: his favourite, faithful little terrier, a staghound, and Wantrouw, 'a large white flap-eared dog, having two or three brown spots, wiry hair, and a bearded muzzle'. Tragically, the terrier ran beneath the shade of the moving wagon to escape the extreme heat and was crushed to death. This sad but common occurrence on many wagon trips through the Cape 'prevented all further enjoyment for the rest of the day'.[40]

Burchell provides a humorous biography of Wantrouw: 'of the canine species [he] was the greatest traveller'. He was born in Tulbagh, but when he arrived at the 'age of doghood', he deserted his owners and attached himself to the missionary Mr Kramer, who named him Wantrouw (Afrikaans for 'distrust' or 'suspect'). During the journey from the Cape, Burchell became Wantrouw's favourite, and at Klaarwater he 'took up his quarters at my station'. But Wantrouw soon acquired a dislike of the 'monotony of his prospects' in Klaarwater, and 'from that time commenced the new era of his life'.[41]

By the time the party left the Ky-Gariep River, the faithful dogs no longer excited that 'painful compassion for their wretched lean bodies'. Instead, 'their sleek and improved appearance, their contented looks, declared them to have been living in plenty and enjoyment, heightened at the same time by perfect freedom'.[42]

Burchell and Jansz the missionary were determined to explore a new route back to Klaarwater from the Ky-Gariep, through a different part of the country, 'but the Klaarwater Hottentots showed no such disposition to oblige':

> They talked of nothing but the difficulties and dangers of the course I wished to take; there was, they said, no beaten road; a certain steep, rocky ascent, would be found impassable; the hook-thorns would tear our clothes to pieces; the lions

would eat up half our oxen; and, finally, the Bushmen, who in that direction were uncommonly savage, would murder us all.

Burchell, however, knew the real reason why some of the Klaarwater people refused to take this route: 'In this manner they are too often in the habit of inventing any tales that may answer their own views; for, the truth was, they wished to join the party of women whom we had left behind cutting rushes.'[43]

The Klaarwater men drove off, taking the road to the part of the river where the women had been left to gather rushes. Burchell returned by a more northerly route, setting out on 13 November, and choosing to pass through Groote Fontein (now Campbell).

Having derived much pleasure from the river and the woods, Romantic Burchell left the river with regret, and while surveying 'its glittering surface, my imagination personified its ever-flowing stream, and warmly apostrophized it with a last farewell'.[44] The return journey from the river was tough. The engraving *Travelling over a plain abounding in ant-hills* illustrates the wagons journeying 'over a country without roads, and the deep track of the waggon wheels over an untravelled soil'.[45] There were storms, prowling lions, Khoisan robbers,[46] predatory '*Wilde Honde*' (wild dogs),[47] wagon trouble when a wheel of the captain's rickety wagon shattered,[48] and an encounter with a puff adder. Indomitable Burchell took on all the challenges with gusto, and, ever the man of science, he devised a process to preserve the skin, and for the benefit of other travelling naturalists, systematically, and in detail, outlines his method.[49]

Travelling over a plain abounding in ant-hills

The party reached Groote Fontein on 14 November, where a path in a kloof led up the mountain. This path proved impassable as torrential rain had eroded it, and numerous holes and ravines prevented a safe passage across. Six men spent two days repairing the road and removing large blocks of stone with spades and pickaxes.

On 16 November, waiting for the men to complete this task, Burchell discovered 'indigent Bushmen' living in a rock shelter.[50] For archae-

A group of the Hunting Hyenas, called Wild Dogs

ologist A.J.B. Humphreys, Burchell's 'eye-witness' description of the San is a historical record of a hunter-gatherer way of life in the Campbell area.[51]

The rock shelter has been called Burchell's Shelter in honour of Burchell and the description he gave of its inhabitants.[52] His account of some of the last of the Stone Age hunter-gatherers has enabled archaeologists to examine the occupation of the shelter from both an archaeological and historical point of view. Altogether, Burchell spent four days with the San. His observation of them merits being quoted in full for its meticulous description of an ancient and fading practice of survival in the southern African wilderness:

In this vicinity, we discovered a kraal of *Bushmen*. Their numbers did not exceed twenty, and their abode was merely a cavern in the side of the mountain, sheltered by huge impending crags. They had no earthly possessions whatever, excepting the miserable bit of dirty skin which hung round them; their bows and arrows, a few hassagays, a knife, and two or three ostrich egg-shells. They had not even a hut, or a few mats, like most of their countrymen. Neither beads, nor any thing intended as ornament, were to be seen upon them: their persons, meagre and filthy, too plainly bespoke that hunger had often been their lot. Except when any game was caught in their pitfalls, which, they complained, seldom happened, the only procurable support of life, was the wild roots which they daily dug up in the plains; and these, not found but by long and wearisome search: the eggs of ants, the bodies of snakes or lizards, a tortoise, or an ostrich egg, met with accidentally, formed the only variety in their wretched food. Their life, and that of the wild beasts, their fellow inhabitants of the land, were the same. Of both, the only care seemed to be that of feeding themselves, and of bringing up their young. The four men who visited us today, exhibited their lank, shrivelled bodies, and dry parched arms and legs, to convince us how much they needed provisions, and how long they had been without grease or animal food. They looked first wishfully at our pots which stood on the fire, and then submissively at us. Truly, these were the most destitute of beings, and the lowest in the scale of man.[53]

Burchell, in precise but lively prose, enlivens and brilliantly illustrates the vanished world of these hunter-gatherers for modern readers.

The four San men, on 16 November, 'squatted on the ground by the fire, with the rest of our people' and with 'dog-like voracity' ate the meat provided by Burchell.[54] The tobacco they were given 'raised their enjoyment to its highest'. Burchell sat among them so he could 'better watch their manners', but 'their smoking absorbed all their thoughts, and created an incapacity, as well as a disinclination, for conversation'. He retired to his wagon and played his flute to see if the 'sound would have any effect upon them'. It did. The San came to the wagon and 'expressed themselves pleased' with the flute.[55] Their chief – an old man who Burchell said looked ten years younger four days after consuming Burchell's plentiful supply of food – was particularly impressed. He 'was considered a good performer on the *Goráh*, an instrument of the greatest antiquity.' Burchell was curious to hear a genuine Khoisan musical instrument and asked him to come back the next day with his gorah.[56]

The musician returned, bringing several women and his entire family. Burchell made sure all were 'well feasted'. His *Portrait of a Bushman, playing on the Gorah* shows the musician sitting on a rock and playing the instrument. In the text accompanying the scene, Burchell compares the appearance of the gorah to the bow of a violin, but when played it is a 'stringed, and a wind instrument combined'. It also resembles a trumpet in the way different tones are produced. The instrument consists 'merely of a slender stick, or bow, on which a string of catgut is strained', and has a flat piece at the end which is applied to the lips and vibrates 'by strong inspirations, and expirations, of the breath'.[57]

Burchell humorously describes the performance of the musician 'resting his elbows on his knees, putting one fore-finger into his ear, and the other into his wide nostril'.

[He] commenced his solo, and continued it with great earnestness, over and over again. The exertion which it required to bring out the tones loudly, was very evident; and, in his anxious haste to draw breath at every note, our *Orpheus* gave us into the bargain, intermingled with his music, certain grunting sounds which would have highly pleased the pigs; and, if any had been in the country, would indubitably have drawn them all round him, if only out of curiosity to know what was the matter.[58]

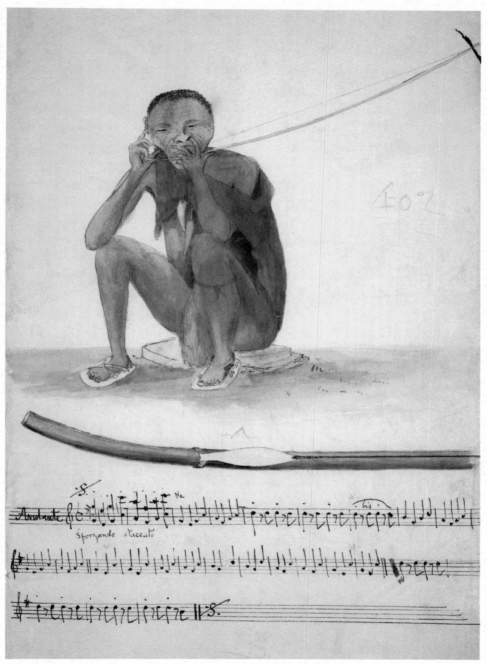

Portrait of a Bushman, playing on the Gorah, 17 November 1811

As Burchell listened to the music, he wrote down the notes played and sketched the man's portrait. Explanatory footnotes in the *Travels* specify the details of the musician's appearance and aboriginal dress.

Of the women who accompanied the gorah player, Burchell says the following:

> Our female visitors, who were past the middle age, were extremely filthy and ugly; their small blinking eyes seemed as if nearly closed, or sunk into their head; wrinkles, filled with dirt, covered their faces and body; their hair was clotted together in large lumps, with the accumulated grease and dust of years, perhaps of their whole lives; and the odor with which they tainted the air, kept me at the distance of a couple of yards, the nearest at which a person having any delicacy of smell, could endure their presence. A wooden bowl, in which was left a quantity of liquid Hippopotamus grease, was eagerly seized upon, and its contents drunk off, with an avidity most nauseous and disgusting to behold; while that which still adhered to the bowl, they carefully scraped out with their hands, and smeared upon their bodies.[59]

Burchell is again unable to separate himself from Eurocentric viewpoints. His vivid and very critical reaction to the physical presence of these women is biased and harsh.

An earnest ethnographer, Burchell was curious to know 'what degree of *intellect* these beings possessed'. Using an interpreter, he asked them what they considered to be good and bad actions, and also showed them a looking-glass, which amused them. In Burchell's opinion, however, this did not excite 'in their minds one single idea'. He was not impressed: 'I may not, perhaps, be doing them an injustice by asserting that, whether capable of reflection or not, these individuals never exerted it.'[60]

For Burchell, the scenes at the shelter triggered comparisons between wild men and famous European thinkers.

> Their miserable poverty-stricken appearance excited the greatest compassion; and as they stood before me, this wretched picture of human nature created a train of reflections perfectly new to my mind. What I had as yet seen of man in a wild state, had amused while it interested and instructed me; but this sad resemblance, in outward shape, to those great, intellectual and elevated characters, whose genius and talents have made their names immortal among us, distressed me to melancholy; and while my eyes were fixed in painful observation on their vacant countenances, I asked myself, What is man? and had almost said; Surely all the

inhabitants of the globe never sprang from the same origin! These men seemed, indeed, the outcast of the Bushman race.

His conclusion:

> I have now, I think, beheld and known the lowest of the human species; and it has taught me a lesson of humility and gratitude; it has rendered still greater, my admiration and respect for men of intellect and cultivated minds; it has also taught me to be thankful to the industrious workman; to feel kind compassion for the uneducated and the uncivilized; and to despise the idle, the arrogant, and vain.[61]

There is nothing of John Keats's 'cold philosophy'[62] of science in Burchell's analysis of the San. A true Romantic, he openly expresses his personal feelings. But, typical of his time, his perspective is inescapably European.

The wagons left Groote Fontein on 18 November and arrived in Klaarwater the next day. The knowledge Burchell had gained on the trip to the Ky-Gariep – especially his 'experience in dealings and converse with wild people' – gave him confidence: 'I thought myself now to be, in some measure, qualified for a journey further into the continent', but at the same time 'was anxious for the arrival of the day of my departure from Klaarwater'.[63] Two months after his visit to the Gariep, Burchell would write:

> The *rainy season* had at length commenced … I had never experienced any thing more refreshing than this alteration of weather, after so long a drought. That constant languor which I had lately suffered from intense heat, vanished at once, and was succeeded by the most agreeable sensations, inspiring an unusual cheerfulness. I know not how to account for the great change it produced, not only in my bodily feelings, but even in those of my mind. My nerves and muscles thus braced and invigorated, I fancied that I possessed the strength to walk the whole length of Africa. Impatient of inactivity, I longed to roam over boundless plains, or climb the lofty mountain; all my troubles and difficulties retired to the furthest distance, where I viewed them diminish almost to nothing.[64]

Burchell feels invigorated and thirsty for adventure after his brief interlude in Klaarwater; the Romanticism and grandeur of his perspective is awe-inspiring and almost contagious. Four days later, however, Burchell discovered that the missionaries in Klaarwater were sabotaging his attempts to recruit men to accompany him to Litakun.[65]

6

'The chief obstacle is the want of proper men'[1]

Klaarwater and Graaff-Reinet
November 1811 to May 1812

BURCHELL'S INTENTION – after his return from the Ky-Gariep on 19 November 1811 – was to remain in Klaarwater for six weeks before setting out to visit the 'Bachapins' (now called the Batlhaping) in the Tswana town of Litakun (now Dithakong), 180 miles from Klaarwater. Two months later, he was still in Klaarwater, having been unable to organise a suitable group of people to accompany him on his journey to the Bachapins.

Burchell was unaware during his Ky-Gariep expedition in October and November 1811 that people in Klaarwater were fabricating stories to prevent men from accompanying him to Litakun. After hearing a great deal of village talk, it was his assistant Gert who eventually informed him of the community's opposition to his journey. Rumours were circulating that Burchell's party would follow the same route as the ill-fated expedition led by Dr Cowan and Captain Donovan in 1808, and that 'all would be murdered by the savages'.[2] The death of the two Klaarwater Khoikhoi who were members of the massacred party still weighed heavily on the whole community. With the death of Mrs Kramer – the wife of the missionary Cornelius Kramer – in January 1812, the shadow of loss looming over Klaarwater grew even larger.

In a letter to Mr Polemann in Cape Town, dated 14 January 1812, Burchell reveals his frustration at his current state of affairs: 'I am situated very unpleasantly owing to want of men.' He rails at the lack of options he has in Klaarwater:

> The people of Klaarwater are, I believe, the laziest men in the world; yet I am
> reduced to the necessity of soliciting some of them to accompany me; which,
> I fear, I shall find great difficulty in doing, as the two men taken from here by the

late travellers, are not returned, and it is suspected that I am not coming back this way again.[3]

Burchell had no intention of pursuing the same course of that fatal expedition, but he was unable to reassure his men and others from Klaarwater of this fact, and was exasperated at trying to convince them otherwise: 'I had the mortification to find that all I could say appeared to have very little effect.'[4]

Always fair-minded, Burchell acknowledged the assistance he received from the missionaries at Klaarwater and the kindness of their wives, believing they could help him smooth away his difficulties and obtain the required number of men. He received 'nothing but the most disheartening representations' in return.[5] The missionaries were unwavering in their scheme to subvert Burchell's plans, and he, understandably, 'could not help giving way to some depression of spirits, the effect rather of anxiety, when I felt myself assailed on all sides by teazing obstructions, and my plans defeated in every quarter'.[6]

By 26 January 1812, three days after Mrs Kramer's passing, Burchell was desperate to leave Klaarwater: 'I was now become impatient to pursue my journey' as 'almost every day brought forth some disappointment, or some disagreeable occurrence'.[7] Determined to travel to Litakun regardless of the resistance he received from the Klaarwater missionaries, Burchell decided to weigh up his options.

Cape Town was one possible location in which to recruit men, but the distance to the town was great. Burchell searched his map for another part of the colony, and 'immediately fixed on the village of Graaff-Reinet', where he could get assistance from the landdrost Anders Stockenström.[8] Burchell did not know at this point that Stockenström had been murdered on 28 December 1811.

An egalitarian leader, he also consulted his own men. All agreed they should undertake the journey to Graaff-Reinet but without the wagons, since the route was unknown and possibly impassable for vehicles. Burchell paid a secret visit to the village of the Kloof and managed to enlist seventy-year-old Cobus Berends, as well as Ruiter, who was very useful as an interpreter.[9]

Armed with a solution to his troubles, Burchell's adventurous spirit felt revived at the prospect of escaping the stifling gloom of Klaarwater to travel and explore once more.

In the *Travels*, the dramatic unravelling of the sabotaging actions of Klaarwater's residents is interspersed with natural history discoveries; an elephant hunt; a vexatious robbery in which he lost his supply of meat; an encounter with an orphaned zebra foal; the splitting of Burchell's flute; the successful distillation of a 'liquor of a strong and spirituous taste' from a 'species of peppermint' Burchell discovered growing wild;[10] and the melancholy death of Mrs Kramer.

In the midst of these difficulties and dangers, Burchell falls back on his love of natural history and exploration, which have always helped in making his 'troubles and difficulties … diminished almost to nothing'.[11] He has faith in the 'Providence of that Great Being whose works and whose wisdom in this remote corner of the creation, I was desirous of studying and making the objects of my meditation'.[12] Through this he discovers the 'the genuine pleasure which Nature bestows only on those who view, with a broad admiring eye, the beauty and perfection of all her works, equally stupendous in the smallest insect, and the glorious picture of the starry heavens'.[13]

The horizon of Burchell's attention while preparing to leave Klaarwater is vast. Bold and creative language shape his descriptions of various incidents, and his linguistic virtuosity ensures that a story is never dull or depressing. Language, to borrow a phrase from the linguist Geoffrey Leech, is used at full stretch,[14] in strikingly different registers. Burchell's verbal creativity enlivens the intense emotional passages and the philosophical reflections in which he engages with the intellectual debates of his time.

The visual idiom at this time, in the form of engravings, is static, symbolic of Burchell's confinement in Klaarwater. It contains no movement until he prepares for his departure to Graaff-Reinet. Instead of wagons travelling over changing landscapes, four still-life vignettes depict a Buchu plant,[15] a grapple plant,[16] some rocks at Leeuwenkuil,[17] and the hut of a Khoikhoi chief.[18]

For the French philosopher Michel Foucault, natural history 'is nothing more than the nomination of the visible. Hence its apparent simplicity.'[19] Burchell, by contrast, is adamant that natural history observations must extend 'beyond the narrow field of nomenclature'; he is critical of naturalists 'satisfied with amassing collections of curious objects, simply for the pleasure of possessing them'.[20] Astronomy, ornithology, botanical seasons, frogs, weather conditions, atmospheric heat, whirlwinds and poisons used on the deadly arrows of the San engage him in Klaarwater. Throughout the *Travels*, Burchell acclaims the indigenous knowledge of the Khoisan, admiring their scientific knowledge of toxins:

This shows how attentively the nation have studied the horrid art, and how well they understand the effect of their combinations: for they must have perceived that the poison of serpents operates in a manner different from that of vegetables; the former attacking the blood, while the latter corrupts the flesh.[21]

Burchell the scientist in action shows a funny side in his observation of the venom: 'On lightly touching the arrow-poison with my tongue, I have, in most cases, experienced a highly acrimonious taste.'[22]

An unexpected circumstance that afforded him much pleasure was 'looking one evening at the planet *Jupiter* through a small pocket telescope': 'I was exceedingly surprised at beholding all the *Satellites*, as clearly as they would have appeared in England through an instrument of many times greater optical power.'[23] He has a transcendent moment on Christmas Day when he compares winter in Europe with summer in Africa. The scientific explanation is simple:

> And these surprising contrasts have but one single cause: it is alone the difference of obliquity with which the sun's rays fall upon the different parts of our globe; or, in other words, the greater or less noon-day height of the sun, which occasions all the diversity of heat and cold, from the burning sands under the equator, to the eternal, never thawing ice of the poles.

It fills Burchell with wonder that the direction of the sun's beams, together with the inclination of the earth's axis, account for the various climates of the world. He exclaims: 'How transcendent and ever-wonderful is the Great Wisdom which planned

Hut of the Hottentot Chief at Klaarwater, 1 October 1811

Rana (Bufo) [toad], 4 September 1812

the universe! How stupendous and noble the scheme; how simple, yet efficient, the laws which govern it ... how admirable! how beautiful!'[24] He experiences and expresses what Isabelle Stengers, a philosopher of science, calls the 'true grandeur of science'.[25]

Similarly, Burchell takes pleasure in the variety of birds at Klaarwater, 'some of which proved perfectly new to the science'.[26] His view on killing a '*Kanari vogel*' (canary bird) to add to his specimen collection is ethical: 'It is not easy to suppress that natural reluctance we feel at taking away the life of anything so innocent and pleasing as the bird that entertains us by its happy warbling. On this account I never shot but one individual of that species.'[27]

Nevertheless, he was an avid collector of specimens. When he wrote to Mr Hesse in January 1812, he had collected 163 birds of 29 different genera.[28] His sketches and paintings of birds and animals have provided a lasting legacy to ornithologists and zoologists, such as the painting of a saddle-billed stork, *Lekollolani* (see page 13), and the watercolour of a green toad, *Rana (Bufo)*.[29]

Frogs enliven Burchell's portrayal of mid-summer in Klaarwater, when everything was 'parched up, and no verdure of any kind was to be seen'. At this time of the year, 'every pool and pond was completely dried up', so the frogs lie in holes in the ground 'in silence and sleep, till the rains again called them forth'. For Burchell the naturalist, the 'most surprising circumstance attending these musicians, is their sudden appearance after the rains':

> No sooner does the delightful element moisten the earth, and replenish the hollows, than every pool becomes a concert-room, in which frogs of all sizes, old and young, seem contending with each other for a musical prize. Some in deep tones perform their croaking bass, while the young ones, or some of a different species, lead in higher notes of a whistling kind. Tenors and trebles, counter-tenors, sopranos, and altos, may be distinguished in this singular orchestra; while, at intervals, some ancient toad, as double-bass, joins in with a hollow croak, the lowest in the vocal scale.[30]

me no more than it was judged we should require for our present journey', Burchell's own men had to beg him to agree to the swimmers' demands, which he eventually did, and the swimmers returned, 'resumed the work and plunged into the stream with another raft-load'. Burchell 'freely forgave them the unfair stratagem', and they happily assisted the party in safely crossing the river by the day's end.[41]

That evening, at the request of Gert, Burchell played his flute. 'Perhaps this was the first time since the creation, that these groves and rocks re-echoed the sound of the flute; and the novelty of the entertainment commanded the attention of the whole kraal,' Burchell said about the occasion. Participating in the amusement of the evening, and making his fellow men happy for a few hours, 'soothed the pains of the more rugged and unkind parts of my road'.[42] Years later, when Burchell was back in civilised society, he relived these moments:

> How often, when far removed from these wild regions, has memory carried me
> back to scenes and amusements such as these, again to try the question whether
> man find not an equal portion of happiness, and feel not equally the care of a kind
> of Providence, in the civilized, and in the uncivilized state.[43]

Unfortunately, the rough journey that lay ahead for the travellers prevented him from taking his flute to Graaff-Reinet.

Burchell's peace-making deed with the swimmers and his compliance with his party's wishes ensured that 'we all parted good friends' the next morning, and the swimmers even helped to bring Burchell's oxen across the river. The wagon, driven by Gert, drove off to Klaarwater as soon as the party landed safely on the southern bank of the Gariep. Now on the other side of the river, they were ready to begin their arduous two-week journey to Graaff-Reinet, without wagons, and in the territory viewed by the missionaries as 'inhabited by tribes of Bushmen the most savage in Africa'.[44]

Through his entire expedition to Graaff-Reinet, Burchell experienced none of the aggression the Klaarwater missionaries claimed made the San the 'most ferocious of savages'.[45] Instead, Burchell and his party were always warmly welcomed. The dangers of travelling in the unknown country of the San 'were much greater than those of any other part of the published journey',[46] Professor Poulton states, yet Burchell met no hostile encounters. Poulton explains how the explorer was admitted freely and intimately into the life of the kraals: 'Burchell owed these unrivalled opportunities not only to his own unique personality and the power of presents, but also to the wise idea of taking with him Bushmen who were known over the track he proposed to pass.'[47]

After leaving the Gariep River on 28 February, the party travelled southward across extensive plains, and at sunset reached a '*Bushman kraal*' where they enjoyed a friendly reception. Communication was not a problem as members of the party, Hans Lucas, Ruiter and Nieuwveld, could speak the San language.[48] Burchell also had the satisfaction of hearing that Riizo, who lived at the kraal, was keen to travel to Graaff-Reinet; and he joined Burchell's party – which had overnighted on the banks of a nearby river – on 1 March. Kaabi, the chief of a large kraal 'which lay exactly in the direction of our course',[49] happened to be at the river as well, and he 'pledged himself for my safety while I remained in his part of the country, and for a friendly reception at his village'. On the way to the village, Burchell's party 'rode forward; our Bushmen friends followed on foot'.[50]

On 3 March, before arriving at Kaabi's kraal, the travellers came upon a San party, mainly women, who invited Burchell to their own kraal.[51] Burchell was shocked at what he saw there: 'Never before had I beheld, or even imagined, so melancholy, so complete a picture of *poverty*.'[52] Pitying the party, he 'ordered a large quantity of [meat] to be cut off and given to them'.[53] But while he engaged with the community, his servants bartered unfairly with the San. Burchell 'felt highly irritated at the ungenerous advantage which had been taken of the folly of these savages, not because favourable bargains had been made, but because they were so very far below the current *rate of bartering* . . . that they bordered closely on fraudulence'.[54]

The party continued their journey and reached Kaabi's kraal on 6 March. Burchell's aquatint, *A natural Obelisk in the Country of the Bushmen*, depicts some of the spectacular scenery enjoyed on the way.[55] It was dark when they arrived, and Burchell slept under a bush, a few yards from where his men had their fire,[56] looking forward to the 'opportunity of studying and knowing the *real character* of this nation'.[57]

Burchell was able to converse about marriage, wife-beating, polygamy and other customs of the San at Kaabi's kraal. He found he could view 'these tribes as they really are' – 'Till now, imagination only had amused my mind; but here the interesting reality itself was before my eyes.'[58]

For Burchell, 'every circumstance and object by which man is surrounded may be viewed in a philosophical light'.[59] At Kaabi's kraal, he had an opportunity to participate in and 'philosophise' about the music and dancing of the San. The spectators were pleased to see him among them, and he, 'in imitation of their own familiar manner,

A natural Obelisk in the Country of the Bushmen

seated myself down in the circle'.[60] A technical description of the dancer's movements follows:

> One foot remains motionless, while the other dances in a quick wild irregular manner, changing its place but little, though the knee and leg is turned from side to side as much as the attitude will allow. The arms have little motion, their duty being to support the body. The dancer continues singing all the while, and keeps time with every movement; sometimes twisting the body in sudden starts, till at last, as if fatigued by the violence of his exertions, he drops upon the ground to recover breath; still maintaining the spirit of the dance, and continuing to sing, and keep time by the motion of his body, to the voices and accompaniments of the spectators.[61]

Dancing rattles used by the dancer, the singing of the spectators and the beating of the drum are all described, and Burchell records the notes and words of the song. He derived as much pleasure from it 'as the natives themselves'.[62]

Comparisons with European dancing follow: 'it would be an injustice to these poor creatures not to place them in a more respectable rank, than that to which the notions of Europeans have generally admitted them'. Rude laughter, boisterous mirth, drunken jokes and noisy talk in Europe contrast negatively with the soothing effect and 'peaceful, calm emotions of harmless pleasure' of the San's dancing and music. Burchell's words show his sensibility, while the imagery adds a strong visual charge:

> Had I never seen and known more of these savages than the occurrences of this day, and the pastimes of this evening, I should not have hesitated to declare them the happiest of mortals. Free from care, and pleased with a little, their life seemed flowing on, like a smooth stream gliding through flowery meads. Thoughtless and unreflecting, they laughed and smiled the hours away, heedless of futurity, and forgetful of the past. Their music softened all their passions; and thus they lulled themselves into that mild and tranquil state, in which no evil thoughts approach the mind.[63]

He was able to sit in the hut, as if it had been his home, and 'felt in the midst of this horde as though I had been one of them; for some few moments, ceasing to think of sciences or of Europe, and forgetting that I was a lonely stranger in a land of wild untutored men'.[64] Burchell reluctantly quit the party at midnight. Cross-cultural engagement of this kind, taking place in Burchell's era, breaks new ground throughout the *Travels*.

The travelogue continues with a successful rhinoceros hunt on 7 March. During the hunt, Speelman shot two rhinoceroses and Burchell commends his hunting skills and knowledge about the animals.[65] Burchell did not accompany the hunters as his priority was to record in his journal 'the observations of the past day, before the impressions which they had made became weakened, or mingled with those of succeeding objects and occurrences'.[66] However, after Speelman shot the second animal on 8 March, Burchell, with 'one of the Hottentots, and some Bushmen as guides, crossed the rocky hills on the west, and descended into a dry and extensive plain' where the 'animal lay in a position very favourable' for scientific observation (see pages 216–217).[67] They only reached Kaabi's kraal after twilight. Burchell had a fever, but recovered by 9 March and the party departed.[68]

They journeyed to the kraal of Oud Kraai-kop (Old Crowhead), the chief who 'wore the head of a crow fixed upon the top of his hair',[69] arriving in the afternoon on 12 March. Here Burchell again 'witnessed the pleasures of the dance' of the San.[70]

Before leaving the next day, Old Crowhead 'ordered an old man and his son' to accompany Burchell. Burchell's men named them '*Oud*, and *Klein, Magerman* (Old, and Young, Lean-man)'.[71] When they finally left the kraal, the party ran into driving 'rain and hail so violent that my horse refused to face it'.[72] For Burchell the ethnographer it was noteworthy that he 'could not discover in our Bushmen any symptoms of fear, though nothing could be more awful than the thunder, which seemed close above us and exploded with a violence almost sufficient to destroy the hearing'.[73]

After travelling over a plain surrounded by mountains, a faint wagon track was discovered the next day – 'a sight, in the highest degree pleasing to us all'.[74] The Khoisan, with their extraordinary ability to interpret signs in the veld, reasoned that 'it must have been about two years since the waggon had passed that way'. Burchell marvels at the extraordinary ability of all Africans to interpret signs 'connected with the habits and mode of life of wild animals'.[75] As a man of science who embraces Western ideals, he still sees the values in their opinions. Where Burchell found himself, indigenous knowledge 'proved of the utmost importance; it is therefore a subject deserving of attention'.[76]

By 15 March, the travellers had advanced towards the borders of the Cape Colony[77] and were looking forward to enjoying the hospitality of Boer colonists. The first colonist they met on 18 March was Jacob van Wyk, who, with his family, was churlish towards the travellers, and unwilling to accommodate them. Burchell and his disappointed men left Van Wyk in disgust, departing 'from a place, the inhabitants of which, were so much inferior in benevolence, to the savages, – men in whose kraals we had been received with artless joy and genuine good-will'.[78]

At this time, Riizo and Oud Magerman left to return to Kaabi's kraal, but the old man was fearful that Van Wyk would 'seize the boy [Klein Magerman] and detain him as a slave',[79] as 'the stealing and enslavement of San children were widespread at this time'.[80] He trusted Burchell, however, and 'resolved to leave him under my protection; begging that he might be kindly taken care of, and restored to him at our return'.[81] Unlike so many early travellers who privileged the colonial vantage point, Burchell focuses on the concern of the father and undertakes to care for 'my young *Bushman protegé*'.[82]

Travelling in the colony, and having direct contact with military commandos, Burchell witnessed and recorded the bitter struggle between the Xhosa, Khoisan and colonists in the Fourth Frontier War. The actions of the veldcornets – government officials responsible for executing orders from the landdrost – are dramatised in the account of his journey from the Sneeuwberge [Snow Mountains] to Graaff-Reinet. These were troubled times for the colony, and Burchell is uneasy after sighting Van Wyk driving off in his wagon on 18 March 1812, 'for the purpose, as we afterwards heard, of reporting to the veldcornet that a party of strange men had entered the colony'.[83] A few days later, on 21 March, Burchell, having been comfortably accommodated by two other farmers, starts the ascent of the Sneeuwberge. He sets the scene:

> nothing presented itself in the prospect around us, but rocky mountains, the summits of which were enveloped in misty clouds. The unsettled state of the weather, assisted in strengthening the character of frowning grandeur which belongs to this scene. The rude and bold features of the wild landscape, and the sublimity of nature, were unmingled with any trace of human works; and the beaten track under our feet, was the only mark which could inform the traveller that these rugged valleys had ever been frequented; or that the abode of man was to be found in a region apparently so deserted and solitary.[84]

With no wagons for shelter, the party complained of being extremely cold. Fortunately, they came to the house of Piet van der Merwe, a hospitable colonist, who 'very readily, and with marked kindness, received us under his roof'.[85] The rain continued, but Burchell was determined to depart so they could reach a warmer region.

As Burchell mounted his horse to continue the climb up the mountain, a man sent by the veldcornet arrived on 22 March with 'orders to discover, who we were, and what were our intentions'.[86] Burchell, recalling Van Wyk's suspicious departure when Burchell and his party had left for the mountains, realised the man's inquiry was instigated by Van Wyk's report on the party: 'some alarm had been excited by the fact of people having come into the Colony, in a quarter where no arrival of the kind had ever been known before'.[87] After a few minutes of questioning the party, and gathering no proof that they were dangerous, the veldcornet rode off.

On the mountains, the entire party suffered from the cold. All 'were now wrapped up in every piece of clothing they possessed'; Ruiter 'had so tied himself up in skins of various sorts and colors, sheep-skins, leopard-skins, and goat-skins, that he looked more like an automaton pile of furs, than a man'. The hope of descending to a lower, warmer level gave them courage to continue, but Burchell found himself in a serious situation. Old Cobus told him the 'cold had seized his heart' and he was 'struck with death'. The little 'Bushboy', nearly naked except for his kaross, was unable to move or

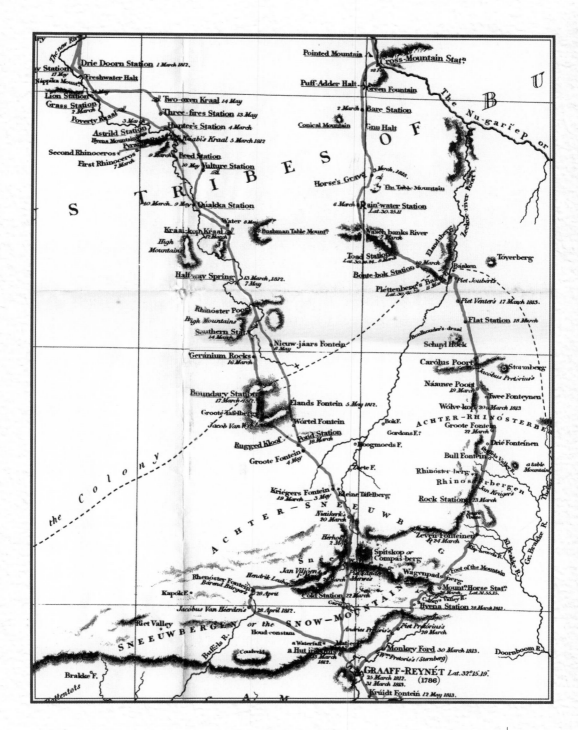

speak: 'It appeared that the hand of death lay already upon him.'[88] Burchell's anxiety increased as such distressing reflections 'crowded on my mind':

> What was I to tell the father at my return! That he had died of cold? This would not have been believed. I should have been accused of being the cause of his death; or having left him in captivity under some of the boors. My return through the Bushmen's country would be impracticable. Kaabi, and the whole tribe, would have considered me no longer as their friend; but as one who had treacherously deceived them and betrayed the confidence of a father. The whole plan of my travels was deranged.[89]

The party halted to find firewood, and with great difficulty made a fire. Burchell successfully restored the child to life, and Cobus and the others 'revived by degrees'.[90]

With warmth came a lightening of the spirits. On 23 March, Burchell had the 'consolation of finding all my people able to bear another day's travelling, and the boy not only alive, but recovered'.[91] Their joy increased, they could now descend the Snow Mountains. The travellers, pack-oxen, sheep and dogs, the 'wild and rocky scenery', and the steep, dangerous descent are represented in the aquatint *Descending from the Snow Mountains*.[92]

But soon another crisis struck the party. Burchell developed 'symptoms of a violent fever' which left him unable to descend further. Serendipitously, there was shelter at the foot of the mountain, a deserted hut in a 'very ruinous state' in which he could recover. Optimistic as always, Burchell considered the ruin 'placed in my way by good fortune'.[93] But in the morning, the fever was life-threatening, and for the first time since leaving Cape Town he was unable to travel.

As Burchell recuperated in the hut, three burghers on horseback, armed with muskets, arrived from Graaff-Reinet, ten miles away, and found Burchell asleep, lying on the ground in the corner of his roofless hovel.[94] Informed that they 'had orders to bring me to the landdrost', Burchell responded in the indomitable manner that was typical of his character, even when ill:

> I quickly replied, that I was unwell; and that I neither could, nor would, remove from this place; that they could have no authority for disturbing me; and that they might inform the landdrost, that it was my intention to come to him as soon as I could conveniently. This, and the tone in which it was spoken, put an end to their importunities.[95]

Descending from the Snow Mountains

Dialogue animates the scene in this encounter. Burchell's authoritative tone 'immediately brought about a revolution in their sentiments and behaviour'; and the burghers became civil and even offered to send for a '*paarde-wagen*' (a wagon drawn by horses) to take him to the village. Ever hospitable, Burchell ordered 'a chop to be broiled for them', and they continued sitting there 'at their ease for two hours'. Before they left, two other visitors 'of a more agreeable kind' entered the hut.

Mr Menzies, the surgeon of the twenty-first regiment of light dragoons, and Mr Oloff Stockenström, the younger son of the late landdrost, had heard that an 'Englishman had entered the colony in an unusual manner' and came to find out whether he was Dr Cowan or Captain Donovan. Burchell enjoyed their company, and being able to speak English helped in his recovery as 'I never once thought of my fever'. The visitors' account of Van Wyk's exaggerated report to the veldcornet astounded Burchell:[96]

> on my account the whole village of Graaff-Reinet had been for several days in
> a state of alarm. *The current report* was, that three hundred of the Klaarwater

Hottentots, under the command of a white-man, were marching to attack the colony, taking advantage of the favourable moment when so many boors were absent from their homes and detained on the commando in the Zuureveld. So greatly had the inhabitants magnified my little party, and so strongly was the report believed, that not only constant guard had been kept; but, on account of my near approach and hourly-expected attack, a number of persons remained under arms, and the guard and night-watch had last night actually been doubled.[97]

Shortly after the departure of Menzies and Stockenström, the acting landdrost and his brother, having established who Burchell was, brought a carriage to convey him to Graaff-Reinet. They pressed Burchell to 'quit the place', but he was too ill to move.[98]

He felt better the next morning, 25 March, learning later that his illness was 'a species of influenza', a flu epidemic rampant in the whole colony. The landdrost, accompanied by Mr Kicherer the clergyman, arrived to take him to Graaff-Reinet. He 'entered the carriage and we drove from a spot which, for some moments during my illness, I thought it possible I might never quit again'. Burchell's men arrived in the evening, 'but *the little Bushman*'[99] was not with them, resulting in yet more anxiety for Burchell.

In Graaff-Reinet, Burchell again struggled to find men for his Litakun trip. The Frontier War and the murder of the landdrost Anders Stockenström in December 1811 made it difficult to secure the services of any travelling assistants. As the new landdrost was away for a month, and would only return 22 April,[100] there was no official with the necessary authority to assist Burchell. Khoikhoi labour was also in great demand as 'the business of the farms cannot proceed without the labor of their hands'.[101]

By 7 April, Burchell's 'search and inquiries for men, ended unsuccessfully';[102] and only by 24 April, persuaded by Mr Kicherer, did Burchell engage two 'Half-Hottentots': Cornelis Goeiman and Jan van Roye. Both were well thought of in Graaff-Reinet as they were baptised, and Kicherer had even exhibited Van Roye in Europe in 1803 as a successful specimen of missionary conversion. In addition to the baptised men, Burchell had to take three 'tronk' (jail) Khoikhoi: Keyser Dikkop, Stuurman Witbooy and Andries Michael – incorrigible scoundrels, who were the 'refuse' of the jail. Juli, the wagon-driver of the late landdrost Anders Stockenström, joined the group too, and proved to be the most faithful and valuable of all of Burchell's men. Finally,

The Drostdy, Graaff-Reinet, 6 April 1812

another man, Platje Zwartland, looking to travel with Burchell, was able to join the party only after Burchell successfully registered him as his servant so he was legally free to do so.

While travelling in the colony, and in the wake of the Frontier War, Burchell's contact with the Boers allowed him to observe their households, individual mannerisms and physical traits; and to record his perceptions of them, both negative and positive, 'faithfully in that light in which they appeared'.[103] Burchell is open-minded and sees both sides of the conflict between the two groups of opponents, and the points of view of both the Boers and the Khoisan are given. The colonists regard the 'savages as a most dangerous race of beings'; but while 'these ideas have not been without cause', the 'Bushmen, in exculpation, declare they rob in retaliation of past injuries'.[104]

Burchell had already witnessed some of the fear the colonists inspired in the Khoisan when Oud Magerman, the old Bushman, had begged him to care for his son Klein Magerman before Van Wyk could enslave him. Instances of colonial brutality were common throughout the Cape that Burchell visited, and it did not take long before he encountered more of it on the Graaff-Reinet expedition.

Advancing towards the colony's borders in the middle of March, Burchell met two men and six women, two with infants on their backs, who had quit working for *Oud Baasje Jacob* because he had beaten one of the women. The young girl of a 'harmless engaging appearance' tells the story, and the other women act out the cruel actions of 'Baas Jacob':

She told me that *Oud Baas* had tied her up to one of the wheels of the waggon and flogged her for a long time. The other women all joined in the tale, and two or three at once were showing me the position in which she was tied, first imitating the act of *flogging*, and then that of crying and supplicating for mercy: but she implored in vain, for no mercy was in his heart, till he had vented his rage.[105]

Burchell was incensed that 'any man had been brute enough to lift his hand against so weak and defenceless a fellow creature'. Not only did the 'baas' assault the young girl, but he also enslaved the child of another woman and did not pay 'the stipulated wages for these people's services'.[106]

The violence acted out by some of the colonists is individualised in the history of Juli, 'a Hottentot of the mixed race'. Burchell first heard Juli's story when he employed him in Graaff-Reinet. The cycle of violence his family suffered is horrific and merits quoting in full:

His father lived in the vicinity of Algoa-bay, but was killed by the Caffres while hunting in the Zuureveld. The mother, induced by distress at her loss, resolved to quit a district which had been fatal to her husband, and removed with her two children, a girl and a boy, to the western side of the colony. Here she was still more unfortunate; for, falling in the way of a brutal colonist who resided on the river which runs through that tract, he seized her children, then nearly grown up and strong enough to be made useful on his farm, and drove her away from the place, as she herself appeared too old to render much service by her labor. He therefore procured Juli and his sister to be registered in the field-cornet's books, as legally bound to serve him for twenty-five years; which was in fact to make them his actual slaves for that time. The mother clung to her children, wishing to resist this unjust seizure, and desiring to be permitted either to take them away, or to live on the farm with them; but the farmer repeatedly drove her off, and at last, with a

Portrait of Juli, a faithful Hottentot

resolution to deter her from coming there again, he one evening flogged her so unmercifully that she died the next morning! This, and the harsh treatment which he himself received, were sufficient to drive Juli to despair; and he, in consequence, took the first favourable opportunity of making his escape.[107]

The heartless practices of the colonist are historically significant, as is the powerlessness of the mother. Aboriginal inhabitants are disadvantaged: 'the word of a Hottentot gains, in general, but little credit in the Colony'.[108]

Even before his arrival in the colony nearly a year and a half before, Burchell, on board the *Harriet*, had wondered about the cruel hand colonialism had dealt to the original peoples of the Cape.[109] The interaction of such vastly different cultures and mindsets, such as those of the European and the Khoikhoi, and the consequences thereof, intrigued and concerned him. Empathising with the Khoikhoi, he attempts to see the new world they found themselves in from their own point of view:

> my imagination carried me back to that period when its peaceable inhabitants, the simple Hottentots, roamed freely over the country, enjoying the liberty of nature, nor dreaming that a day could ever arrive when they must resign all to some unknown race of men, coming upon them from the ocean, an element which no tradition had ever told them could be travelled on by man. Their arms and their watchings had no object besides their inland enemies; the turbulent surface of the 'Great Water' and the noisy shore, seemed the only side whence no danger was to be dreaded.[110]

Burchell recognises the cruelties inflicted by colonialism on the native inhabitants of the lands conquered (despite being a citizen of one of these empires himself); and he questions the actual benefit they have reaped from the colonist:

> But it is not at the extremity of Africa only, where treachery has surprised men from a quarter where it was least expected. I was wishing, for the honour of Europeans, men enjoying the blessings of civilization, and illumined by the superior light of arts and science, that I could have persuaded myself that these natives had been rendered happier by their communication with them: I longed to be amongst them, that I might ascertain so important a fact by my own experience; and my fondest wish was, to be able to bear witness to the truth of it.[111]

Eager to ascertain the effects of colonialism on the traditions and lives of these indigenous peoples, Burchell is naturally grateful when he finally makes direct contact with them. Two years after his philosophical wonderings aboard the *Harriet*, and numerous exchanges with the various inhabitants of the colony later, he can finally formulate an answer to this driving question:

> I now could give myself the answer to that question which I had long marked as one of the *desiderata* of my travels: but, alas! it is in the negative; and I must believe, that these savages have *not* been rendered happier by their communication with Europeans; I must too, believe, that they have *not* been made better or morally wiser; and I fear I must conclude that the present state of all the Hottentot race, is far less happy, far less peaceful, than it was before our discovery of the Cape of Good Hope.[112]

Burchell left Graaff-Reinet for Klaarwater on 28 April 1812 in Mr Kicherer's vehicle, drawn by six horses: 'We flew past every object, and, hardly had I turned my eyes to anything remarkable by the roadside, than it was already behind us.'[113] For four days Burchell was hospitably accommodated in the Sneeuwberge by various Boers, and was able to avoid the troubles he experienced on his first trek through the mountains. His party, who left separately, met him on 2 May near one of these farms. With them were unwelcome hangers-on and Burchell turned them away. However, Juli's wife Truy and their three-month-old baby girl Windvogel, joined the group. Mother and child were always allowed to ride, either on Burchell's horse or on one of the oxen.[114] Like her husband, Truy proved to be a valuable member of the party.

Klein Magerman was also among the party waiting for Burchell at the mountains. A farmer, Piet van der Merwe, had found him when he absconded, kindly taken him home and employed him to tend sheep. Burchell 'felt relieved of much anxiety',[115] and at Kaabi's kraal Klein Magerman was safely returned to his father.

The colonial boundary was reached on 6 May without any mishaps.[116] '[T]he northern boundaries of the colony,' according to historian Nigel Penn, 'were so vague as to be virtually non-existent.'[117] Burchell gives a traveller's impression of the boundary in 1812:

> we considered that we had crossed *the boundary* of the Colony, a line very ill-defined, especially along the northern border, and marked by no appearance

which can inform the traveller precisely when he has quitted the settlement, or when he enters the wild country of the Bushmen; both being equally wild, and, excepting immediately around the boors' dwellings, equally destitute of every trace of cultivation or human labor.[118]

The party successfully traversed the *'pathless desert'* and found the remains of their shelter from their journey to the Gariep two months before.

Burchell's return to Klaarwater took another ten days. A lion killed two dogs, and crossing the Gariep was dangerous – Burchell, his horse, and Truy and her child almost drowned. Most ominously, the 'baptized' men from Graaff-Reinet, Van Roye and Cornelis, made continual attempts to undermine Burchell's authority. He 'watched therefore with a jealous eye, every attempt at disobedience, and considered nothing of so much importance as the preservation of my authority over them'.[119] Notwithstanding these ordeals, Burchell 'had the satisfaction of having accomplished my journey, without accident to any one, and with the gratification of knowing that no one was the worse for having accompanied me'.[120]

The travellers arrived in Klaarwater on 24 May 1812. According to colonial custom, 'twenty discharges of our muskets' saluted the missionaries 'announcing our return'.[121] But the salutation remained unanswered, the missionaries nowhere to be seen. At last, Mr Anderson came forward,

and in an admirably calm manner, and without the least expression of any emotions, such as worldly men might naturally indulge in, on witnessing the return of a person whom he might consider as having risen from the dead, received me with; *So, you're come back again.*[122]

The missionaries 'preserved a silence well becoming men whose minds were occupied with better things'. This sect, he writes, suppresses and even destroys 'every lively emotion' as 'they strive to become *serious people*'. For his part, 'I never could bring my mind to so serious a state as to avoid being extremely glad at finding myself, with all my men, safely arrived at Klaarwater, or to avoid being equally rejoiced at getting away from it.'[123]

Burchell intended on leaving Klaarwater a week after his arrival, but his departure was once again 'prolonged from day to day, by various difficulties and obstructions arising in one quarter or another'.[124]

7

'Broils and discords'[1]

Journey to Litakun
June to July 1812

ALL PREPARATIONS AND ARRANGEMENTS FOR the 183-mile, north-east journey to Litakun were complete by 6 June 1812.

The welfare of Hannah and Truy, the two Khoikhoi wives remaining at Klaarwater,
concerned Burchell: 'It was settled that they should take up their residence at Groote-
doorn, where our friend Hans Lucas, and Hendrik, very readily promised to give them
protection.' These were trustworthy men from Klaarwater who had accompanied
Burchell on the hippo excursion. Mr Anderson was asked to see that 'they were not in
want' and Burchell 'engaged to repay whatever might be advanced on their account'.[2]
Always sensitive to the emotions of others, Burchell reassured the women that he 'would
not take their husbands where there was evident danger, and assured them that we
should return safe'.[3] He cautioned them that the party might be absent longer than
expected.

Before setting off, the first calamity struck when '*Wilde Honden*' (wild dogs) bit
off the tails of three oxen. Abraham Abrams,[4] appointed by Burchell to take care of
his oxen in his absence, had not secured the oxen in the cattle pound. Burchell's men
would continue to neglect their duties and challenge his authority during the journey
and in Litakun.

Departing from Klaarwater, Burchell, a lone Englishman venturing into the
unknown interior, reveals his feelings: 'it was not without some emotion, that I finally
bade farewell to the last Europeans with whom I could possibly converse, for a long
period'.[5] Several Klaarwater Khoikhoi wished him a safe journey. At Gert's request,
Burchell authorised the customary farewell salute: a dozen discharges were fired, and
'seven or eight from different quarters, were given us in return'.[6] Anticipating that the
five-week trip would be full of incident and interest, Burchell declares: 'Having set
my foot in a new region, I prepared for examining with attention all its features, and

for enjoying the feast of novelty and instruction, which lay spread before me in every quarter.'[7]

In Klaarwater, Burchell's patience was put 'severely to the trial',[8] but early in the journey, vexations continued. One wagon, carelessly driven, almost overturned; oxen wandered off; and on the second night of the journey, Van Roye, Speelman, Platje and Keyser, with '*Hottentot unconcern*',[9] distressed Burchell by not informing him they were passing the night in Khoikhoi huts some distance from where Burchell camped. 'Broils and discords' loomed and intensified. Historian Elizabeth Green Musselman, considering Burchell in the context of collaboration between European naturalists and African employees, states: 'A closer look at his extended interactions with Africans during his multi-year journey can give a more detailed picture of the reasons for both Euro-African collaboration and its erosion by mid-century.'[10]

In Musselman's view, the 'deterioration of trust between Burchell and the Africans around him resulted in part from his and the other imperialists' tendency to magnify personal and practical frustration into a civilization-level struggle'. She accuses Burchell of 'a tirade' about the 'simplemindedness of "Hottentots"',[11] and of fuming about 'the hopelessness of ever improving the barbarian'.[12] But a careful reading of his journal entries gives a more nuanced picture of Burchell responding to negligent or confrontational acts of specific individuals. It is not surprising that Burchell, a highly intelligent European man travelling with incompatible servants, and often in harsh conditions, would be bothered by such behaviour and prone to outbursts of irritation.

Muchunka, the interpreter hired for the excursion to Litakun, joined the travellers on 13 June. With his arrival, Burchell 'was glad to add to my party, not only an interpreter, but a person whose manners were a little more lively than those of the Hottentots'.[13] Muchunka had been hired in Litakun in November 1811 with the assistance of Mr Jansz the missionary (even though he and the other Klaarwater missionaries refused to help Burchell find any other men for his journey). It was imperative for Burchell to have an interpreter in Litakun, and Muchunka, who was born there, was fluent in the languages of the Kora and Bachapins; he could also speak Dutch, having lived in Klaarwater.[14] While Muchunka refused to accompany Burchell to Graaff-Reinet when he was first employed, he offered to go to Litakun, and then no further. Before he joined the party, he had been residing in the Langeberg.

Another invaluable addition to the party was a pack of dogs of 'about five-and-

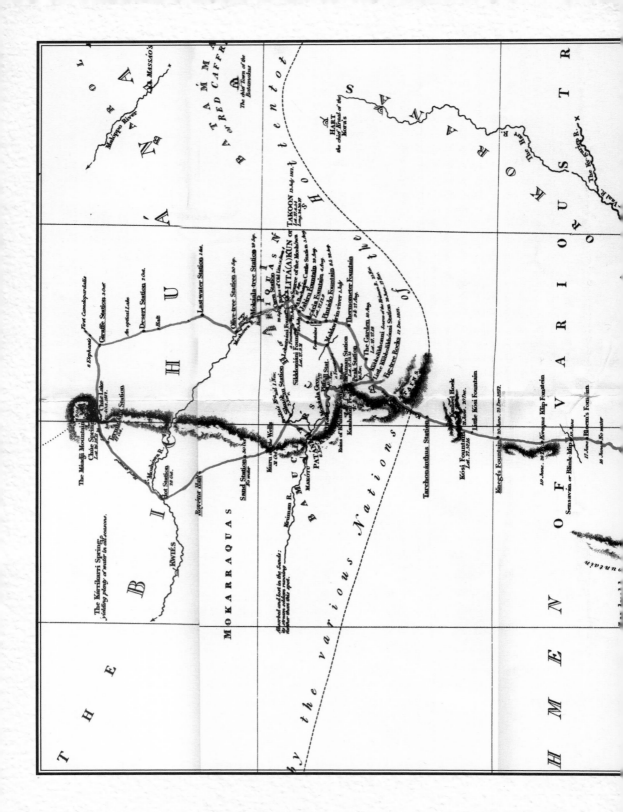

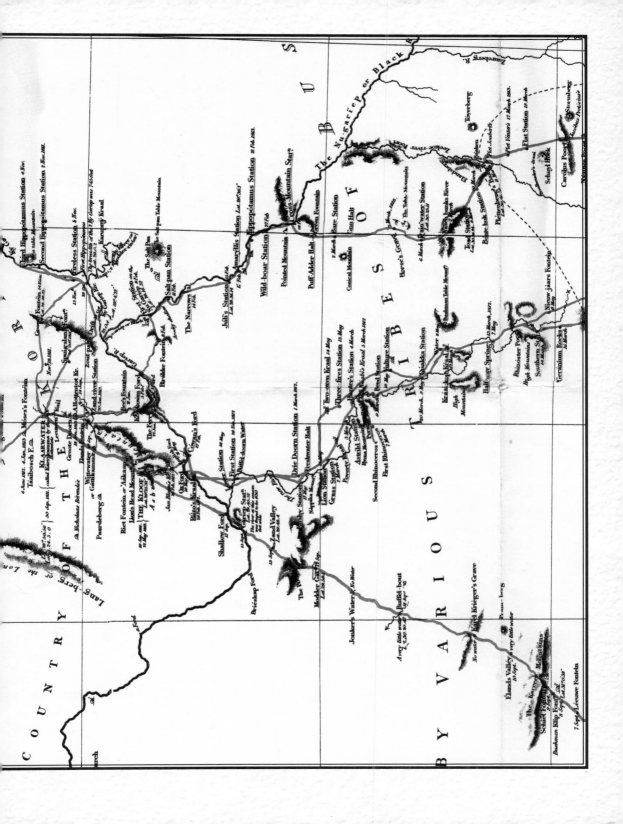

twenty of various sorts and sizes'.[15] Burchell, in tune with canine behaviour, was able to interpret the *'various tones of barking'* which gave notice of danger:

> Some were more disposed to watch against men, and others against wild beasts; some discovered an enemy by their quickness of hearing, others by that of scent: some were useful only for their vigilance and barking; some for speed in pursuing game; and others for courage in holding ferocious animals at bay.[16]

Burchell esteemed them 'for their social inclination to mankind'. When 'wandering over pathless deserts, oppressed with vexation and distress at the conduct of my own men, I have turned to these, as my only friends, and felt how much inferior to them was a man when actuated only by selfish views'.[17]

Burchell's disparaging views of human nature are scattered across uplifting journal entries that describe items of scientific curiosity, transcendent spiritual moments, aesthetic pleasures in the landscape, and an account of him learning to speak and write Sichuana (Setswana), the language of the Bachapins. The sighting of a huge acacia giraffe tree delights him;[18] a Khoikhoi family moving their hut from a spot 'swarming with *fleas*'[19] amuses him; and geological changes and animals encountered are precisely recorded, often with excitement. A highlight of the trip was the sighting of 'the track of the tallest of all the quadrupeds in the world'. 'No person who has ever read, even the popular books of natural history, could, I think, behold for the first time, the ground over which he is walking, imprinted with the recent footsteps of a *camelopardalis*, without feeling some strange and peculiar interest at the sight.'[20] Burchell's party did not see the giraffe, but a day later, on 17 June, they encountered a lion, a lioness with two cubs, and a buffalo at Bloem's Fountain, a spring named after Jan Bloem, who led a 'lawless life'.[21] Philip shot the buffalo for the pot.

Buffalo – Head, 17 June 1812

For readers 'who have acquired a taste for zoological information',[22] Burchell provides a detailed exposition of the animal and its characteristics: the name of buffalo is a 'misapplication' of the European name; the animal is only found in 'the extratropical part of Southern Africa'; 'its countenance exhibits a savage and malevolent expression'; the horns 'are so unusually broad at their base as to cover the whole forehead, and give it an appearance of a mass of rock'; and it is 'of a fierce and treacherous disposition'. Further anatomical details follow, and a drawing shows the 'distinguishing characters of this remarkable species of buffalo'.[23]

Sandwiched between two entries about the buffalo is a list of words from the '*Kora dialect*', tabulated in two columns. On the left-hand side, in English, are numbers ranging from one to twenty; the words 'yes' and 'no'; a list of pronouns; and nouns, such as sun, moon, clouds, rain, hail, lightning, thunder, wind, water, fire smoke, mountains and 'spring or fountain'. In the right-hand column are the Kora translations of the words, and a pronunciation guide is provided. Burchell's knowledge of Greek, Dutch and French phonetics appears in a technical footnote on the correct pronunciation of the vocal sounds in the Kora language.[24] The range and richness of his multilingualism is extraordinary.

On 18 June, the travellers stopped over at the foot of a hill called Blink-klip (Shining Rock) by the Khoikhoi in Klaarwater, and Sensaván by the Bachapins of Litakun. In 1892, the town Blinkklip was renamed Postmasburg. The engraving *Sensaván, the Sibílo mine*[25] depicts the mine at the foot of the rock. *Sibílo*, used extensively by the Bachapins, 'is a shining, powdery iron-ore of a steel-grey or blueish lustre, and soft and greasy to the touch'. The ore is ground together with grease and smeared over the body and head. Burchell observes a parallel between this and European customs, amusingly writing:

> A Bachapin whose head is thus covered, considers himself as most admirably adorned, and in full dress; and indeed, to lay aside European prejudices, it is quite as becoming as our own hair-powder, and is a practice not more unreasonable than ours; with which it may in some respects be compared. There is however a real utility in it, or rather in the grease … it protects the head from the powerful, and perhaps dangerous, effects of a burning sun, as it equally does, from those of wet and cold.[26]

In St Helena, Burchell produced paint from samples of earth; in southern Africa, he 'succeeded in preparing from the *sibílo* a very singular kind of *paint*, which may be used either in water-color drawing or in oil-painting, by grinding it either in gum-water

Sensaván, the Sibílo mine

or in oil'. Burchell would later paint portraits in Litakun, and used *sibílo* to give the exact colour of the 'peculiar glittering which it would be impossible to imitate by any other means'.[27]

The party had to leave Sensaván on 19 June as there was no water for the cattle. Burchell called the voyage from the area the 'most rocky of any between the Gariep and Litakun'.[28] Dr Roger Stewart notes that Burchell was the first traveller to describe glacial pavements,[29] after the wagons 'suffered the most violent jolts' travelling over a 'natural pavement of pure rock' and 'a primitive limestone'.

Throughout the expedition, Burchell had to endure Khoikhoi cooking. Their habit of cutting meat into lumps before throwing it into a large iron pot of water caused it to be 'boiled and exceedingly hard' as a consequence. He is pragmatic about the situation, however, wisely observing that 'as it was not easy to change the system and notions of these men, I found it less troublesome to accommodate my palate to their cookery, than to pretend to teach them an art of which I knew as little as themselves'. Acknowledging that a change in diet is 'necessary to health and strength' – both absolutely essential to a traveller – he confesses this was 'a point of prudence which, among my preparations, was never once thought of, because the full enjoyment of health induced me to regard it as very unimportant and quite unnecessary'.[30] Prudence, a quality highly thought of in the eighteenth century, is practised assiduously by Burchell. He repeatedly points out instances when his men have 'neither prudence nor foresight'.[31]

Burchell's party were told a cautionary tale of 'imprudence', which elicited varying reactions. Seven years earlier, the story went, two Khoikhoi and their families were returning home from Litakun with a wagon loaded with elephant tusks when Bushmen attacked and killed the two men. In Burchell's opinion, the 'two unfortunate Hottentots were certainly to blame for their *imprudence* in venturing, with so little probability of being able to defend themselves, to traverse a country of lawless savages, with a large quantity of property, by which the wretches were too strongly tempted to attack them'. This fatal occurrence infused the minds of Burchell's men, and he 'had the vexation of witnessing their effects on several occasions'.[32] Gert, 'under the impression, probably, of this story', came to Burchell's wagon to discuss the 'course and extent' of the journey. On being told that he must not expect it to terminate at Litakun, Gert announced, 'Then, Sir, we shall, not one of us, ever come back; we are all murdered men!'[33]

Having left Sensaván because of the lack of water for the cattle, Burchell clearly displays prudence in his care for animals. He castigates hasty travellers who deny oxen time for grazing and resting. The oxen are consequently driven violently, and without food sink 'under the yoke' and are heartlessly left to perish. Burchell, in contrast, regarded his oxen as 'faithful friends whose assistance was indispensable'. Characteristically, he is humane and opposes the 'coldness of hearts' in those who possess a hard nature.[34]

The party reached the Kosi Fountain at the close of day on 19 June. Burchell writes admiringly about the springs, revealing his aesthetic appreciation of its distinctively African beauty:

> In the character of the *landscape* and its peculiar tints, a painter would find
> much to admire, though it differed entirely from the species known by the term
> 'picturesque'. But it was not the less beautiful: nor less deserving of being studied
> by the artist: it was that kind of *harmonious beauty* which belongs to the extensive
> plains of Southern Africa.[35]

Burchell, an artist trained in the European pictorial arts has acquired 'an African eye', to use J.M. Coetzee's words.[36] African colours, topography and shrubs please him immensely. Using principles of 'picturesque' composition, or what Wordsworth calls 'the cold rules of painting',[37] he translates this appreciation of African beauty into a word picture:

> The pale yellow dry grass gave the prevailing color, and long streaks of bushes as it seemed, parallel to the horizon and gradually fading into the distance, sufficiently varied the uniformity of a plain; while clumps of the soft and elegant acacia, presented a feature which relieved these long streaks by an agreeable change of tint, and by the most pleasing forms backed by low azure hills in the farthest distance. Our horses and oxen grazing close at hand, added a force to the foreground, and, by contrast, improving the tenderness of the general colouring, completed a landscape, perhaps altogether inimitable; but which, if put on canvass, would form a picture of the most fascinating kind, and prove to European painters, that there exists in this department of the art, a species of beauty with which, possibly, they may not yet be sufficiently acquainted.[38]

After Burchell's lyrical description of Kosi Fountain, the tenor of his journal changes dramatically in his account of Cupido Kok, who stopped at the fountain on 27 June. Kok, who was from Klaarwater, had been to Litakun to barter for ivory and oxen, and Burchell 'was exceedingly glad at falling in with this man, as I now expected to get back my *great rifle*'.[39] Burchell had lent Kok the heavy gun before he went to Graaff-Reinet, on the understanding it would be given back to him upon his return to Klaarwater. The rifle being too heavy to carry, Kok supplied Burchell with a lighter musket.[40] While Kok did return the rifle, he did so without the bullet mould. Annoyed, Burchell describes the incident:

> He was therefore told that, as the rifle was the most important of all our guns, and its use absolutely indispensable for the prosecution of my journey, I would wait at our present station till he returned home and despatched a man on horseback to me with *the mould*; that I would not proceed without it, and that as soon as it was received I would return him his own gun, which I had brought with me in expectation of meeting him at Litakun.[41]

Kok made no objection, and Burchell concluded the matter was settled. However, he ended up waiting six days at Kosi Fountain 'in expectation that *Cupido Kok* would send the bullet-mould'. His men were 'clearly of the opinion that we should hear nothing further from him, and that it would be fruitless to remain here longer'.[42] Burchell vents his irritation about the affair:

> Seeing myself thus, for the whole of my journey, deprived of the proper use of my best gun, by an ungrateful Hottentot whom I had formerly shown myself desirous of obliging, and whom I treated in a manner which proved my good-will towards him, I could not but feel irritated, in whatever light I viewed his conduct. But, as no remedy was now to be had, I resolved to consider this privation as one of the inevitable accidents of my journey.[43]

Ever the Enlightened man of reason, Burchell sees the futility in dwelling on the subject.

The two baptised Khoikhoi servants, Van Roye and Cornelis, ended an 'interval of tranquillity' when they refused to follow Burchell's instructions for making cartridge boxes.[44] Hired on the recommendation of the clergyman Mr Kicherer, they 'were considered to be of a much superior class, as having been baptized and taught to read', and 'on this account I agreed to pay them a salary double that of my ordinary men'.[45] But to Burchell's disappointment, they 'were as stupid, and as unwilling to adopt improvement, as the rest'. They were the laziest of his men and had done no work; yet 'on account of their being *Christemensch*, they rated themselves so high, that they actually regarded it as degrading, to do the same work as a Hottentot'. Their attitude shocked Burchell: 'It was disgusting, though ridiculous, to hear these two woolly-headed men, call their companions, *Hottentots*, as an appellation of inferiority good enough for Heathens, and proper for making these sensible of the superiority of Christians.'

Their belligerence, which began to influence the other servants' behaviour, became a source of continual anguish for Burchell:

> This unbecoming spirit was frequently the cause of broils and discords; and their tempers and conduct, so very different from what I had expected, were the source of continual vexation to me, and the germ from which many of my difficulties and disappointments sprang; an example of laziness and insubordination which in time infected the others, and required the utmost vigilance and resolution, to check it.[46]

The image of an embryonic germ evolving into a full-blown infection would materialise later in Litakun.

In the evenings, Burchell was tutored in Sichuana by Muchunka, and he reduced 'an oral language to a written form'.[47] His notes on the structure of the language and the dictionary he compiled are not included in the *Travels*: 'the inconvenience which would attend an increase in the bulk of this volume beyond its present size, compels me to omit the Dictionary'.[48] (The dictionary is lost.) Of interest is Burchell's insight into a pejorative European view of African languages:

> Those, whose minds have been expanded by a European education, cannot readily conceive the *stupidity*, as they would call it, of savages, in everything beyond the most simple ideas and the most uncompounded notions, either in moral or in physical knowledge.[49]

Burchell, unlike his fellow Europeans, understands that languages are structured by different world views: 'But the fact is; their life embraces so few incidents, their occupations, their thoughts, and their cares, are confined to so few objects, that their ideas must necessarily be equally few, and equally confined.'[50]

Prevailing Western attitudes inform Burchell's views of local inhabitants and their concerns, which he considers narrower than those of Europeans. He criticises Europeans for their opinions of African languages, distinguishing between 'the absurdity of seeking in their language for that which was not to be found in their ideas' and the 'civilized society' and 'cultivated minds' of Europe. Burchell implies that Muchunka's 'faculty of thinking' is deficient, and uses this to explain why he did not have Burchell's stamina for the lessons: 'that exertion of mind ... soon wore out his powers of reflection, and rendered him really incapable of paying any longer attention to the subject'. For Burchell, the 'mode of expressing those abstract qualities and virtues, and those higher operations of the intellectual power' belong to Europeans.[51]

On 28 June, the travellers reached the range of mountains that formed the boundary between the country inhabited by the San and the territory of the 'Bichuana nations'.

Burchell, in a footnote, explains that Bichuana is used 'when speaking generally of those tribes of the Caffre race, who speak a language which they call *Sichuána*, and inhabit the countries comprised in the northernmost part of the map'. Bachapin and the Khoikhoi word 'Briqua' (signifying 'Goat-men') are intended only for the tribe governed by Chief Mattivi, in the town of Litakun.[52]

Taking his leave of the Bushmen, 'those hordes of *wild men*, as they are justly called', Burchell reflects on 'men who are moved by various motives either to hostility or to friendship':

> to the former, often by feelings of revenge or retaliation, and too often by a spirit
> of plunder; to the latter, often won by trifling acts of kindness, and by treatment
> founded on a due and reasonable view of their untutored state and of the
> comfortless existence of a nation without a head, without laws, without arts,
> and without religion.[53]

Christian values take precedence for Burchell, and he reveals his 'European-ness' in how he cooperates with people of such vastly different cultures to his own: 'Towards such men, vengeance and punishment, however justly merited, should be mitigated by pity and forbearance, such as we are taught by the mild and genuine spirit of Christianity.'[54]

Entering this new region, Burchell imagined the inhabitants to be a 'superior race of men, a nation among whom I was to find some traces of industry and art, and who, by living in fixed abodes and in large communities and by following agriculture, had advanced the first steps in civilization'. These musings excited him and 'chased from my mind every vexatious sentiment, and banished every thought of those troubles and difficulties which naturally attend a traveller venturing into these countries under circumstances such as mine'.[55]

Burchell's men did not share his enthusiasm about this unknown area of the interior, fearing both its people and their customs. Muchunka continually helped to raise the morale of the party, praising the pastures, water and abundance of game in his native country, and persuading the men that they need not fear the 'unknown tribe to which we were about to commit ourselves'.[56]

The next day, the travellers arrived at the Kuruman River: 'a sight so delightful for African travellers, had not been seen since we left the Gariep'.[57] Here, Muchunka, sitting by the fire with others in the party, spoke Dutch, the 'Hottentot' language, and then several times held 'a *long oration* in Sichuana'. Burchell, perplexed at first, soon discovered the object of his theatrical performance was to persuade Bichuanas in the vicinity that 'we were friends'.[58]

The first Bachapins that Burchell encountered, the day after arriving at the Kuruman River, were two herdsmen. They annoyed him by giving him a false report that 'a body of white men were coming to take revenge for the alleged murder of the last English party which had visited their country'. In Burchell's words:

> Thus, at my first entrance into their territory, I began to experience some part of the *deceit* and disregard for truth, which, although pervading more or less every African tribe, seem scarcely to be considered by the Bichuanas as a vice or disgraceful practice; and which, in these countries, so deeply contaminate every class of society, that I afterwards proved by too many trials, that no man's word, not even a Chief's, could be relied upon in any case where the least advantage was to be gained by falsehood.[59]

Burchell points out 'that contradictory facts and sentiments will occasionally be met with' when travellers are 'reduced to getting' information from 'the mouths of others'.[60]

En route to the Bachapins, on 30 June, Burchell passed the location where the original town of Litakun stood in 1805, when it was visited by Burchell's friend Dr Lichtenstein, a professor from Germany. After crossing the Kuruman River on 1 July, Burchell's party travelled over the '*Great Plains of Litakun*'[61] and halted at the Makkwarin River, where they remained for several days to prepare for their arrival in Litakun. The area surrounding the river was of scientific interest to Burchell as it was situated in the vast area north of the Gariep River, which he named the 'Transgariepine'.[62] Observations of the landscape and its fauna were a welcome distraction from the tedious task of organising his journey.

Burchell found the geology of the Transgariepine to be primitive: 'its most remarkable feature, is the undisturbed, and generally unbroken state of its great strata', which 'lie in, what may be supposed, their original position, and present rarely any evidence of those violent convulsions of nature which, beyond all doubt, have once, at some immeasurably remote period of time, shaken the whole fabric of the globe'.[63]

For Burchell, astronomy and geology lead the human mind to the 'most sublime prospects of the creation' and present 'for man's reflection, the most interesting subjects which can engage the attention of a liberal and enlightened understanding'. Like

Travelling over the Great Plains of Litakun

Darwin, he believes in 'deep time', which is the scale of geologic events, and not the Genesis account of Earth's history: 'It places before our eyes, and in our hands, the clear and legible record of an antiquity, compared with which, all other records are but the tale of yesterday.'[64] It is the tangible proof

> of the aweful power of that inconceivably Glorious, and Incomprehensible Being, by the spirit of whose Wisdom, all which we behold has risen into existence; and which may sink into chaos, whenever, at His nod, a similar convulsion may happen again.[65]

Helen McKay suggests Burchell differed from Darwin 'only in that he turned invariably to the supernatural for an explanation of the phenomenon he encountered'.[66]

Burchell, the English Romantic, compares the 'dawn of an African day' with the 'superior beauty of that hour in Europe'. In scientific terms, the 'inferiority of the *African Aurora*' is caused by the 'aridity of the climate and clearness of the atmosphere' – there are no 'rosy and golden tints, and those beams of light, which decorate the morning sky of European countries'.[67] Yet, the African dawn is also pleasing:

> While watching the cold darkness of night, the eastern sky becomes less obscure, a faint light gradually increases; the stars seem to fade away, though the earth still continues in night; a warm glow is perceptible, and soon spreads itself over the vault of heaven; the trees along the horizon become visible, and, backed by the sky, the upper branches of those which are nearer, are seen more distinctly; the

landscape begins to show its outline; the light has reached the west; the forms of objects are visible, but as yet, present a painting in one color only, a sombre brown, equally strong in the distance and in the foreground; the whole atmosphere is illumined, and reflects its light upon the earth ...[68]

The light changes and 'the azure of the sky is everywhere suffused with a warmer light; Nature is awake; and, unattended by cloud or vapour, the sun himself is seen rising above the horizon in noontide brilliancy'.[69] Burchell brilliantly depicts visual perception in slow motion, moving beyond the European aesthetic ideal of beauty.

On 6 July, the death of one of the dogs, run over by a wagon, sparks off a lengthy philosophical passage about vultures in nature. Crows and vultures discover the body and 'immediately began to tear it to pieces'. Burchell believes that vultures – along with every other creature – have been ordained 'to perform very necessary and useful duties on the globe'. The formation of a vulture is adapted to 'clearing away putrid or putrescent animal matter, which might otherwise taint the air and produce infectious diseases'; their own flesh smells strongly of carrion and other animals will not eat it, 'a quality of importance to their preservation'; and vultures often 'feed in company with hyenas, and other beasts of prey ... but so nicely is the mutual relation of all things balanced, that none of these animals, nor the domestic dog, show the least inclination to take away the life of these birds'. Vultures are tolerated 'because they never harm the living'.[70]

Still, the vulture is a symbol of the cycle of life and death. Matter circulates through the whole system of living objects, but so does destruction: 'This picture of a succession of destruction among the animal creation, though natural and immutable, is not an agreeable one.'[71] Rapacity and death, warfare and bloodshed, result from natural laws:

The Limong, or *Vultur occipitalis* – White-headed vulture

the Power which made things so, has implanted in the human mind a sentiment which, if not stifled, causes this prospect, however interesting and instructive, to appear unpleasing; and, from the view of rapacity and death, warfare and bloodshed, even though the result of natural laws, we gladly turn towards that part of animated nature where more peaceful scenes present themselves: from the tiger to the lamb, from the hawk to the dove, we turn with pleasure. Or, if more tranquil thoughts delight us, we change to the contemplation of the beauties and perfection of inanimate objects; to the verdant foliage of the spreading trees which clothe the mountain-foot, or to the lively hues of the fragrant flowers which adorn the valleys.[72]

Burchell's philosophical reflections end with a striking, harsh judgement on Man: 'In him terminates this scale of rapine and destruction; in him, this graduated tyranny reaches its height.'[73]

At the Makkwarin River, Burchell and his party undertook various mundane preparations for the journey to Litakun. The store-chests were opened, and 'beads and other things which were intended as *presents* to the Bachapin chief' were selected. Opening the chests before arriving in Litakun would prevent 'the natives from knowing how large a stock I had of these things', a practice that security-conscious Burchell followed everywhere he went.

> To have allowed them to see the contents of the chests, would have been, to tempt them to rob me; or, should their sense of honesty restrain them from such an attempt; still the sight of so much riches might render them covetous, and induce them to practise every extortionate and unfair stratagem to get possession of them.[74]

Burchell's narrative of his wearisome preparations at the Makkwarin River is interspersed with a number of humorous anecdotes. On one cold evening, he finds himself enlivened by an African tale Keyser relates at the campfire of a 'Hottentot of *Sneeuwberg* being pierced by so many arrows that when they found his body he looked more like a porcupine than a man'.[75] Burchell would again delight in the poetic talents of his men, when, in Litakun, his interpreter Muchunka described Bachapins assembled for war:

> And in order to give me a suitable idea of the magnitude and power of the *Bachapin nation*, he added, that if, their chief were to order the whole of his

people to assemble for a great war, I should behold so countless *a multitude*, that my eyes would open wide with wonder. His men would stand, he said, so closely together that they would tread on each other, and the ground all about us would be crowded with them, like reeds on the bank of a river.[76]

Burchell 'could not but admire the beautiful *simile* which he employed, and which so expressively conveyed the idea of multitude'.[77]

Muchunka amused Burchell and three visiting Bichuana herdsmen, who joined Burchell's party on 9 July, the night before his departure from the Makkwarin River. Once the visitors had enjoyed meat, snuff and tobacco, Burchell took the opportunity to observe 'in them the workings of an untaught mind', and to observe the performance of Muchunka, 'whose simple brain seemed not yet to contain a true idea of the nature of writing or of the real purport and utility of our evening exercise at the dictionary and vocabulary'.[78]

With Muchunka at his side, Burchell tested his knowledge of Sichuana by reading words and sentences, written down in his book, during his tutorial sessions with the interpreter.

These were readily understood by them, who at first, supposing me to have a tolerable knowledge of that tongue, talked a great deal, to which I could give no answer; but when they at length discovered that I could speak only when I looked in the book, they stood with eyes and mouth wide open; wondering both at the book and at myself, and unable to conceive how it could be, that 'the white thing in my hand,' told me what to say; or how, by only looking at it, I could know more than when I did not.[79]

Muchunka told Burchell that he was surprised at him 'remembering so well every thing he had taught me, and even those words which he had never told me but once'.[80] Burchell had to explain to Muchunka and the three Bachapins that the 'black scratches' in the book showed him what to say. Muchunka, very surprised,

laughed most heartily, and desired to see the very words which I was pronouncing. On pointing them out, he laughed again; and his three countrymen, whose mouth and eyes had by this time recovered from their expression of surprise, joined in the laughter …[81]

Burchell, as he shut the book, 'was unable to resist the impression which their ludicrous appearance and distorted countenances' made upon him.[82]

All preparations for the trip to Litakun finalised, the travellers departed from the Makkwarin River on 10 July. Two days later they were 'within a very moderate day's journey' from Litakun. Burchell strategised it would be best to arrive in the morning, when there would be 'sufficient time to have an interview with the Chief; and make some arrangements before the night came on'.[83] It was Burchell's intention to stay at Litakun for some time so he could study the character of the people and observe their customs.[84] Before entering the town on 13 July, Burchell gives his own expectations of what he hopes to find in Litakun:

> I need not describe my own sensations at so interesting a point of my journey; they
> may easily be conceived by those who have ever felt a desire to visit a foreign land
> that they may view and contemplate the human character in some new light; and
> that, by tracing the gradations and shades of notions and ideas, through the various
> customs of different nations, and even to their first feeble source in uncivilized
> life, they may better understand themselves, and learn by the comparison, to form
> a juster estimate of that society which more immediately surrounds them, and to
> which they more properly belong.[85]

The good humour of the welcoming crowd in Litakun instantly 'banished every uneasy sensation which the uncertainty of our reception might have created'. In a triumphant mood, feeling that the numerous difficulties experienced on the journey had been successfully overcome, he voices his excitement:

> I caught a spirit of enthusiasm which seemed like some fascinating power
> emanating from the strange objects which everywhere surrounded me, and
> excited feelings which rendered my first view of the town of Litakun, a moment,
> which, in its peculiar gratification and delight, was never surpassed by any other
> event of the journey.[86]

8

'Breathing the air of Africa'[1]

Litakun
July to August 1812

'IT IS IMPOSSIBLE,' Professor Poulton points out, 'to speak in any detail of Burchell's residence, from July 13 to August 3, 1812, in the chief town of the Bachapins, or of his admirable and precise account of this primitive semi-civilization, as yet unmodified by contact with European nations.'[2]

Indeed, the amount of information Burchell collected on the Bachapins and their way of life is so extensive that his research findings are not part of the travelogue, but collated into two chapters at the end of Volume II. History, architecture, population demographics and the climate of Litakun are outlined in the first chapter; while politics, warfare, trade, religion, moral character, mental capacity, customs, food, arts, amusements, agriculture and artefacts are covered in the second. The data on the Bachapins was 'extracted principally from the subsequent parts of the journal'; 'added for the purpose of completing the work as an account of the inhabitants of the interior regions of Southern Africa, and more especially for conveying as much general information as may be sufficient for filling up the description of the Bachapins'.[3]

The three turbulent weeks Burchell spent in Litakun underline his Enlightened character in the resilience and open-mindedness he showed the people of the town. He believed that 'a resolute opposition to encroachment, and a determination not to be intimidated, were the safest and most prudent measures' to govern his dealings with the Bachapins, and balanced peaceful dispute resolution and fact-finding with good will, humour and art.[4] Burchell's clear-eyed, but at times Eurocentric examination of the Bachapins provides an interesting perspective on the similarities and differences between the greatly differing cultures of the Europeans and this small traditional African society. Burchell's daily journal entries in Litakun cover a number of topics: his reception upon arriving in the area; interactions with the chiefs and villagers; problems with his employees; bartering disputes with locals and constant harassment from begging; hunting expeditions; the music and dance of the Bachapins; a conversation on a Sunday with Mollémmi, a brother of the chief, Mattivi, on religion and morality; the town in a state of alarm; a futile inquiry into the fate of Dr Cowan's expedition; portrait painting of various individuals; and data on the town and its occupants. The travelogue ends abruptly when food shortages force him to leave Litakun on 3 August 1812 to go on a hunting expedition.

In Stephen Watson's opinion, in Burchell's account of the Bachapins, it is his 'art of writing that *makes* for interest'. For Watson, 'every writer's consciousness may be likened to some custom-built prism through which light from a common source will be differently absorbed and refracted. What one of them may notice may well remain below the horizon of another's attention.' Applied to his observations in Litakun, Burchell's 'individual sensibilities and angles of vision',[5] to use Watson's words, make 'for the interest and importance'[6] of the place and its people.

A skilled story writer, Burchell brings the cast of characters he meets in Litakun to life. On his arrival, he wishes to discover the character of Mattivi, the chief of the Bachapins:

> *Mattivi* in outward appearance differed in no respect from those of the crowd by whom he was surrounded. Compared with the rest of his nation, he was in stature of an intermediate proportion, and of a good figure; neither tall nor short, neither thin nor corpulent. In his countenance there was little expression of openness, or of that good-natured easy disposition which might be seen in the features of several who stood near him.... [Mattivi] stood perfectly still, with his hands before him folded in each other, and with his eyes directed downwards, but now and then looking up and showing that he was attending to all that was said. He spoke very little or almost nothing; and left the conversation to Serrakútu and his brothers.[7]

Burchell's ethnographic lens then focuses on the chief's brothers, Mollémmi, Molaali and Măhúra, taking note of familial divisions: Mollémmi and Mattivi were the sons of a Kora, whereas Molaali and Măhúra had a Bichuana mother. The brothers' striking physical features also stand out for Burchell. Mollémmi 'was a tall thin man, of a countenance most remarkable for its long and disproportioned features'; Molaali 'was a fine well-proportioned young man of genuine Bichuana countenance and complexion, approaching somewhat to the negro'; the younger brother Măhúra 'was remarkably handsome as a black, ... he was of fine proportions, and in limbs and

View on entering the Town of Litakun

figure, not unlike the well known statue of Antinoüs, though somewhat fatter'.[8] In the allusion to Antinous (using the modern spelling), Burchell's angle of vision extends to European readers familiar with the statue of the Greek youth, a lover of the Roman emperor Hadrian.

Artworks portray the unique visual qualities of Litakun. The aquatint *View on entering the Town of Litakun*[9] shows the division of space in the town in its portrayal of a man carrying a parasol made of ostrich feathers, two women and a child, and large camel-thorn trees. Burchell recreates the features of a typical house in an engraving, *Houses at Litakun*.[10] In another, his first meeting with Litakun's chiefs on the day of

his arrival is depicted:[11] Burchell and the chiefs are seated in a circle on the ground, surrounded by crowds of people standing 'as close as it was possible for them to crowd together'.[12] While Burchell felt 'perfectly at ease' in his conversation with the chiefs, he

> could not, on viewing the assembly and snatching in the midst of these transactions a moment to reflect on my situation, a solitary Englishman wandering among lawless nations in the heart of Africa, to gratify a desire of beholding human nature in its uncivilized state, I could not but feel sensible of the risk I incurred.[13]

His adventurous spirit is what ultimately takes precedence and helps to quiet his unease: 'every hour at Litakun presented some new and interesting fact to my observation; and, even in the midst of all the confusion of novelty, the care which my situation created and the watchfulness which it demanded could not prevent me from enjoying the contemplation of the strange scene to which this day's journey had brought me'.[14]

Burchell's curiosity in the Bachapins never diminishes; nor does his goodwill towards them – even when put severely to the test. During the occasion he labelled 'the affair of the gun', Burchell indicated his singular ability to handle unique and tricky cross-cultural situations.

On Burchell's first evening in Litakun, Mattivi, his two brothers Mollémmi and Molaali, and Adam, a Bachapin they brought in as an interpreter, joined Burchell in his wagon. Burchell asked his own interpreter Muchunka to join the group as well, and, after they had enjoyed the coffee Burchell provided, the ice-breaking desultory conversation turned to an '*important subject* which it seems had occupied their thoughts long before my arrival, and had been a matter of national consultation'.[15]

With great authority, and to Burchell's horror, Mattivi requested that their visitor give him a gun:

> So unexpected a demand, and of such a nature, for it had more the character of a demand than of a request, and made on the very moment of my arrival, was a circumstance exceedingly unpleasant, as the earnestness with which it was made, convinced me at once of the difficulty of the situation in which it placed me.[16]

Houses at Litakun

First interview with the Chief of the Bachapins

Burchell, prudently, did not wish to put 'into the hands of this people a weapon which in the event of any future misunderstanding would be used against ourselves; so that we might lose our lives by the very instrument which we had brought for the purpose of defending them'. Being outnumbered by the Bachapins, however, meant that if he refused, the gun could be 'taken by force or by stealth'. He had 'but an instant for reflection; my answer must follow the question'; so he resolved not to grant the request, knowing this 'would produce some unpleasant consequences'.[17]

Burchell told them that all the muskets in his possession were used by his men, who had to be armed while travelling through dangerous country inhabited by Bushmen. He added that their food supply depended on guns too, unlike that of the Bachapins, who 'had an abundance of corn, milk, and cattle'. Diplomatically, he assured Mattivi of his 'most friendly sentiments towards him and all his people', and emphasised that, if he had more muskets, he would 'willingly let him have one, but that it was impossible to think of disarming my own men'.[18]

His words had no effect, and Burchell eventually 'begged them to wait till the morning'[19] to continue the deliberations. But waiting one night did nothing to quell Mattivi's wishes, and he 'obstinately persisted' in demanding a gun the next day. Burchell, noting the relentlessness of Mattivi's demands, and to amuse his erudite nineteenth-century readers, wryly slips in a line from Oliver Goldsmith's poem 'The Village Schoolmaster': 'e'en tho' vanquished, they could argue still'.[20] Realising 'it was in Mattivi's power ... to take without permission, not one gun only, but all',[21] Burchell judged it imprudent to continue resisting his wishes. He capitulated, on the condition that the Bachapins could have just one musket, but only when he returned to Klaarwater after travelling into the interior. Burchell conceived that by making such an agreement with Mattivi, 'I was dealing with him in his own way, by outwitting him; as it was of course not my intention to return to that village, but to proceed onwards farther into the Interior'.[22] Despite Burchell's offer, the chiefs' demand that they be given a gun at once continued relentlessly; and on 15 July, two oxen and two large elephant tusks were presented as payment, and the next day, four oxen were produced, which Burchell rejected, since 'their intention was to establish a claim to have immediate possession of their purchase'.[23] He was aware, though, that he was powerless 'to break off the negotiation', and the chiefs knew they could insist on the gun on their own terms: 'there is little doubt that they were emboldened to act in this manner, by observing the symptoms of fear which the looks and behaviour of my own men, had, from the first hour of our arrival, but more especially during these transactions, too visibly betrayed'.[24]

The 'violent debates' respecting the gun had 'strongly excited' fear in all of Burchell's men besides Burchell's best servant Juli. Speelman, Philip and Gert 'begged' Burchell to leave the circle, and urged him to let the chiefs have the gun at any price. Professor Poulton sums up the no-win situation:

> In the great controversy about the gun Burchell, urged to yield by his terrified attendants, was pitted single-handed against Mattivi with his chiefs and people. He resisted with extraordinary courage, resource and ingenuity, but was met with arguments, it must be admitted, equally ingenious, and ultimately had to give way.[25]

Burchell, in a conciliatory manner, asked Muchunka to tell the chiefs that 'I should dispute with them no longer' and would let them have the gun, 'as I desired nothing so much as their friendship'.[26] Mattivi then wished to see the gun fired, and asked that Molaali be allowed to fire it. Molaali did so, but instead of returning it, he 'was ordered by the Chief to take it home to his house'. Burchell was furious:

> At so flagrant an act of bad faith, I loudly expressed my dissatisfaction, as it was an open breach of our agreement; but he, in his turn, pretended to be equally dissatisfied with me for wishing to detain what he had now bought and made his own; the whole party at the same time crying out, that they ought not to give it out of their possession. At this moment I felt exceedingly irritated at their conduct, so

deficient in honour and every just principle; but I suppressed my feelings as well as I was able, since a glance at the crowd and my own men, showed me too truly that I was completely in their power, and that my gun was irrecoverably gone. They must have read in my countenance, what I thought of their dealings; but they walked away, exulting in the success of their cunning, and even, perhaps, inwardly proud of their superiority over a white-man in this essential qualification, the possession of which seems in their eyes, and, I am ashamed to confess, in the eyes of many Europeans, to constitute a man of talents.[27]

Burchell's conclusion about the incident is significant: many Europeans are no different from the scheming Bachapins. Characteristically, his point of view reaches beyond Litakun to Europe.

Mattivi celebrated his cunning procurement of the gun by dedicating a whole day to music and dancing. Burchell's journal entry focuses on the sound of the music played on reed pipes; the technicalities involved in the dance; the 'grace and ease of motion'[28] of the '*the dancers*, who were all men'; and the 'clapping hands' of the women and girls regulating the steps of the dancers.[29] The harmony of the celebration briefly relieved the tension of the gun affair. An astute strategist, Burchell, 'while affairs were thus going smoothly', used the opportunity to send 'some of my men out to hunt', as provisions were exhausted and no food could be purchased at Litakun.[30]

The fiasco with the gun was just one of many ordeals Burchell suffered on his first days in Litakun. While he 'beheld everywhere, a harvest of new ideas',[31] he soon realised his animals and their attendants, Andries and Stuurman, were nowhere to be seen. Keyser was also absent.[32] He felt exasperated too: having come to Litakun for scientific inquiry, and to observe its people and their customs, he was understandably upset at being repeatedly distracted from these pursuits:

These Hottentots, it now appeared, had again neglected their duty; and thus, at a moment when so many other subjects demanded my attention, were my cares increased by their worthlessness; nor could I, under the pressure of these feelings, scarcely avoid the wish that those who reduced me to the necessity of hiring such people, and those who prevented better from engaging in my service, might someday be placed in a situation to feel all those anxieties and difficulties which their ungenerous dealing caused me for so many months to suffer.[33]

Frustrated, Burchell sardonically remarks that the loss of the horses was 'a more serious misfortune than that of the men; who by this conduct, proved that they would be of little value in time of danger'.[34]

Sending Philip and two others to search for the three men, they were eventually discovered a mile or two away from Litakun, 'sitting together under a bush, with the horses near them'.[35] Burchell viewed the desertion of his attendants in a serious light, understanding that his authority as leader had been jeopardised. Burchell wished to conceal 'this affair', but it was 'soon made known to the Chief and the whole of the town, who, most unfortunately for me, were now convinced that I was accompanied by men who would be ready to desert me on the first appearance of danger'.[36]

A brief phase of tranquillity followed this incident, but on 22 July, Burchell discovered the horses had again gone missing through Andries's neglect. Furious, Burchell ruthlessly sums up the character of his servant: 'The disposition of this Hottentot, was either so careless, so worthless, or so stupid, that no reprimand had any effect in causing him to pay more attention to the duty which had been allotted to him.' As the loss of oxen and horses 'would have put an end to my journey',[37] Burchell decided to appoint Van Roye and Cornelis to take charge of the cattle.

But his troubles with his men would not end there. Since arriving in Litakun, they had constantly found ways in which to defy his wishes; and this became a matter of greater concern when the neglect of their duties led to the mishandling of Burchell's property and animals. It also weakened his authority among the Bachapins, who would see him as incapable of controlling his men. Therefore, upon giving Van Roye and Cornelis the responsibility of caring for the cattle, Burchell hoped they had entered upon this 'new duty … with perfect willingness'.[38] However, in the presence of the chief and other chieftains, they seemed intent on challenging Burchell's authority, frequently exhibiting insolence, disobedience and defiance towards him. To prove he could check the defiance of his servants, and simply tired of their insubordination, Burchell – the day after transferring the care of the cattle to Van Roye and Cornelis – 'resolved at all hazards to maintain my authority; and, buckling on my pistols and cutlass' followed Cornelis, who had contemptuously walked out of the cattle enclosure. Burchell ordered Speelman and Platje to 'bring him back', but they were too afraid to: 'But as [Cornelis] was the tallest and stoutest man of our party, they declared that they were afraid to approach him.'[39] Burchell was obliged to

support the step which I had taken, by hastening alone towards him; and on overtaking him, commanded him instantly to return to the waggons. He was at the first moment, on the point of refusing obedience; but observing me to be armed, and seeing me determined on enforcing my words, he thought it more advisable to obey; and with a slow and reluctant pace, walked before me to the enclosure.[40]

At the wagons, Burchell assembled his men, and in front of them demanded an apology from Cornelis. If he did not 'beg my pardon', Burchell would have him instantly punished.

> He seemed to hesitate. At this moment I felt myself placed in that critical situation which was balanced between violent measures and all the dangers of ineffective authority. Nothing could be more discordant to my disposition, or wishes, than the former, nor more fatal to the expedition, than the latter. While I assumed the appearance of a firm resolution to have my threats put immediately into execution, I in reality made a delay of a minute or two, in order to give him time to reflect on the dangerous position in which we all stood. This had the effect so much hoped for; and he at length begged *pardon* for his conduct.[41]

Nonetheless, Burchell's firm yet forgiving approach towards his servant soon proved inadequate as well. Cornelis was clearly only apologising because he felt compelled to: 'He did it, however, in so unwilling a manner, that it was evident that I had preserved nothing more than the bare appearance of my command.'[42]

Cornelis quickly 'recovered his *refractory spirit*' and again confronted Burchell, who stifled his anger and reminded him that he was a servant and 'bound to be obedient'. Cornelis, 'seeing therefore no prospect of gaining the mastery by intimidation … walked quietly away'.[43]

Burchell, victorious, felt he had shown it would be perilous for any man to resist his orders, and he 'thus ended one of the most turbulent days which I had experienced since the commencement of my journey'.[44]

The next day, Burchell was pleasantly surprised by the 'rattling of two waggons driving into the town' and the arrival of his old Klaarwater acquaintances, Berends the Khoikhoi captain and Jan Hendrik.[45] This pleasure was short-lived when, on 24 July, Van Roye put him 'into a state of irritation and uneasiness' by manifesting 'a determination not only to resist my authority by disobedience, but even to act in open defiance of it'.[46] Van Roye had brazenly ignored Burchell's instructions to take proper care of the cattle, and 'in order more clearly to show me his disposition, and his inclination to *disrespect*, he conducted himself before me with a gait and looks, which were too clear and visible to the rest of my men and the natives, to admit of my pretending not to see and understand them'.[47]

Burchell resolved to confront his servants' rebellion once and for all, and organised a formal trial for Van Roye with all of his men as witnesses. Laying out his pistols and sword on the chest in his wagon, to have them close at hand, he set out 'to impress more strongly on my people the serious nature of the affair'. He requested Captain Berends and Jan Hendrik to witness the 'proceedings with one of my men who had dared openly to disobey me'. Burchell 'desired their presence' so that he had some credible witnesses and 'impartial judges whose opinion' he valued.[48]

The formal proceedings began with Burchell reading aloud the written agreement in which Cornelis and Van Roye 'had legally bound themselves in the obligation to go with me wherever I should think advisable, and punctually to obey every order, under penalty of all his wages, and of legal punishment'. Next, he called on his men 'to declare freely, and without any apprehension of gaining my displeasure by giving an opinion against me, whether I had ever issued to Van Roye or any of them, orders to which they were not bound, or not able, to conform'. His attendants confirmed that no harsh orders were ever given and agreed that Burchell had 'just cause of complaint against that Hottentot for having done so much less work than any of the rest of my people, that he might be considered as having done nothing'.[49]

Van Roye was required to defend himself and take the 'usual oath to relate the truth'. He proceeded to 'relate his story and reply to my questions; but, in so contradictory a manner, and with so much hesitation and *prevarication*, that I failed in my endeavours to obtain from him the truth'. Burchell warned him of 'the dreadful crime he would commit by uttering a falsity at the moment when he called God to witness his veracity'.[50] Eventually, after Burchell repeated to him 'the substance of several passages in the New Testament ... Self-conviction instantaneously operated on his mind':[51]

> I then asked him, in a tone which might encourage him to give the answer I wished, if he now felt disposed to conduct himself in future as his duty demanded: to which he readily replied, Yes. To conclude: I told him, that if he did as, in the presence of all, he had now promised to do, I was willing in the same manner to promise forgiveness; and would, according to his fulfilment of this promise, even forget all past cause of complaint.[52]

Thus, Burchell, as a natural-born leader, used the 'court case' to affirm his authority – a very Enlightened solution. Van Roye converted to 'a becoming humility and obedience:

and although, unfortunately, this change was not permanent, yet it continued for some time to produce a good effect'.[53]

Burchell used the court case to underline the importance of his leadership and authority, which would ensure the safety and success of expeditions. He believed it essential that the leader 'should be fortified with *special power* to enforce, if occasion required, the obedience and due co-operation of its members'. The individual 'case' of Van Roye led Burchell to reflect on human nature, which without the guiding force of reason or scientific inquiry, has no other course to follow but that of discord and hostility: 'For, the perverseness of human nature when uncontrolled, seems every-where alike to seduce men from unanimity, and strangely to mislead them to prefer turbulence to peace.'[54]

The perverseness of human nature – 'This is Man, without morality or religion!'[55] – is tragically represented in the case of a San child Burchell encountered in Litakun. The boy had been seized in an attack upon a San kraal and carried off as a 'prisoner of war'. The Bachapin who now 'owned' the boy clearly had very little regard for him, informing Burchell that the child was 'his by right' and that Burchell could buy him for a sheep. About five or six years old, the child, on the evening of 26 July, stood 'by our fire … anxiously watching my men in hopes of getting a piece of meat'. Burchell's heart broke at the sight of the suffering boy: 'But I never beheld an object which more strongly excited my compassion: the sight of this wretched poor little creature, pained me to the heart, and I stood for some minutes shocked at the view of its emaciated and more than half-starved figure.'[56]

Deep, personal feelings of compassion and shock on Burchell's part are followed by his chilling realisation of the boy's condition, and one of the most callous, incom-prehensible acts of cruelty that can be carried out by a human being – starving an innocent child to death. Burchell's harrowing eyewitness account of the crime of this Bachapin man against a San child indicates that not only the colonists were respon-sible for the genocide of the San.

Those who have seen a human skeleton of that age, may obtain an idea of this child's form, not greatly exaggerated, by imagining the bones of the body and limbs, to be wrapped round with a wet cloth. Those rounded shapes which are given to the human figure by flesh only, had dwindled quite away. The legs and arms were merely straight sticks; the calf was entirely gone; the *fibula* and *ulna* were plainly distinguishable; and the knees and elbows were comparatively large knots. The abdomen was contracted in an extraordinary degree; and behind, scarcely any flesh concealed the shape of the bones termed *os sacrum*, and *os ilium*. The collar-bones seemed to project unnaturally; and the blade-bones, the spine and the ribs, were in appearance covered only with skin. In short, this miserable little boy, who from his age could not have been capable of harm, or guilty of offence, was on the point of being *starved to death*.[57]

Burchell, enraged, takes a broad view on human depravity, and what could cause a human being to abandon compassion and sympathy for brutality and general wickedness.

This is Man, without morality or religion! This is the selfish savage, without feeling! … Alas! Man who vaunts himself the noblest work of the creation; how closely does he approach to Brute, when reason lies dormant, or when the passions usurp its place! The power of speech forms but a weakly distinctive character, for him whose intellect is never exerted. The boasted human form will hardly raise him in rank above some quadrupeds, when it serves no better purpose than that only of ministering to animal appetite.[58]

For Burchell, the qualities of speech and language, traditionally distinguishing humans from animals, are negated when they succumb to savage passions and instincts. When reason and intellect are quiescent, the margin between 'brute' and 'man' dissolves.

Dogs were victims of human cruelty as well, and had to survive by scavenging; they were 'generally very thin and meagre, as their masters themselves devour all the offal which should fall to the share of the animals'.[59] The maltreatment of dogs in Litakun deeply distressed Burchell, who was tormented at the sight of half-starved, malnourished dogs, driven by hunger, prowling around and devouring 'every piece of animal substance which they can find', even shoes.

Herbivorous cattle in Litakun were more advantaged, merely by a circumstance of what they could eat: 'That the cattle belonging to this nation, are more fortunate, with respect to food, than the domestic animals, is to be accounted for solely by their living on grass, and not on any substance which their owners can convert into food for themselves.'[60] Burchell provides another scathing allusion to heartless, human covetousness: the cattle were not subjected to the same abuse as the dogs, only because their masters had not found a way to use their food for themselves.

Notwithstanding the darker encounters of his stay in Litakun, Burchell's enthusiasm, resilience and facility for making friends with the Bachapins is extraordinary. When he walked through Litakun, 'everybody seemed pleased at my paying a visit to their quarter of the town'.[61] As the only 'portrait-painter' there, he amused the 'models' and the crowds: 'At the sight of these likenesses, the crowd were again as much delighted as when they first saw them: they examined them for a few moments with the same surprise and attentiveness, and then laughed most heartily, as if unable to conceive what caused the drawing to look like those persons.'[62] The portrait of Massisan, 'a good specimen of Bachapin [female] beauty',[63] 'excited a strong curiosity among that sex, who seemed to consider it an important mark of respect to them, that I had put *women* "into my book," as well as men'.[64] Burchell's portraits of individuals in Litakun are carefully annotated, describing clothing, hairstyles and ornaments, and can be considered precious, pictorial records.

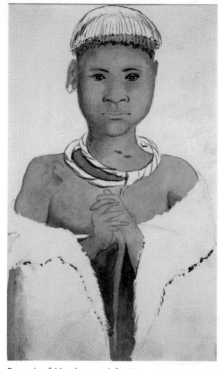

Portrait of Massisan, 29 July 1812

The aquatint *A View in the Town of Litakun*[65] gives an idea of the 'appearance of this strange and singular town'. Burchell is spiritually uplifted in Litakun:

> yet nothing but breathing the air of Africa, and actually walking through it and beholding its living inhabitants in all the peculiarities of their movements and manners, can communicate those gratifying, and literally indescribable, sensations, which every European traveller of feeling, will experience on finding himself in the midst of so interesting a scene: – a scene not merely amusing; but highly instructive, for a contemplative mind.[66]

He compares Litakun society with a European metropolis's 'intellectual and exalted characters, and its pure knowledge of the Deity':

> Let us, in short, contrast piety with atheism, the philosopher with the rude savage, the monarch with the Chief, luxury with want, philanthropy with lawless rapine:

Portrait of Chaasi, a Bachapin,
19 August 1812

let us set before us in one view, the lofty cathedral and the straw-hut, the flowery garden and the stony waste, the verdant meadow and the arid sands. And when our imagination shall have completed the picture, and placed it in a light which may invite contemplation, it will, I think, be impossible not to derive from it the instruction of the highest class. If that truly wise but difficult precept, *Know thyself*, has been judged so valuable and important, as to deserve being inscribed in letters of gold on one of the greatest temples in the world; most certainly, a precept which should command men to seek wisdom by gaining a knowledge of human nature and of the globe which they inhabit, cannot be less important or less deserving of being inscribed on the tablet of the mind.[67]

In spite of his delight in the 'pure air of Africa', Burchell's contrasting images privilege the benefits of a European social order over what he believes is the intellectual and spiritual poverty of an African way of life. His travels have been driven by his quest for knowledge, and, in the spirit of the Enlightenment, he is reflecting on human nature in Europe and Africa.

The insatiable covetousness of the Bachapins detracted from Burchell's stay in Litakun – 'they are all beggars of the meanest kind'.[68] He eventually developed a strategy to stop them begging:

> As an experiment, I adopted his own style of solicitation … and therefore begged he would every day send me a large quantity [of milk] … I was induced to make this demand, by having discovered that *the art of begging* follows one of the rules of an algebraic equation; that, like-quantities on both sides annul each other, and may be expunged, as not affecting the result. Whenever I began to beg of the Bachapins, their begging ceased immediately, and thus, neither party gained nor lost.[69]

As a man of small stature, and the only European in Litakun, it was imperative for Burchell to prove his muscular power to the Bachapins. On a visit to the houses in the town on 21 July, an elephant's tusk was dragged out of a storeroom in the hope that Burchell would purchase it. Instead, he used the opportunity to lift the tusk, which weighed between eighty and ninety pounds (about forty kilograms) to show his strength:

> Desirous of gaining, among these people, the character of being *múnŏnă tatáaïo* (a strong man), I confess that in this instance I exerted my utmost force with a view to induce them to suppose that the tusk was, to my hand, comparatively light; for as I knew that, guided by outward appearances, they judged themselves to be my superiors in muscular power, I regarded it as an important point of prudence and policy, to give them the impression of my being personally able to defend myself against any attempt on their part, should they ever feel disposed to offer open violence.[70]

Portrait of Mahuta, 31 July 1812

'When the natives saw me heaving it up and down with apparent ease, they seemed greatly surprised, and considered me to be a person of extraordinary strength,'[71] continues Burchell humorously. The undercurrent of potential violence is strong, yet he remains gregarious, genial and good-humoured.

The next day, a chieftain, Serrakútu, invited him to see the house of his younger wife, who had painted animal figures on the front wall. While observing the wall, a person behind Burchell cautiously felt his hair, 'which being rather unfashionably long, admitted of their doing this, as they supposed, without being perceived'.[72] The chief's wife then begged Burchell to take off his hat:

> I did so; and had it been a man with eyes in every part of his head, who had thus unexpectedly appeared before her, she could not have expressed greater astonishment. She lifted up both hands with amazement; involuntarily drew herself back a pace, as though fearful of a strange animal; and remained for a minute or two fixed in silent wonder. The greater part of the crowd also stood gazing with

A View in the Town of Litakun

surprise at the extraordinary sight, and seemed scarcely to credit the testimony of their own senses, that there could exist on the earth a race of men whose heads produced a similar covering.[73]

Burchell left 'them all exceedingly pleased at my visit, which, I doubt not, furnished them with abundant matter of conversation during the remainder of the day'.[74]

The cheerful mood in the town changed considerably on 2 August when marauders threatened Litakun's cattle stations. In Burchell's words:

The uproar and clamour soon became general, and confusion reigned in every quarter. The vociferations of the men denouncing vengeance against the invaders, and the cries and lamentations of the women, filled the air and reached the ear in every direction. Amid these tumultuous sounds, the violent howling of some of the women, was heard above the rest, and impressed the mind with sensations which may be more easily conceived than described, and which were well suited to give a complete idea of a state of warfare among savages.[75]

Panic seized Burchell's men, and, as he had done on so many former occasions, he endeavoured to 'inspire my people with confidence in our own strength and resources, and to convince them that the most certain way to escape from danger, was by keeping their minds cool and free from agitation.[76]

Burchell and his men 'kept watch during the whole night'. In the morning, calm returned and Burchell cross-examined Muloja, 'an eye-witness to the murder of the former party of travellers under *Dr. Cowan* and *Captain Donovan*'.[77] His story was inconsistent and contradictory: 'it would be useless here to repeat a fabricated tale of events which never took place'.[78]

As soon as the investigation was over, Burchell informed Mattivi that his provisions were exhausted and he was going on a hunting excursion to acquire more food. He would therefore be away from Litakun for two or three weeks.[79] In light of the current hostilities in the area, Burchell took the precaution of informing Mattivi that 'any party of men approaching us under suspicious appearances' would be fired upon. The Bachapins, however, would always be welcome, but should 'be careful not to visit us in large bodies, lest we should unfortunately mistake them for the enemy'.[80]

Before leaving, Burchell fulfilled his promise to the chief's wife, Kibbukiili, to paint her portrait. He retains his sense of the comic in the midst of turmoil: she 'dressed herself in her best Nuakketsi hat, to set herself off, as she supposed, to the greatest advantage, and to give her an air of importance becoming so great a personage'. His portrait succeeded in 'obtaining as good a likeness of her'.[81]

Burchell drove out of Litakun on 3 August 1812, an hour after sunset. The departure was nerve-wracking: Mattivi 'jumped up behind the great waggon', as did another man wanting tobacco. The 'innumerable crowd' surrounding them alarmed Burchell:

> Not knowing whether so large a body of men was to be viewed as a friendly escort or as a preparative for some act of intimidation or treachery, I armed myself with a cutlass, and buckled on two braces of pistols, as though my usual travelling accoutrement.[82]

Fortunately, 'no other molestation, however, than begging, was offered to me'. Once the crowds turned back, Burchell and his party pursued their 'journey unmolested and alone'. His men relaxed, 'freed from a place where they had been living in a state of fear and uneasiness, regained, in proportion as we increased our distance from it, somewhat of their usual mood, and began to encourage a hope that I should ultimately relinquish all intention of returning'.

Burchell, however, was committed to his knowledge-gathering pursuits:

But, as I was desirous of completing my knowledge of this tribe, or, at least, of collecting information on many subjects with which I considered myself as not yet sufficiently acquainted, I had resolved not to allow the troublesome manners of the inhabitants to deter me from an abode among them as long as there appeared a prospect of obtaining there any portion of the principal object of my travels, or of acquiring that kind of experience which I deemed necessary to the success in my future progress through the unknown regions of the Interior.[83]

Kibbukiili – Portrait, 3 August 1812

With his departure from Litakun, Burchell's voice and his own intimate narrative of the remaining years of his journey in the Cape comes to an end. Most significantly, this final, personal account of his expedition concludes with the timidity of Burchell's men, set against his characteristic vision, courage and daring for future exploits. Burchell's thirst for new knowledge and discoveries does not diminish with the prospect of further perils. Instead, the idea of future adventures, regardless of the dangers they posed, only gave him the impetus to pursue his quest for enlightenment with greater enthusiasm – not an uncommon trait in an Enlightened man of science. From this point on, biographical material and artworks are used to piece together the continually absorbing and very human story of Burchell's life.

9

'Keep moving!'[1]

Litakun to Cape Town, via the Maadji Mountains, Graaff-Reinet and the Garden Route
August 1812 to April 1815

IN 'THE DELINQUENT TRAVELLERS' IN 1824 – the same year that the second volume of Burchell's *Travels* was published – Samuel Taylor Coleridge made fun of the contemporary vogue for travelling:

> Keep moving! Steam, or Gas, or Stage,
> Hold, cabin, steerage, hencoop's cage–
> Tour, Journey, Voyage, Lounge, Ride, Walk,
> Skim, Sketch, Excursion, Travel-talk–
> For move you must! 'Tis now the rage,
> The law and fashion of the Age.[2]

There are no wagons and oxen in Europe, and Burchell is definitely not a 'delinquent traveller'. But Coleridge's 'rollicking, wittily rhymed verse'[3] brilliantly conveys the pulse of Burchell's constant travelling and sketching. 'For move you must!' was a lifelong passion wherever he went.

Burchell travelled in the Cape interior for five years, from 1810 to 1815, mapping, sketching, painting, writing and collecting as he went. Although his travelogue stops after his departure from Litakun in August 1812, the rest of his journey can be reconstructed from his map and his artworks. These offer different levels of engagement with Burchell's aesthetic perceptions and scientific curiosity. Through his artistic creations, he continues to demonstrate the correlation between art and science as mediums of instruction and enlightenment.

While Burchell's travelogue ends prematurely, his large fold-out map – a cartographic masterpiece – provides a record of the entire expedition. The map exemplifies Burchell's scientific eye for detail and the extent of his artistic genius. It represents rivers, mountains and other topographical features, and shows the route in red, as well as arrival dates and the occasional brief description of an event. (See the maps on pages 132–133, 121 and 174–177 for the route of Burchell's journey from Litakun back to Cape Town.)

Dr Roger Stewart has meticulously researched Burchell's map-making and the routes he charted. Using present-day landmarks as guides, he outlines Burchell's route from Litakun to Cape Town:

> [From] Litakun (now Dithakong, 60km north-east of Kuruman), he took a northerly loop towards the Botswana border, to Heuningvlei in the south-eastern Kalahari, and, via Hotazel, back to Kuruman and then Klaarwater. He continued his return by travelling to De Aar, Graaff Reinet, Somerset East and Grahamstown to the mouth of the Great Fish River. He proceeded through Albany to Uitenhage, on to Humansdorp, along the Langkloof to Avontuur and via the initial course of the Keurbooms River to Plettenberg Bay. He continued through the Garden Route forests to George and Mossel Bay, from which he proceeded along the wagon highway, to the north of the N2, to the base of Garcia Pass near Riversdale and on to Grootvadersbosch and Genadendal. He continued along the northern bank of the Riviersonderend, crossed what is now the Theewaterskloof Dam and took a unique route on a forgotten pass adjacent to Viljoen's Pass, past Grabouw and down Gantouw Pass (replaced by Sir Lowry's Pass). He went through Somerset West, Stellenbosch and his final return leg passed through Bottelary, Tygerberg and the Salt River outspan (now part of Ndabeni).[4]

Stewart's use of modern terms, in place of Burchell's obsolete nineteenth-century names, means that Burchell's cross-country routes can be accessed on Google Earth. Adventurous Burchell enthusiasts in 4 x 4 vehicles or on motorcycles have retraced his trek, following the route on his map, and described and photographed the places he visited – selecting scenes painted or mentioned by Burchell on his travels.[5] It is fascinating to see the juxtaposition of modern photographs with Burchell's illustrations. They can be viewed on the internet, and are a fun and informative way of becoming acquainted with the captivating journey Burchell took two centuries ago.

Cape Cobra, 26 August 1812

The map is complemented by pictures Burchell drew throughout the expedition. The artworks typically have a date, number and a brief title, and can be matched with the dates on the map. These paintings and sketches reveal the power and diversity of the eye of Burchell the artist as he moved across this diverse landscape.

On 26 August, Burchell completed the watercolour *Cape Cobra*, depicting 'a young & small Bruin Capel or Geel Slang more venomous even than the Cobra Capel'.[6] Also striking are the watercolours of two plants from the Kuruman region: *Morea papilionacea*, found at Pintado Fountain, dated 29 August 1812; and *Nananthus aloides*, spotted at Jaburi Fountain on 31 August 1812. Plant representations provide visual evidence of Burchell's botanical discoveries.

On his route from Litakun to the Maadji Mountains in Bechuanaland (now Botswana) – the most northerly point of his journey – Burchell encountered a giraffe for the first time. The giraffe was an animal that inspired passionate interest in Europeans,[7]

Giraffe – Head, 4 October 1812

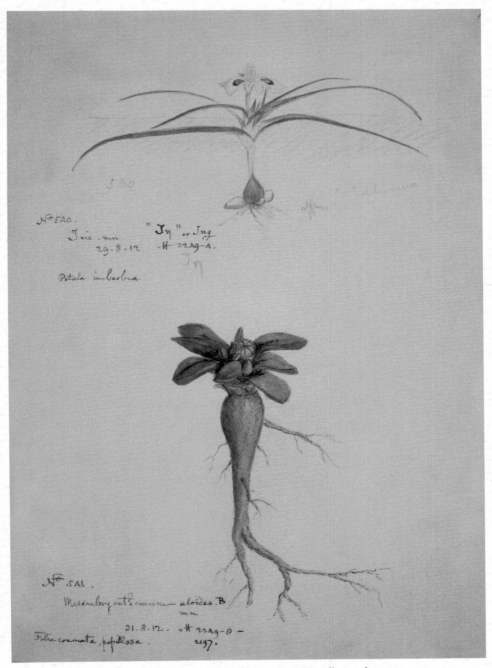

Morea papilionacea, 29 August 1812 [top]; *Nananthus aloides*, 31 August 1812 [bottom]

including Burchell. With scientific precision, he sketched a female giraffe head. Marion Arnold, while discussing botanical art, explains the complexity of scientific representation: 'These representations indicate the complex interactions between seeing and interpreting, an elaborate process of translating and transforming personal vision into signs and objects that are understood differently by different communities.'[8]

Not noted on the map is Burchell's first encounter with a white rhinoceros on 16 October 1812 at Chue Springs[9] – one of his greatest zoological discoveries. The rather faint drawing, *Rhinoceros – Sketches of Heads*, is another demonstration of Burchell's

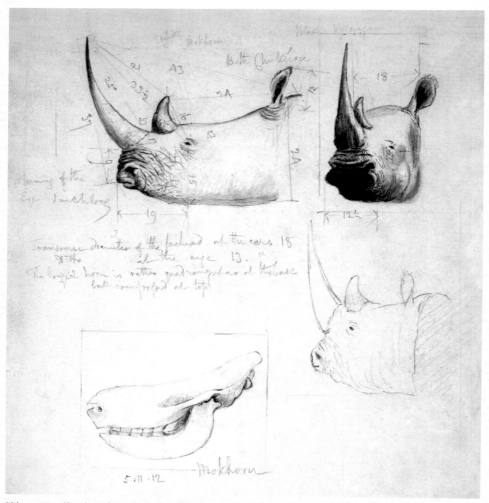

Rhinoceros – Sketches of Heads, 5 November 1812

Elephants, 2 October 1812

process of scientific observation, and the interplay between Burchell the artist and Burchell the scientist. In this illustration of a white rhinoceros, he transforms his personal vision into a scientific record. The inscription specifies the aboriginal names: '(top left) "White mokhoru"; (centre) "Both Chukuru"; (top right) "Black kilanjon"; (bottom left) "Mokhoru" and measurements'.[10]

Science, in Arnold's words, 'claims to be concerned with intellectual objectivity and empirical reality', whereas art 'aims to move the mind through the imagination and senses'.[11] In Burchell's painting of elephants, both of these elements blend together in a perfect whole: art – in the visual structuring of the scene – meets science, portrayed in the habitat and habits of elephants, their heights, and the damage they do to trees. The light and shade in the monochromatic painting are eye-catching. Burchell prominently includes himself in the foreground, in the centre, gazing at the elephants. He holds a cutlass and stands with three marksmen with guns, who are preparing to shoot. This immediately sparks the imagination of the viewer, who is forced but fearful to ask, 'Are humans about to harm Nature and kill elephants?' For Arnold, the 'silent eloquence of [the] visual form moves the mind in powerful ways'.[12]

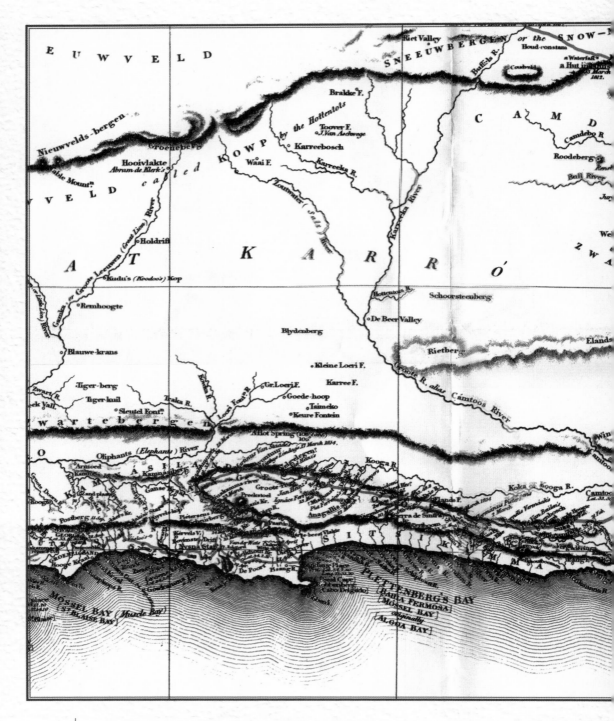

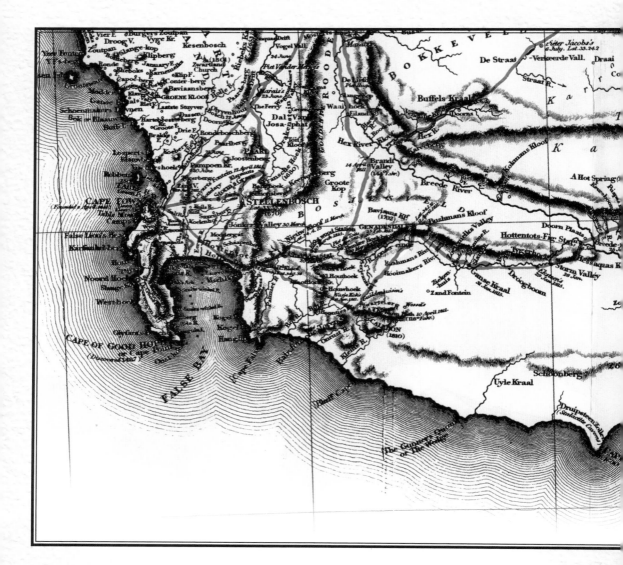

On 22 September 1813, Burchell reached the mouth of the Great Fish River. In April 1814, he was in Plettenberg Bay, where he stayed for nine days.[13] The painting *Plettenberg Bay Panorama*, dated 20 April 1814, shows the stone VOC beacon erected by Governor Joachim van Plettenberg in 1778.

Roger Stewart has reconstructed Burchell's journey through what he calls Burchell's Garden Route, the stretch of formidable terrain with mountains, rivers and forests from the source of the Keurbooms River to Mossel Bay.[14] The pace of this journey was

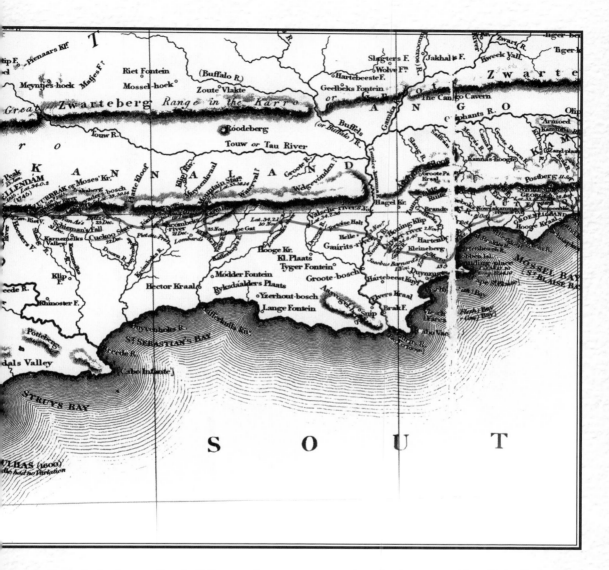

relatively slow, as Burchell frequently went on excursions in the area to identify indigenous trees, to collect snakes, insects, plants, birds and animal specimens, and to walk over sand dunes and climb mountains. Stewart observes that Burchell, ironically, 'took three months to travel about 875 km from Cape Town to Klaarwater, but he took one year and two months to travel the 780 km from Uitenhage to Cape Town; half of this time was spent travelling about 200 km from the source of the Keurbooms River to Mossel Bay'.[15]

Plettenberg Bay Panorama, 20 April 1814

Altogether, Burchell's journey through the Garden Route consisted of about 3 per cent of the distance of his entire trek and a little more than 15 per cent of its duration, but yielded 40 per cent of his South African botanical collection. Stewart calculates that Burchell collected 20 840 botanical specimens during the fourteen months he took to travel from Uitenhage to Cape Town.[16] Like the English artist-traveller Thomas Baines, Burchell – to use Marion Arnold's words – looked at the natural world with the 'curiosity of a scientist and with the sentiments of an Englishman who never questioned that natural resources were available for collection and exploitation'.[17] Burchell's dedicated collection of botanical specimens, catalogues and artworks are a treasured record of the natural history of the Garden Route two hundred years ago.

Stewart makes the point that identifying, preserving and documenting specimens was time-consuming, and was probably the reason Burchell 'produced few drawings and paintings of people and landscapes along the Garden Route: less than twenty of the 500 he produced during the almost five years he was in South Africa'.[18] The paintings show the beauty of the rural landscape, two centuries ago, before its erosion by rampant urbanisation and development.

Burchell arrived in Knysna in the last week of April 1814 and remained there until the beginning of August – his longest stopover during his entire trek.[19] The painting of Melkhout Kraal, produced on 31 May 1814, provides a view of houses in the area and George Rex's well-known garden, and includes handwritten notes below the depiction of the houses. In ink is written 'Radius 8¾ inches', referring to the cylindrical method Burchell used to ensure good perspective. Faint pencil marks denote the

Knysna – Melkhout Kraal, 31 May 1814

names of the houses and other features of the scene from left to right: 'Scholehuis – Schoolmaster's room – Groote Huis – Kombuis – Store room – French's shop – Lit wag – Saddle rail – Gr wag – Melkhuis – Mouth of the Knysna – Garden'.[20] ('Lit wag' and 'Gr wag' refer to Burchell's wagons.)

Sylvan Station, 3 October 1814

Hottentots Holland Kloof – Summit, no date

A few days after painting Melkhout Kraal, Burchell left for George, on a treacherous route that Stewart regards as 'arguably, the most challenging section of road in the Colony'.[21] He camped for more than a month in George. The painting *Sylvan Station*, completed on 3 October 1814, clearly shows the location of the wagons with George Peak in the background, named Postberg by Burchell. In September 2014, a commemorative bust of Burchell, with George's Peak forming its backdrop, was unveiled in the Garden Route Botanical Garden in George.

Zonderend Mountains – Summit, 16 February 1815

In December Burchell reached Grootvadersbosch, in January 1815 he stayed in Swellendam for three weeks, and by February he was in the Zonderend Mountains. A painting shows Burchell and a companion on the summit beside huge boulders. His final landscape painting at this time is of the wagons on the summit of Hottentots Holland Kloof (known today as Sir Lowry's Pass) looking towards Cape Town.

Burchell returned to Cape Town in April 1815. In the preface to his *Travels*, he writes in the third person:

> Of the party which set out from Cape Town, he was the only one who returned to that place; the rest having quitted him, and been several times replaced by others during the journey. In a course of four thousand five hundred miles, exclusive of numerous smaller excursions, regions never before trodden by European foot, were explored and examined.[22]

Burchell sailed from Cape Town, with forty-eight packages of specimens, on board a small trading vessel named *Kate*, on 25 August 1815. The ship reached St Helena on 13 September and four days later sailed for England. Burchell finally arrived in Fulham on 11 November 1815.

10

'In the full vigour of manhood'

England and Brazil
1815 to 1830

A YEAR AFTER BURCHELL'S RETURN FROM Cape Town, his portrait was etched for inclusion in a collection of 'a hundred portraits of great men'. The drawing, observes Professor Poulton,

> brings back to us Burchell's features in the full vigour of manhood. The face is highly intellectual and indicative of strong purpose and resolution, yet singularly attractive, even winning. We see in it evidence of the ample fund of humour which led Burchell to appreciate and to describe many a quaint incongruity in his great 'Travels in the Interior of Southern Africa.' In the drooping eyelids we probably see the result of four years' exposure to the African sun.[1]

The original picture is housed in the Victoria and Albert Museum in Kensington, London, and the Cape Archives possess a copy of the portrait.

The period between Burchell's return to England in 1815 and his departure for Brazil in 1825 was, as Professor Poulton observes, marked by an outpouring of creative energy in diverse directions – 'nearly everything he gave to the world in his whole life was written and published in these ten years'.[2] In the first four years of Burchell's return to Fulham, however, he put most of his energy into horticulture, botany and botanical art.

The horticultural industry flourished in Europe in the nineteenth century. Plant collectors were famous, while the work of distinguished scientific travellers to the Cape – such as the university-trained Swedes Thunberg and Sparrman – did not attract the same public attention. Burchell, unlike famous plant hunters such as Francis Masson and William Paterson, never supplied Kew Gardens with new plants from southern Africa. He chose not to jump 'on this flower-laden bandwagon', as Mike Fraser puts it,[3] and instead planted 276 bulbs and 2 000 different seeds[4] gathered in southern Africa in Fulham. Helen McKay remarks that the 'Cape Colony was famous as the home of many bulbs cultivated in Europe' long before Burchell's time.[5] Burchell, however, was the first traveller to gather specimens from the arid inland of the colony, successfully grow them and describe them scientifically.

Burchell's bulb collection was highly acclaimed, and eminent horticulturalists – including Prince Leopold of Saxe-Coburg, Lord Carnarvon and members of the aristocracy, such as Lord and Lady Caledon – would visit him to see it.[6] He diligently documented the history of individual plants

William John Burchell in 1816, the year after his return from southern Africa

and bulbs in his *Hortus Fulhamensis*, now in the library of the Herbarium at Kew. There are more than two thousand entries recording, McKay notes, the 'locality where the seeds or bulbs were gathered, the dates when they were collected when sowed, came up, and in several cases, died'.[7] Botany as a science is exemplified in the *Hortus*, while botany as a visual art is apparent in his paintings completed in the ten years after his return from Cape Town.

Of particular interest is the care with which he records the places in South Africa where he discovered the plants, as well as how patiently he monitored their flowering in his Fulham nursery. On the south bank of the Gariep River, at the station he named Amaryllis, he collected bulbs of the lily *Amaryllis riparia* on 17 February 1813. Professor Poulton had access to Burchell's botanical notebooks and documents Burchell's thirty-six-year-long wait for the flower to grow in English soil:

These he planted at Fulham after his return, and they flowered in 1817, 1818, 1820 and 1821. On August 3, 1818, he notes that they 'ripened very fine bulbous seed', which was sown with the following results: 'The seed of *Amaryllis riparia* sown in 1818 did not flower (at Fulham) till June 1854.'[8]

In 1816, Burchell was introduced in the second volume of *The Botanical Register*,[9] an illustrated horticultural magazine that promoted exotic plants cultivated in British gardens. Although he excluded the *Amaryllis coranica* in his *Travels*, Burchell's painting of the exquisite lily was exhibited in the magazine, the caption of the picture spotlighting the famous supplier: 'Besides being new and ornamental, the present species has a claim to our interest as the first fruit offered to the public from the long and arduous expedition of Mr. W.J. Burchell.' An account follows of Burchell's work and his forthcoming book, expected to be 'one of the most instructive and amusing books which have appeared'.[10]

Chronicling Burchell's botanical exploits in England and Brazil, McKay cites Burchell's verbal portrait of the flowering bulb:

> I discovered this beautiful plant in the Corana country, in the interior of Africa, several days' journey beyond the Orange River … It grew in a grassy plain of sand, in such profusion as to remind me of a vast bed of choice flowers. The air was perfumed by an odour from the blossoms resembling that of the Tuberose. It begins to open its flowers in succession about sunset, and continues in beauty for about a week or fortnight. The bulbs as they stood when I found them were nearly nine inches in diameter, of a spherical form … I should judge the larger bulbs the growth of not less than 200 years, probably 300 … Notwithstanding, those I have brought home have been three years and three months out of ground, they are now growing in my garden in as flourishing a state as on their native spot, and have flowered in perfection. In their own climate the bloom is produced in

Amaryllis coranica, 24 June 1816 [left] and *c.* 1816 [right]

December, and it is not unworthy of remark how readily they have yielded to the reversal of the seasons in this part of the globe by flowering in June.[11]

Hypoxis obtusa, 6 July 1816

Burchell seamlessly threads together a vast array of verbal images in his portrayal of the lily: arid, sandy Africa; the scent of the blooms; their flowering at sunset and the duration of their beauty; the speculated age of the bulbs; and their successful cultivation in Fulham. The visual description harmonises perfectly with Burchell's watercolour of a specimen in his garden. A second watercolour provides more botanical detail.

Burchell had a particular gift for making plants available for posterity – a talent reminiscent of the words Andrew Marvell attaches to the Gardener in his poem 'The Garden': 'How well the skilful gardener drew / Of flowers and herbs'.[12] In his feats as a botanist – his collection and growing of plants – Burchell was the epitome of the 'skilful gardener'.

With the help of his sister Mary, he produced watercolours and sketched many of the South African plants that flowered in Fulham. Some of the paintings housed in Museum Africa are stained and damaged (a reminder that they were painted two hundred years ago). They are of interest for the notes they contain on the localities of the South African plants Burchell cultivated in Fulham.

The illustrations of these plants are diverse and detailed. *Hypoxis obtusa* was also included in *The Botanical Register* in the same volume in 1816,[13] labelled as 'An unrecorded species discovered by Mr. Burchell during his late travels ... on the sandy plains in the vicinity of Litakoon'. The *Gethyllis ciliaris* (commonly known as Kukumakranka) from Cape Town is described and illustrated in the *Travels*;[14] *Crassula versicolor* was another plant from Cape Town; and *Haemanthus incarnatus* was gathered in the Uitenhage district in February 1814. Burchell's plant portraiture needs to be more widely displayed for the appreciation of botanical art enthusiasts.

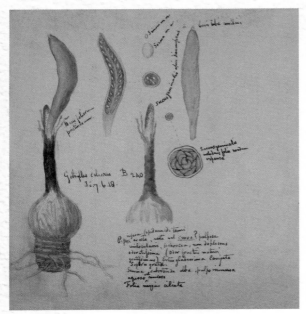

Gethyllis ciliaris [Kukumakranka], 7 June 1818

Crassula versicolor, 14 June 1818

In 1820, Burchell was recognised as an 'artist of distinguished merit' when his painting, *Inside of my African Waggon*, was exhibited at the prestigious Royal Academy in 1820 (see page 66). The still-life painting measures only 19 by 13⅝ inches,[15] and 'yet into that space', declares an admiring Professor Poulton, 'the painter has introduced everything characteristic of his life so far as it was spent within the wagon, and typical of the collections he made'.[16] Over eighty articles are visible in the painting. Burchell listed them and the order in which they were finished, as shown in this small extract of the list:

Tortoise	12/2/20
Elephant's grinder	12/2/20
Hippopotamus tusk	12/2/20
Press Screws	14/2/20
Memorandum Book	14/2/20
Flute	14/2/20
Shell	14/2/20

In total, Burchell worked on the painting 'for thirty-one days (or about 120 hours' work on the whole)', which comprised 'In sketching 4 days; In colouring 27 days'.[17] His notes to the painting attest to his numeric fixation with dates and measurements.

The subjects of his publications ranged widely. They include the scientific 'Description of R. *simus* (the white rhinoceros)' in French, in the *Bulletin des sciences par la Sociétè philomathique de Paris* in 1817, and *Hints on Emigration to the Cape of Good Hope* in 1819. This article argued that an English colony might be formed in the easternmost part of the Cape of Good Hope, and it played an important role in the recruitment of 1820 settlers to the Cape.[18] Burchell initially argued this idea before a committee of the House of Commons in London on the question of emigration to the Cape Colony as a relief to the distressing increase of pauperism from want of employment. He also published a catalogue, *A list of quadrupeds brought by Mr. Burchell from*

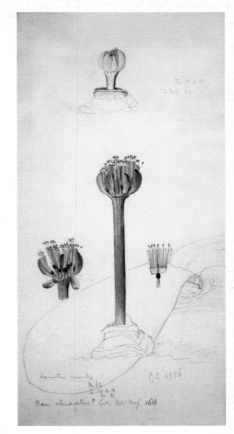

Haemanthus incarnatus, 24 August 1818

Southern Africa and presented to the British Museum on 30th Sept. 1817, around 1824. But his main achievements, of course, were his *Travels in the Interior of Southern Africa* and the accompanying map.

In 1819, Burchell 'retired to a quiet spot near Sevenoaks, Kent' according to McKay, and began writing and illustrating his *Travels*,[19] using material from the journals he meticulously kept during the expedition. Professor Poulton gives a glimpse of Burchell's literary method: the original journals contained pencil marks, which contain 'the material worked up by the author into the smooth, continuous narrative of the *Travels*'. Poulton adds:

But the same markings are continued beyond the date at which the published work closes, to the very end of the journal. This strongly suggests that Burchell prepared the manuscript for a much longer work, perhaps indeed for the whole of his African journey.[20]

The journals are now lost, and Burchell never published the projected third volume of his *Travels*. Volume I was published in 1822 and Volume II in 1824.

Having written his travelogue[21] in a four-year period, from 1819 to 1823, it is not surprising that events which rankled Burchell as he completed the book slipped into the published work, or that he used it to lash out against those who disregarded or criticised his scientific contributions. He targets the British Museum, which had, in April 1817, received forty-three quadruped skins that Burchell had collected in South Africa. When Burchell visited the museum in July 1822, he found the skins 'swarming with live moths and maggots, and their hair dropping off'.[22] While writing about his expedition's dogs in the narrative about the excursion to the Ky-Gariep River, Burchell switches to satire, using the playful canine Wantrouw to lampoon the museum's neglect of his specimens, and insinuates that the dog could have taken better care of them:

> *Wantrouw* had prepared and cleaned a large collection of bones of rare quadrupeds, which would have been to any museum a valuable present. Or, to the great extension and benefit of science in England, they might have been deposited in the cellars of the British Museum, to receive the same honours with his master's skins. But as they would require no stuffing, and consequently would not put that establishment to any expense, it is very probable that the public would soon be gratified with the sight of them.[23]

Burchell's attack on the museum is justified, and he found some relief in using the *Travels* to vent his understandable bitterness and irritation at the disrespect shown for his specimens: 'it would have been less vexatious to have left them to be eaten by maggots in the deserts of Africa, than in the British Museum'.[24]

Burchell also used Wantrouw satirically to attack Sir John Barrow, a colonial civil servant and geographer, who was in the Cape Colony from 1797 to 1804, and authored the popular *An Account of Travels into the Interior of Southern Africa in the Years 1797 and 1798*.[25] Burchell read Barrow's travelogue aboard the *Harriet* when he sailed to Cape Town in 1810,[26] and found much to criticise in Barrow's chronicle of his African expedition. Burchell mocks Barrow in this account of Wantrouw's adventures:

His numerous adventures, hair-breadth escapes, and observations on men and manners, would form a pretty thick quarto, if dished up in good language by some writer acquainted with the art of book-making, and published by a bookseller at the West end of the Town; at the same time taking care to have it properly recommended in the Quarterly Review. Although *Wantrouw* had not the least notion of drawing, yet a few coloured aquatinta plates, or lithographic prints, should, by all means, be inserted; these, his publisher could easily get designed by some artist, who must be told to take especial care that the words *Wantrouw delineavit, or, From a sketch, by Wantrouw, Esq.* appear conspicuous at the bottom corner. Such a work, if rightly and humbly dedicated, and well advertised, would be sure to sell.[27]

As Professor Poulton remarks, the nineteenth century was 'an age of embittered and not too scrupulous controversy' and, in his opinion, 'there is little doubt that Burchell was struck with the humorous inappropriateness of the name Barrow, or Bar-row, for one who made so unprovoked an attack. Wantrouw, or Want-row, seemed much more suitable.'[28] Stylistically, the satirical Wantrouw episode is strikingly different from the 'strict journal'[29] format of the *Travels*. It is of autobiographical interest, as these antagonistic feelings surface in the journal entry describing Burchell's excursion from Klaarwater, and long after his travels in the colony.

Burchell first took issue with Barrow after his 1819 pamphlet, 'Hints on Emigration to the Cape of Good Hope', came under Barrow's unfavourable scrutiny.[30] Barrow misrepresented and savagely attacked Burchell's view in the November 1819 *Quarterly Review*, a popular literary and political journal:

Mr. Burchell, it seems travelled far into the interior and passed some years among the natives … and we are surprised that, under such circumstances, his book should contain so scanty a proportion of factual information. He was, we understand, a culler of simples, and he certainly seems to have culled little else…. Mr. Burchell might as well talk of planting a settlement behind the Himalaya mountains. He means well, however, but we do not see that his book can be of any use to those who are about to emigrate.[31]

Throughout his *Travels*, Burchell criticises Barrow in footnotes – an aspect that exposes his caustic wit and the more resentful side of this usually enlightened traveller.

Burchell also insulted Sir John Barrow's map, which was released in 1801. 'As to the miserable thing called a map, which has been prefixed to Mr. Barrow's quarto, I perfectly agree with Professor Lichtenstein, that it is so defective that it can seldom be found of any use.'[32] Barrow's map only encompassed the areas he visited in his six years in the Cape. For Professor Martin Lichtenstein, who released the English edition of his *Travels in Southern Africa* in 1812, the map – considered 'the most up to date in existence' by Jacob Abraham Uitenhage de Mist, the Batavian commissioner-general to the Cape in 1803 to 1804[33] – was neither accurate nor ground-breaking.[34] Burchell never specified his own issues with Barrow's map. It should be noted, however, that the first volume of the *Travels*, in which Burchell pronounces his condemnation for the map, was published in 1822 – three years after Barrow's attack on Burchell in the *Quarterly Review*.

Burchell's own map was an extraordinary achievement. In the appendix 'Remarks on the Map; and Geographical Observations', he explains his cartographic project:

> It must, in the first place, be stated that *my own track* is laid down *entirely* and *solely* from my own observations, made during the journey. These observations consist of daily distances travelled; the courses from station to station; the bearings and trigonometrical intersections of distant and remarkable mountains; the bearings of various places remote from the track, and their distance, according to the concurrent information of the native inhabitants; very frequent astronomical observations for the latitude; and many sets of lunar distances for the longitude. These, whenever my time permitted, were laid down during the journey, from day to day, on a large scale; and various details added from ocular observation.

When Burchell returned to England, he carefully checked all his distances and created a map measuring 'seven feet and a half by eight and a half; and from this the present map has been reduced and engraved'. The engraver gets 'the greatest credit for accuracy and fidelity to the original'.[35] For publication in the *Travels*, the 'large scale map [2.28 x 2.59 metres] was reduced to about a sixteenth: to 27½ x 32½ inches [70 x 82.5 centimetres]'.[36]

The 'Explanations' at the top of the map cover the subject matter of:

> the entire track of the journey; stations where the party halted with the date of arrival; Colonial farm houses and names of the colonists; springs of water; Kraals or Villages of Colonial Hottentots; Kraals or Villages of Kora Hottentots and Namaquas; Kraals or Villages of Hottentots comprised under the term Bushmen; Towns of Bichuana Nations; Missionary Villages; Colonial Villages with the year in which they were founded; the boundary of the Cape Colony.[37]

Artworks in the *Travels* portray colonial, Khoisan, Khoikhoi and Bichuana dwellings, while the map specifies the exact locations of heterogeneous inhabitants two hundred years ago. Marion Arnold points out 'the most noticeable evidence of European colonialism in Africa is settlement – the construction of villages and towns – denoting the permanent occupation of the land and establishing social relationships that are reflected in the built environment'.[38] Burchell's map documents such colonial and aboriginal settlements, providing a rare visual record of imperial history.

Throughout the text, indigenous names are favoured by Burchell, who disapproves of the imposition of modern European names on aboriginal inhabitants. A glossary at the top of the map gives the meanings of Dutch and Khoikhoi words. The names of stations along his routes – Giraffe Station, Sand Station, Olive-tree Station, Hot Station, Cold Station, Robber's Station, Spuigslang Fontein – are loaded with meaning and record salient discoveries, weather conditions, vegetation, hardships, events and so on. The names are an instant repository of memories for Burchell – for a viewer of the map, a glance shows Burchell's conceptualisations of the importance of specific places.

Amazingly, Burchell also mapped parts of the country he did not visit: he 'undertook the task of forming sketches of the routes' from the narratives of travellers in whom he had confidence, such as Thunberg, Sparrman, Lichtenstein and William Paterson.[39] He never relied on any one map: 'the positions I have assigned … are the mean result of all the maps and journals combined'. This task was described by him as 'the most troublesome part of my labour'.[40] Burchell did not, of course, include John Barrow's 'defective' map among the maps that he used.

Randolph Vigne, who compares the two maps in 'Mapping and promoting South Africa: Barrow and Burchell's rivalry', admits that Burchell's map 'surpassed Barrow's in many respects' because it covered a greater amount of territory and detail.[41] Helen McKay writes that the map was removed from a number of volumes of the *Travels* because it was 'in great demand during the South African war by the army and intelligence department, and naturally the map and the text about it were of special value.'[42]

By the time Burchell finished writing the second volume of his *Travels*, he was restless and ready to travel again. In 1824, he set off for Scotland to visit his friend Sir William Hooker, professor of botany at the University of Glasgow. On Burchell's return, he went to the Lake District, and then visited the famous naturalist William Swainson in Elm Grove near Liverpool.

Swainson had returned from Rio de Janeiro in 1819, and Helen McKay suggests

'Brazil was now the chief topic of [their] conversation', one which rekindled Burchell's desire in St Helena to visit South America.[43] In his *St Helena Journal*, Burchell frequently recorded conversations with sea captains praising Brazil, and he was bitterly disappointed when he missed out on an opportunity to travel there in July 1810: the '*Camperdown* sailed today for Rio Janeiro … I was very vexed that I was not ready to take my passage in her'.[44] Fifteen years later, Burchell was finally able to journey to Brazil.

Jane Pickering clarifies that Burchell's journey to Brazil was not a 'planned expedition, but an opportunistic use of being able to travel with a special Foreign Office mission to Rio, led by Sir Charles Stuart'.[45] The mission was only formally announced in the middle of January 1825, but Burchell, as late as 28 January 1825, did not mention plans to travel to Brazil in a letter complaining about the British Museum and the British government's lack of support for scientific work. The first written record of his trip appears in a letter to William Swainson on 15 February 1825, which relates Burchell's plans: 'affairs begin now to wear the appearance of my going to South America'.[46]

In two subsequent letters to Swainson, a frenetic Burchell conveys his anxieties regarding the preparations for his Brazilian trip. On 15 February 1825, he writes:

I am in fact very busy in making preparations, and in so much bustle as scarcely to have a moment to spare; for hours are now as valuable as days were a short time ago. All arrangements are completed excepting that of the passage, and the Embassy will most assuredly sail in a few days. I shall in this case, see the Brazils, and long to have some conversation with you. All must be done quickly. If I could but have got the insect boxes in time![47]

A few days later, on 22 February, he writes again to Swainson:

I am worn off my legs and quite exhausted with the fatigue of collecting together the things I want. Do pray get for me the Recipe for "Arsenical Soap", or rather give it at once to a Chemist to make up for me about two pounds weight and send it quickly [to] Fulham. I hope the Insect boxes are come. Send them down with [no] loss of time.   Your's in the greatest haste —[48]

Burchell left Fulham on 10 March 1825, hopefully with the insect containers, to sail with the mission from Portsmouth. They left on board the *Wellesley*, bound for Lisbon, on 15 March.

Burchell's party landed at Lisbon on 25 March 1825, and remained in the city until 25 May. During these two months, McKay writes that Burchell 'botanised, sketched and took regular lessons of a Portuguese Master for the Portuguese language, to get a right pronunciation'.[49] A day was spent at Funchal, Madeira, and two days at Santa Cruz, Tenerife.

Burchell landed at Rio de Janeiro on 18 July 1825. According to Pickering, Brazil at this time 'was a sparsely settled country, dominated by transatlantic trade, with the majority of the population living within 100 kilometres of the coast'.[50] Many things had changed in the country since Burchell first expressed a desire to visit in 1810. King John VI of Portugal – who had been exiled in Brazil – returned to Lisbon in 1820, leaving his son Dom Pedro as regent in Rio de Janeiro. The Brazilian states subsequently installed Pedro as emperor, and he declared Brazil's independence from Portugal in 1822. Britain had economic ties with Brazil, and Britain's foreign secretary sent a special mission to Rio to negotiate an Anglo-Brazilian commercial treaty, led by Sir Charles Stuart. Pickering states that Sir Charles's task was to go to Lisbon to 'persuade the Portuguese to come to terms with Brazilian independence', and then to proceed to Rio de Janeiro.[51]

In a letter to Swainson, written on 31 August – more than a month after his arrival in Rio – Burchell laments the miserable conditions of his living quarters:

> Dear Swainson
> I landed at this place on the 18th of last month, and have found so much difficulty in getting into convenient quarters, that I am obliged still to continue at the dirty crowded hotel where I first took shelter. I cannot therefore pursue my scientific operations with much facility but I endeavour to make the best of my time in every way that circumstances permit.[52]

Burchell worked hard to make the most of his Brazilian expedition in spite of the hardships. It is noteworthy that years later, he still possessed the same fortitude and optimism that helped him tackle so many adversities on his South African expedition. In great detail, he informs Swainson of his progress in Brazil, exclaiming about the 'rich scenery' in Mandioca which delighted him, and the specimens he collected in the vicinity of Rio. The letter ends with his hope that when he returns to Fulham, he'll 'have the long-looked-for gratification of publishing all my African discoveries myself, and which I reserve as one of the most pleasing results of my toils in that country'.[53]

In Rio, Burchell considered himself independent of Sir Charles, but he remained on friendly terms with him. Because of the war between Brazil and Argentina over Uruguay (which began the year Burchell arrived in Brazil, and ended in 1828), travelling to Rio was difficult and expensive. Sir Charles had most certainly helped Burchell obtain the required documents for travelling in Brazil, and for this Burchell would have owed him a great deal of gratitude. Sir Charles left Rio in May 1826.[54]

Burchell ended up spending over a year in Rio. He made two short excursions in this time into the province of Minas Gerais, and to the Serra dos Órgãos mountains. It is clear from his letters that he never intended to spend much time in the city, but 'endless delays in sorting out the paperwork and equipment he would need for his journey kept him there'.[55] Typically, he was philosophical about these setbacks, using the opportunity to improve his Portuguese. Pickering observes that he enjoyed a busy social life in the city as well: 'his letters to his family speak of regular social engagements, particularly whilst the rest of the Embassy party were there'.[56] Much of his time was occupied painting the many things he saw in Rio: its landscapes, rivers, buildings, streets, trees and islands.

Burchell had a tent made for him in the city. The inscription on his illustration of the tent reads, '8 feet high – 11 feet long – 8 feet wide at bottom'; and on the back: 'Plan of the tent I had made for me at Rio & which I take with me'.[57] Interestingly, Burchell's wagon in the Cape was not much larger than his Brazilian tent: the wagon's length was only fifteen feet, and the breadth at the bottom two feet, nine inches. The height, from the bottom of the wagon to the top of the tilt, was five and a half feet.

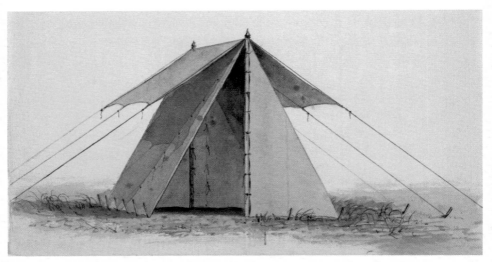

Burchell's Tent, *c.* 1829

Sheet 4, Looking North-east, Rio de Janeiro – Panorama, 1826

Burchell's famous panorama of Rio, probably painted in May and June 1826, exemplifies his method of perspective drawing on the cylindric principle, which he describes in great detail in his *Travels*.[58] R.F. Kennedy, compiler of the catalogue of artworks in Museum Africa, explains how the eight numbered sheets comprising the panorama pass through the full 360 degrees of the Rio landscape: 'it starts looking due west and proceeding clockwise finishes looking south-west. The right edge of No. 1 fits perfectly with the left of No. 2 and so on. No. 8 joins perfectly with the right of No. 7 and the left of No. 1.'[59]

Sheet 4, titled *Looking North-east*, is inscribed with a description of its subject: '85 boats under sail to dist. parts of bay'. The panorama, which Burchell completed in five to six weeks, attracted 'a great deal of interest with many people coming to visit him to see it', according to Pickering.[60] Unfortunately, the drawings are not well preserved, as sealing wax, used to attach the sheets to a display board Burchell used when he showed the panorama to friends and visitors in Rio, has left stains. Burchell's 360-degree view of Rio inspired the London panorama painter Robert Burford to paint his own famous panorama of Rio, which he presented in Leicester Square in London in the nineteenth century.[61]

In Rio, Burchell's artistic subjects vary constantly. Strikingly different from the vast Rio panorama are *Roofed Bridge over River*, dated 6 February 1826; *Street Scenes c. 1826*, showing chained convicts, a padre and a soldier; and a sloth, produced in October 1826. Pickering cites the praise that visual art critic Gilberto Ferrez – who wrote a book in Portuguese about Burchell's art in Brazil – bestows on Burchell, who, unlike many foreigners, 'always spelt the names of places and buildings correctly' in his notes and on his paintings.[62] Interestingly, of Burchell's 257 Brazilian drawings and paintings in Museum Africa, only thirty-three are of plants and animals.[63]

Travelling with his gear and collections was cumbersome: he had '33 packages, most of them weighing (with the box) about a hundred pounds'.[64] In a letter to Sir William Hooker, Burchell writes that 'the conveyance of collections, baggage, and instruments, over a country like this is attended by difficulties that nothing but patience can overcome; especially as I travel in the same solitary, unassisted manner as in Africa'.[65]

Burchell kept notebooks on Brazilian natural history (now lost), but published nothing about his Brazilian travels. Sir William Hooker, however, published 'Mr Burchell's

Roofed Bridge over River, 6 February 1826

Street Scenes, c. 1826

Brazilian Journey'[66] in a botany magazine in 1831. In this article, Hooker cites, almost verbatim, two letters he received from Burchell. 'This intelligent and persevering traveller, and accomplished naturalist, so well known by his valuable "Travels in Africa" has recently returned from Brazil,' he begins.[67] In one of the letters, written on 1 November 1830 when he was back in Fulham, Burchell gives a riveting synopsis of his adventurous, scientific expedition in Brazil.[68]

Sloth, 6 and 13 October 1826

Having sailed from Rio to Santos on 10 September 1825, Burchell landed two days later, and stayed for three months in a small house on the outside of town. From there, he moved to a solitary hut at the foot of the Sierra da Cubatão mountain range before travelling north to São Paulo, where he resided for seven months, and purchased mules and engaged muleteers to transport his baggage for the next leg of the journey inland to Belém, the northern port and capital city of Pará.[69] On his way, he passed the rainy season of 1827 in the city of Goiás (formerly Goyaz), designating himself the first and only Englishman to enter that province. After nine months in Goiás, he continued moving northwards and, in November 1828, he reached Porto Nacional on the river Tocantins. Here he had to wait until 28 April 1829 to go north along the river. Burchell described this part of his journey as 'being very dangerous due to numerous rocky falls, rapids and whirlpools'. But at last, nearly four years after setting out from Rio, and seemingly unfazed by the duration and difficulty of the expedition, Burchell reached Pará.[70]

Finally, I arrived at the city of Para in June 1829, and while waiting till February for a convenient opportunity of embarking for England, added largely to my collections both in zoology and botany. Of this city I made a panorama, which, with that of Rio, I hope perhaps to succeed in getting engraved, together with my landscapes, &c. Of insects I found from sixteen to twenty thousand specimens (at a guess). Of birds I shot and preserved 362 species. In other classes a proportionally smaller number.[71]

Clearly Burchell's Brazilian journey has not worn him out, and he continues tirelessly in his quest to discover and preserve scientific knowledge. The massive size of his collections in Brazil attests to his energy and dedication to scientific pursuits, often in hazardous circumstances and in terrain where no scientific traveller had ever been before.

A true Romantic, Burchell was enchanted with the New World. In letters about Brazil, his voice is vigorous and his spontaneous impressions of Brazilian landscapes, flora and fauna are fresh and engaging. Writing to the botanist R.A. Salisbury from Rio on 14 August 1825, Burchell expresses his enthusiasm for the scenery, plants, birds and insects he is seeing for the first time:

> As to the Botanical riches of this country (at least what little I have hitherto seen) you cannot form an adequate idea, even though you pictured to yourself all the fine plants of our hothouses growing wild and clothing the hills and valleys with their utmost luxuriance. At the Cape of Good Hope you are walking in a richly stored greenhouse: here you walk into one of the great hothouses of Nature … Mountains and rocks, forests and rivulets and plants of remarkable forms, combined in the most picturesque manner, tempt one to turn often from Natural History to Painting.[72]

As he did in St Helena and South Africa, he continues to make the link between natural history and the Creation, articulated in this letter to Hooker, dated 1 November 1830:

> I cannot bring my mind to abandon any branch of natural history for the sake of giving more time and attention to any one in particular: although I know this is wrong and can never lead to perfection in any. Still, the contemplation of the whole system of created objects, is so fascinating, that it is very difficult to turn away from all but a few.[73]

Resonant with science and Romantic sensibility is Burchell's response, in the same letter, to Hooker's request for a description, in general terms, of Brazil's vegetation:

> You have from all quarters heard the most animated descriptions of the luxuriance and richness of the vegetation of Brazil: and with these I most warmly agree. But this is become almost a fashion, and in Europe, it seems the general opinion that the *whole* of that country is covered with the most magnificent forests, and of gigantic growths. This idea, though correct with respect to all the maritime districts, the courses of the rivers and the greater part of the country lying under the equinoctial line, is, however, not at all applicable to vast tracts in the provinces of San Paulo and Goyaz.[74]

Palm Tree, 14 October 1826

He soon switches to scientific description, using botanical names for the grasses and plants growing in the 'boundless plains or open regions' of Brazil. He then compares the botany of South Africa and Brazil: the arid groves of Brazil 'have sometimes reminded me of the Acacia groves so predominant over the plains in the interior of Southern Africa'.[75] Empirical observations and Romantic feelings coalesce in his appreciation of Brazilian forests, and how they compete with those of the Cape:

> Yet it is rarely that one can compare African with Brazilian botany: their character, in many particulars, differs so widely: but I was a long time in Brazil before I saw such large trunks of timber as I have observed in some of the forests of the Cape Colony. I allude to the Podocarpi. These forests are indeed of no extent compared to those of America: but they afford specimens of sylvan scenery for the painter not less grand and beautiful: although they are generally deficient in that most splendid and noble feature, the Palm.
>
> When, however, we descend towards the low latitudes of Brazil, the glorious magnificence of the forests is truly astonishing, and none but those who are born in the midst of them can view such imposing productions of Nature without a feeling of awe or respect. She overloads herself, and one object oppresses and smothers another in the general struggle for luxuriance.[76]

Brazil's palm trees enthralled Burchell, and, like English biologist and writer Colin Tudge, he marvels at their splendour: 'they are among the wonders of the world'.[77]

When Charles Darwin travelled in Brazil a few years later, he experienced 'the higher feelings of wonder, astonishment, and devotion' for Brazilian forests. Palms caught his eye: 'the contrast of palm trees, growing amidst the common branching kinds, never fails to give the scene an intertropical character'. Darwin's description of the cabbage palm – 'with a stem so narrow that it could be clasped with the two hands, it waves its elegant head at the height of forty or fifty feet above the ground' – could easily be a caption for Burchell's watercolour, *Palm Tree*, produced on 14 October 1826. Burchell also painted *Palm Trees*, on 30 April 1826, growing 'amidst the common branching kinds'.[78] Burchell, in his letter to Hooker, affirms his delight in this splendid tree: 'we can never be silent with respect to the Palms: they abound in every latitude and situation, and their variety is far greater than any one traveller can form an idea of'.[79]

When Burchell travelled from São Paulo to the city of Goiás in August 1826, he had a black slave with him.[80] Pickering writes:

> this is confirmed (together with an interesting description of Burchell) in the 'Register of Foreigners of 1823–1830' which, 25 August 1826, notes that Burchell, a 'British subject, 39 years of age, of medium height, long face, full beard, blue eyes, thick eyebrows, leaves for Santos, taking Joaquim, a Congo slave, short, long face, beardless, large mouth and has certificate'.[81]

In letters to his family, Burchell often referred affectionately to his 'Negro boy', and in his final letter, dated 1 December 1829, to his mother from Belém, he told her 'he was bringing the boy back to England with him'.[82] Professor Poulton, while trawling through Burchell's notebooks, discovered the existence of this 'native attendant named "Congo", who seems to have been as good a naturalist in Brazil as "Speelman" was in South Africa'.[83]

William Swainson's wife Mary had seen Burchell in Fulham, in 1830, with a 'live black servant'.[84] Unfortunately, not much more is known about Burchell's relationship with Congo aside from

Palm Trees, 30 April 1826

A Church and Ships, 11 October 1826

these observations, leaving us with only a tantalising area of silence from which to draw inferences.

In Brazil, Burchell covered much less ground than in South Africa: approximately 2 500 miles compared to 4 500 miles.[85] His journey was characterised by long waits in cities and delays caused by inclement weather. He admits in a letter written in June 1826, to his mother, that he was depressed, and 'found the people dilatory and wearing out his patience when dealing with them, "for what might be done in a day they often required a month"'.[86] In the five years he was in Brazil, the total time spent actually travelling was only seven and a half months. He writes of this shortcoming of his Brazilian travels to Hooker:

> In this country of illiteracy, no one is found to whom notions of science are intelligible. Here Nature has done much – man nothing: here she offers him innumerable objects of admiration and study, yet he continues to vegetate in the darkness of ignorance and in extreme poverty, the consequence of laziness alone.[87]

As in St Helena and South Africa, Burchell observed and suffered the dire consequences of idleness in Brazil.

In spite of these issues, Burchell continued to document Brazilian scenery and attractions in his artworks, and he had a particular flair for accurately depicting Brazilian buildings and houses. Indeed, in Brazil, Ferrez has acclaimed Burchell as 'supreme among those who best depicted our architecture'.[88] Two examples of Burchell's focus on architecture are the watercolours *A Church and Ships* and *Rua Dircita at Santos*; while landscape is accented in *General View of Santos*.

After the end of his expedition in Pará, Burchell planned to travel to Peru and Buenos Aires, and from there sail to England. He explains his reasons for curtailing his trip to Hooker in a letter written from Goiás in April 1828: 'letters from Fulham overtook me, stating that my dear father's health, from the infirmities natural to his age, was gradually declining, and that it was his wish and that of the rest of the family that I should return directly to England'.

Burchell immediately cancelled his future plans to explore Peru. His deep love for his father, and a wish to see him again before his passing, ruled out any regret on Burchell's part on cutting his South American tour short.

Rua Dircita at Santos, 25 November 1826

General View of Santos, 8 October 1826

Whatever regret I may feel at thus relinquishing my American travels, and whatever disappointment I may experience from a premature return, I have no hesitation whatever in preferring filial duty to science and the gratification of my own inclinations. I have therefore greatly altered my plans, and instead of ending this journey at Buenos Ayres, shall, *Deo volente*, end it at Pará, where I shall embark for England.[89]

Reaching Fulham on 25 March 1830, he was heartbroken to hear that his beloved father had died in 1829. Burchell had to assume legal responsibilities for which, to use Helen McKay's words, 'he was little inclined, but which he faithfully and dutifully performed'.[90]

While in Brazil, Burchell collected a prodigious quantity of material. He shipped collections back to England, in boxes, whenever he had the opportunity. Remarkably, all of his boxes arrived safely. By the time he returned to Fulham, he had

collected 7,022 plant species (including a few from Madeira, Tenerife and Portugal). He also told Hooker he had 16–20,000 specimens of insects and had shot 362 species of bird, whilst also commenting that 'I have nowhere beheld an herbarium so large as my own'.[91]

There simply was not enough space at Churchfield House to unpack the collection. The Brazilian herbarium alone consisted of 132 packages, which Burchell only started unpacking in February 1847, seventeen years after his return from Brazil. He finished dealing with the specimens three years later.[92] Relabelling 49 000 specimens took another four years. He says despondently (again in the same letter to Hooker) about the entire process: 'while writing of such glorious things as I have met with, I lose all patience on feeling my hands, as it were, tied up from beginning to work on them'.[93]

It is not surprising that Burchell – who enjoyed the movement of travelling and collecting scientific information – 'lacked the persistence and patience to prepare his observations for publication'.[94] The dearth of published material ultimately meant that his extensive scientific work in Brazil was unknown to other students of science. It is tragic that, nine years after his return to England, in 1839, he wrote to Swainson:

For my part I have lived only to learn that man is born ~~only~~ for care & disappointment – What have I travelled and laboured so hard for! only to sit still in years of inactivity to grieve at the sight of my unpacked boxes, and patiently submit to those circumstances which have so long rendered all my hard labours abortive.[95]

11

'A life of science'

England and the Continent
1830 to 1863

BEFORE HE SAILED TO BRAZIL, Burchell wrote in a letter to William Swainson, 'A life of science, is a life of endless labor; without any other reward than the pure exalted enjoyment which it brings to those minds who pursue it from a real love of its superior character: and I could wish that circumstances allow me always to dedicate my time to these pursuits.'[1] This was a prescient statement, for in the remaining three decades of Burchell's life, the 'endless labor' required to arrange his collections single-handedly overwhelmed him, and adverse circumstances continually thwarted him.

Shortly after Burchell's return to Fulham, in September 1830, he wrote to Swainson about a horticultural disaster, in which '500 pots of plants [were] killed by the last winter'.[2] Domestic and legal affairs burdened him. His father had died, Salisbury had died, and Burchell had to manage their estates: 'but alas my days are still consumed in law matters & unavoidable domestic affairs which nobody but myself can arrange'.[3] Disturbingly, his letters expose recurrent, incapacitating bouts of illness, and there is an alarming hint of depression in this letter to Swainson, dated 24 January 1831: 'To confess the truth I have been for a long time past in so strange & idle a state with regard to correspondence, that I disliked writing a letter more than any other occupation whatever. However I hope this fit will soon pass over.'[4]

On a positive note, Burchell partook in many pleasant and uplifting experiences in Europe as well. The passing years were enlivened by regular attendance at professional meetings, and frequent trips in England and on the Continent comprised visits to eminent botanists, many of them noted for their work on plant classification systems.

Burchell attended the meeting of the British Association for the Advancement of Science (founded in 1831) in Oxford on 18 June 1832, where he was elected as a member, dealing with zoology, botany, physiology and anatomy.[5] Burchell served on the committee for two years before becoming a life member in 1835. It is clear he enjoyed the opportunities to meet with the association; he regularly attended its annual meetings, and cheerful letters to friends and family confirm the pleasure he gained in his visits to Oxford, where he was always, to use McKay's words, 'received as an honoured guest'. Burchell, together with the other erudite members of the committee, revolutionised the teaching of botany at Oxford University, where they helped it gain the distinction of becoming a science: 'the subject was receiving attention from a viewpoint other than that of the herbalist, and that the gathering of plants was now regarded as more than just a harmless and elegant occupation of the female sex'.[6]

In May 1834, the university awarded Burchell the degree of Doctor of Civil Law (*Honoris Causa*). This, as McKay pronounces, 'was a remarkable honour in those days for a man who was not a graduate of Oxford'.[7] Burchell greatly appreciated this distinction, but, Professor Poulton points out, he was hurt that he did not receive the recognition, in the form of a pension from the British government, 'accorded to far less distinguished men'.[8] A few years later, Swainson, who had published brief biographies of other naturalists, condemns in his biography of Burchell, this blatant disregard for a man who had travelled to distant and unknown lands, and had acquired a mountain of scientific knowledge of use to all in the process:

> One of the most learned and accomplished travellers of any age or country, –
> whether we regard the extent of his acquirements in every branch of physical
> science, or the range of the countries he explored. Science will ever regret that
> one whose powers of mind are so varied, and so universally acknowledged
> throughout Europe, should have been so signally neglected by his government –
> the most thankless and ungrateful one, to unpatronised talent under Heaven....
> A Government which bestows honours upon writers of novels, and pensions for
> licentious ballads, cannot be expected to regard modest worth or unobtrusive
> talent.[9]

Swainson decided to honour Burchell himself by dedicating the third volume of his book, *Zoological Illustrations*[10] (published in 1833), to him. Poulton notes that 'bitter resentment' on behalf of his friend breathes in the dedication.[11]

Surprisingly, Burchell – who was so healthy in southern Africa – in England, at the age of forty, suffered from fever, lumbago and rheumatism in the early months of 1831. During his illness he took pleasure in visits from John Henslow, professor of botany at Cambridge (famous for initiating Darwin's round-the-world voyage on the *Beagle*); Dr Peter Mark Roget, physician and writer of the *Thesaurus of English Words and Phrases*; Major General Thomas Hardwicke, who had collected specimens in Calcutta for the East India Company; and his closest friend, Swainson. Burchell showed no signs at this stage of being a recluse, even in the midst of his ill health – his friends were leading men of science, and Burchell enjoyed their company exceedingly. Intriguingly, in a letter to Swainson, there is an intimation that he perhaps would have liked having a family: 'I am really glad to hear that Mrs Swainson & all your little ones are well, these are blessings which ought to make you consider yourself far "more fortunate" than I am.'[12]

On 19 September 1832, Burchell and his sister Anna embarked on a two-month tour of Europe, combining sightseeing with scientific networking. As Burchell stated in the *Travels*, innovations in botanical and zoological nomenclature were rife at the time of his African journey.[13] Helen McKay considered Burchell a taxonomist, and he certainly pursued his taxonomic interests on the Continent. In Geneva, a week was spent with the plant taxonomist A.P. de Candolle. In Paris, he visited Adrien-Henri de Jussieu, professor of botany at the Jardin des Plantes, and son of the author of *Genera Plantarum* – one of the fifty scientific volumes Burchell kept in his wagon.[14] When Burchell visited Basel, he was entertained by Carl Meissner, professor of botany at the University of Basel. While Burchell had seen himself as a 'solitary Englishman wandering among lawless nations'[15] in Africa, his travels in Europe indicate he was revered as an esteemed traveller and man of science. He and Anna returned to Fulham on 22 November 1832.[16]

By the end of 1837, Burchell was on the move again – this time on his own – on a ten-month tour of Europe. He went to Hamburg and Hanover, where he met Olaf Hesse, the son of his Cape Town friend Reverend Frederick Hesse. In a one-horse open carriage, they travelled to the Harz Mountains and climbed Brocken, the highest peak of the mountain range. Amusingly, when Burchell spoke German, 'he produced a mixture of Dutch and French with Portuguese to give it a flavour'.[17] In Prague, Mozart's opera *Don Giovanni* was a highlight, and in a letter to his sister Mary, he praises how it was 'performed in the greatest perfection possible'.[18] In December, in Vienna, Burchell was entertained by Archduke John, who had travelled extensively in England and Turkey; and he met Stephan Endlicher, professor of botany at the University of Vienna and an expert on plant classification. From Vienna, Burchell travelled to Naples via Venice, Padua, Bologna and Rome; he then sailed to Genoa. Throughout this tour, he comes across as energetic, sociable and physically fit.

He was unable to extend his journey after Genoa, as his frail mother and sisters 'were anxious for his return' to Fulham. He returned to England in 1838 and 'was plunged into family cares and worries'.[19] In a letter written to Swainson from Fulham, on 29 January 1839, he says that he was 'reduced to live a very secluded life owing to the daily & hourly care [of] our dear Mother'.[20] Burchell's mother died in 1841, the same year Swainson immigrated to Van Diemen's Land (the name Europeans gave to Tasmania). The death of his beloved mother and the departure of his closest friend were followed by yet another sad loss: the death, in Van Diemen's Land, of John Butcher, the husband of Burchell's sister Sarah.

It is clear from a farewell letter Burchell wrote to Swainson shortly before the latter's departure that he is depressed:

> I hope my dear friend that happiness & a new life of prosperity await you in your far distant home. This must console me for the sad presentiment that I shall never see you again – These melancholy feelings are rendered more sensible by intelligence just received that my brother-in-law in Van Dieman's Land has left this world.[21]

The next sentence in the letter strongly suggests Burchell was finding life in England hard:

> You may there very probably lead a much happier life and enjoy greater health than in England, where all must be done by struggling and scrambling; for which neither you nor I were ever fitted by nature.[22]

The whole tone of the letter is one of dejection and suggests that Burchell, grieving for his late mother and the loss of Swainson, no longer has the emotional resilience he showed in all his arduous travels.

When, following her husband's death, Burchell's widowed sister and her family returned to England from Van Diemen's Land, his troubles were exacerbated as there was no space for him to unpack his Brazilian collections in the family home.

In spite of the seemingly endless family and professional troubles that plagued Burchell in Fulham, he 'kept moving'. In 1849, he rambled in the New Forest.[23] With his sister Mary, in 1850, he visited France and Belgium. Burchell was sixty-nine years old at the time of this trip. Four years later, he was in Derbyshire – where he visited Matlock Bath in Buxton – before travelling to Manchester. The following year, in 1855, he was in the Lake District.

William Burchell, aged 73, 1854

Thomas Herbert Maguire, the famous English artist well known for his portraits of prominent Victorians, painted Burchell, aged seventy-three, in 1854. Burchell, in this portrait, has the same intellectual spark, gravity, fine features and tousled hair that were so striking in the portraits of him aged nineteen and twenty-six. However, his facial expression is, perhaps, more serious and enigmatic.

Burchell's last visit to Oxford was in 1860, when he attended the famous meeting of the British Association following the publication of Darwin's *On the Origin of Species* in London in 1859. The biologist Thomas Huxley, who called himself 'Darwin's Bulldog', challenged Samuel 'Soapy Sam' Wilberforce – 'a bulky, vigorous, self-assured man' – on the theory of evolution. In her biography of Darwin, Janet Browne crystallises the confrontational tone of the meeting: 'Bishop Wilberforce argued with Huxley. Huxley argued with Bishop Wilberforce.' She also emphasises the significance of the meeting:

> the debate between Huxley and Wilberforce famously came to symbolise the perceived conflict between science and religion, such a powerful contemporary image that it, in turn, contributed materially to the doubts many Victorians felt about their faith, while reinforcing the convictions of as many others.[24]

There is no record of Burchell's reaction to the debate. But undoubtedly for this staunch Creationist, 'evolution was a sealed book,' as Professor Poulton puts it.[25] In Burchell's view, there was never any conflict between faith and science.

Interestingly, the director of Kew Gardens and leading botanist Sir W.T. Thiselton-Dyer considered Burchell as 'being closely on the track along which Darwin travelled … He differed from Darwin only in that he turned invariably to the supernatural for an explanation of the phenomenon he encountered.'[26] Poulton – reviewing Burchell's insect collection in the Hope Department at Oxford University Museum of Natural

History – shows an example of this link to Darwin, in the extraordinary powers of observation Burchell displayed in his work on mimicry and the sound-producing apparatus in insects: 'Up to the present time Burchell is the only naturalist who has observed an example which still exhibits this ancestral stage in the evolution of mimetic likeness.'[27] Burchell's careful natural history observations and fact-finding explorations in South Africa and Brazil were praised by Darwin. In a letter written aboard the *Beagle*, on 14 July 1833, Darwin asked his sister 'for more books; those most valuable of all valuable things', and includes 'Burchell's travels' on his list.[28]

From 1847 until 1861, Burchell 'laboured at the details of his herbarium and zoological collections'.[29] There is evidence that he became increasingly possessive of his specimens, but McKay suggests many of the 'accusations of hoarding, because of bitterness and jealousy' were false, and 'applied to him by some who seemingly misunderstood his actions'.[30] Burchell's happy participation in the British Association for the Advancement of Science is proof that his reclusiveness has been exaggerated. Sadly, though, it cannot be denied that Burchell's relevance in the scientific arena diminished as he grew older. As Poulton regretfully comments:

> the man who had started as a traveller admirably equipped with a knowledge of every science of the time was left behind by the onward sweep of scientific work. Mighty discoveries shook the world, but left him unheeding in his study. 'I well remember,' Sir Joseph Hooker writes, 'one conversation with him … when he told me he had never even heard of photography, and showed great interest in my account of it!'[31]

By 1861, Burchell was an invalid; by 1863, he was dead. Professor Poulton describes his death on 23 March 1863: he 'shot himself under the large cedar tree in front of Churchfield House. The wound not proving fatal, he terminated his existence by hanging himself in a small outhouse at the back.'[32] Although a highly religious man, he was denied a churchyard burial after a jury determined his death a 'Suicide during temporary insanity'.[33] Sometime later, he was 'pardoned' and interred in the family tomb in the graveyard of All Saints, Fulham.

Sir Joseph Hooker – in a desperate attempt to understand Burchell's state of mind before his death – suggested to Poulton that Burchell could not make up his mind either to publish his own labours or to let others do so, or join him in his work. This and the reproaches of a sensitive mind and highly strung nervous system in a shy man of great mental power and resources, coupled with the memory of great deeds as a traveller, collector, artist, musician and scientific investigator, may well have led to despondency and suicide.[34]

Hooker's description of Burchell as 'highly strung' and nervous when he was an old, frail man, exposes the dramatic and pitiful transformation of this courageous, intrepid traveller, who climbed mountains and traversed perilous tracks in St Helena, southern Africa and Brazil. Throughout his travels, Burchell proved himself to be a 'man of steel'; gregarious, determined and confrontational when necessary.

For Professor Poulton, Burchell's state of mind was indirectly influenced by 'the close of the long labour upon his collection': his life's work was over, and 'it was manifestly impossible, when he was over eighty, to undertake an entirely new line of work, which, moreover, could not be even begun without the co-operation of other naturalists, the very men whose companionship he had shunned for the long years in which he was resolutely working upon his collections'.[35]

There was no treatment for depression in Burchell's lifetime.

Burchell's life ended tragically; the depression he suffered in his last few years certainly was at variance with his former energy and optimism as a younger man, when his mantra was 'I hope. I go.'[36] Being an invalid would have been traumatic for eighty-two-year-old Burchell as well. Always sensitive to changes in the climate, he would have found the weather in March, when he ended his life, severe. According to Robin Castell, his sister Anna, unbeknown to Burchell, had 'refused permission to friends and family to visit him'.[37] The isolation this would have imposed on him, along with his depression, may have, understandably, led him to suicide.

Burchell's sad ending should not eclipse the magnitude of his literary, intellectual, artistic, scientific and humanitarian achievements. He considered himself a botanist and scientific traveller above all other things; and in these two fields, he was a true pioneer. All of his scientific endeavours were marked by the 'high adventure so characteristic of the Romantic spirit' described by Richard Holmes in *The Age of Wonder*.[38] He explored routes never travelled before; and a botanical trailblazer, he was dedicated to discovering and cataloguing new plants for science. Astronomy and accurate measurements were passions of Burchell's, while the languages and customs of the aboriginal inhabitants he encountered during his travels were a priority in his quest for knowledge. His vast collection of specimens – of plant material, quadrupeds, birds, reptiles, insects and cultural artefacts – attests to his confluence of interests. In all of his adventures, Burchell seemed engrossed by human nature, evident in his observations of primitive societies in southern Africa, Brazil and St Helena. And perhaps in his later, more secluded years, the absence of such social interaction contributed to his melancholy and weariness.

For J.M. Coetzee, 'in a larger sense all writing is autobiography'[39] and 'all autobiography is storytelling'.[40] Burchell, writing about himself, has propelled this book, and we find his autobiography is embedded in his story, in his own voice. Intellectual daring, courage, resourcefulness, moods, humour, humanitarian values, prejudices and ethics filter through textual extracts from his *Travels*, his *St Helena Journal*, and letters to friends and family. He was entrenched in the English culture of his day – the English flag, hoisted on Sundays on a bamboo cane fixed to his wagon, symbolised 'That predilection for one's own country, which has been implanted by Nature in the human heart'.[41] However, he still consciously endeavoured to pursue 'an unprejudiced investigation of facts'[42] when encountering other peoples and cultures. Through such open-mindedness, he was able to provide candid, balanced judgements of the people he met – some of which, naturally, reflect the Eurocentric debates and values of his time.

Travels in the Interior of Southern Africa is a book of substance: humour adds the 'lightness of being', to use Milan Kundera's famous words;[43] philosophy inspires abstract reflections; Romantic language creates immediacy; and the story of the adventurous journey sustains dramatic tension all the way from Cape Town to Litakun. No other South African nineteenth-century travelogue can compare with Burchell's masterpiece; no other travel writer of that time integrates science and religion so seamlessly, and creates the sense of wonder which radiates in Burchell's transcendent moments.

William Wordsworth, in his autobiographical poem 'The Prelude', wrote a line about Sir Isaac Newton: he has 'a Mind for ever / Voyaging through strange seas of Thought'.[44] Burchell's life of science certainly rewarded him with exalted enjoyment, and his 'voyage through strange seas of thought' is a lasting legacy for all to celebrate. By reading Burchell's own words and delighting in his artworks, we can recall Wordsworth's famous 'spots of time' when 'our minds are nourished' and we are ultimately uplifted.[45]

Station on the banks of the Nu-gariep; and making presents to a party of Bushmen

Acknowledgements

BURCHELL'S TRAVELS DRAWS EXTENSIVELY ON Dr Roger Stewart's varied publications. My warmest thanks are due to him for all the illuminating discussions, his generosity in sharing his expertise with me and, above all, for introducing me to Burchell's paintings and sketches. Robin Castell's *William John Burchell (1781–1863) St. Helena 1805–1810*, with his transcription of Burchell's St Helena journal, enabled me to write the St Helena chapter. I owe a great debt to his scholarship.

For the use of copyright materials my grateful thanks are due to the Royal Botanic Gardens, Kew (Lynn Parker); the Oxford University Museum of Natural History (Kate Santry); The Linnean Society of London (Elaine Charwat); Museum Africa (Diana Wall); Western Cape Archives and Records Service (Erika Le Roux); and the Library of Parliament (Lila Komnik). My thanks, too, go to Alex D'Angelo and Clive Kirkwood, University of Cape Town Libraries.

At Penguin Random House I would like to thank Robert Plummer for his editorial guidance and for synchronising text and images with artistic flair; Genevieve Adams and Bronwen Maynier for their skilful editing and proofreading; and Colette Stott for her invaluable assistance with the visual material. It was enlightening to be part of a superb professional team.

A special word of thanks must go to Mary Bock, Gail Fincham, Lesley Marx and Judy Broom – their input has much improved this book. For their support, encouragement and humour, I'd like to thank Kathie Buley, and hiking friends Loes Nas, Judy Ross, Adré Marshall and Wendy Woodward. And it gives me personal pleasure to thank my sons, Jonathan and Matthew Marks, for always seeing the lighter side. My husband, Richard Buchanan, did additional research, checked quotations and insisted that I accurately cited Burchell's idiosyncratic punctuation, and transcribed corrections with precision – my deepest debt is to him.

SUSAN BUCHANAN
JUNE 2015

A rhinoceros hunt, 8 March 1812

Picture credits

All paintings, sketches and engravings © Museum Africa, except for:
pages 18 and 19: source unknown
pages 29 and 37 (top and bottom): © Royal Botanic Gardens, Kew
page 66: © Oxford University Museum of Natural History
pages 183 and 210: © Western Cape Archives and Records Service, Elliot Collection (E2850 and E2859)
pages 216–217: © Library of Parliament

Notes

INTRODUCTION

1 T. S. Eliot, 'Little Gidding' in *Collected Poems 1909–1962*, London: Faber, 1963, p. 222.

2 The following edition is used in this book: William J. Burchell, *Travels in the Interior of Southern Africa*, 2 Vols. (1822 and 1824), edited by A. Gordon-Brown, Cape Town: Struik, 1967.

3 Isaac Schapera, Introduction to the London: Batchworth Press edition of *Travels in the Interior of Southern Africa*, 1953, p.x.

4 Ibid.

5 Helen Millar McKay, *The South African Drawings of William J. Burchell: The Bachapins of Litakun*, Vol. 1, Johannesburg: Witwatersrand University Press, 1938, p. xiii.

6 Mary Elizabeth Barber, 'Wanderings in South Africa by Sea and Land, 1879', *Quarterly Bulletin of the South African Library* XVII, 1962–1963, p. 51.

7 Jane Pickering, 'William John Burchell's travels in Brazil, 1825–1830, with details of the surviving mammal and bird collections', *Archives of Natural History* 25, (2), 1998, p. 245.

8 Ibid., p. 244.

9 Robin Castell, *William John Burchell (1781–1863) St. Helena (1805-1810)*, St Helena: Castell Collection, 2011.

10 Pickering, 'Burchell's travels in Brazil', p. 238.

11 Ibid., p. 237.

12 Ian D. Colvin and Frank Rosslyn Bradlow, *Introduction to Africana*, Cape Town: A.A. Balkema for the Friends of the South African Library, 1979, p. 48.

13 Pickering, 'Burchell's travels in Brazil', p. 247.

14 Burchell, *Travels*, Vol. I, Preface, p. viii.

15 Pickering, 'Burchell's travels in Brazil', p. 243.

16 R.F. Kennedy, *Catalogue of Pictures in the Africana Museum*, Vol. Six, Johannesburg: Africana Museum, 1966–.

17 Pickering, 'Burchell's travels in Brazil', p. 247.

18 E.B. Poulton, 'William John Burchell: The materials of a lecture delivered before the British Association on August 17, 1905', *Report of the British and South African Associations 1905*, III, 1905, p. 45.

19 Ibid., p. 3.

20 Schapera, Introduction to the Batchworth Press edition of *Travels*, pp. xvii–xviii.

21 J.M. Coetzee and David Attwell (ed), *Doubling the Point: Essays and Interviews*, Cambridge Mass.: Harvard University Press, 1992, p. 19.

22 Burchell, *Travels*, Vol. I, p. v.

23 J.M. Coetzee, *Youth*, London: Secker & Warburg, 2002, pp. 136-8.

24 Kai Easton, 'Coetzee, the Cape and the question of history', *Scrutiny2: Issues in English Studies in Southern Africa* 11, no. 1, 2006, p. 15.

25 Burchell, *Travels*, Vol. I, 10 April 1811, footnote, p. 98.

26 Ibid., Preface p. vii.

27 Ibid., 14 September 1811, p. 310.

28 Ibid., 14 February 1811, p. 63.

29 Roger Stewart and Brian Warner, 'William John Burchell: The multi-skilled polymath', *South African Journal of Science* 108, no. 11/12, 2012, p. 4.

30 Roger Stewart, 'A meticulous cartographer: William Burchell's map of South Africa', *IMCoS Journal* 125, 2011, p. 12.

31 This map will be published in David Attwell's forthcoming book on J.M. Coetzee.

32 Burchell, *Travels*, Vol. II, 28 April 1812, p. 171.

33 Knysna Historical Society, Outeniqua Historical Society, Stigting Simon van der Stel, George Heritage Trust.

34 Maria Cristina Wolff de Carvalho, 'The Landscape Art of William John Burchell (1781–1863)', *Arquitetourismo*, 2013. Accessed May 2015 at http://www.vitruvius.com.br/revistas/read/arquiteturismo/07.073/4700/en_US.

35 Ibid.

36 John Rourke, 'Beauty in Truth: Botanical Art in Southern Africa – A Brief Historical Perspective' in Marion Arnold, *South African Botanical Art: Peeling Back the Petals*, Vlaeberg, South Africa: Fernwood Press in association with Art Link, 2001, p. 39.

37 Ibid.

38 Colvin & Bradlow, *Africana*, p.36.

39 Rourke, 'Beauty in Truth', p. 32.

40 Burchell, *Travels*, Vol. I, Preface, p. vi.

41 Ibid., 30 October 1811, p. 411.

42 Burchell, *Travels*, Vol. II, Chapter XVIII, p. 563.

43 Colvin & Bradlow, *Africana*, p. 69.

44 Helen Millar McKay, *The South African Drawings of William J. Burchell: Landscape Sketches*, Vol. 2, Johannesburg: Witwatersrand University Press, 1952, p. xv.

45 Richard Holmes, *The Age of Wonder: How the Romantic Generation Discovered the Beauty and Terror of Science*, London: Harper Press, 2009, p. xvi.

46 Ibid.

47 Patrick Cullinan, *Robert Jacob Gordon, 1743–1795: The Man and his Travels at the Cape*, Cape Town: Struik Winchester, 1992, p. 9.

48 Burchell, *Travels*, Vol. II, 13 July 1812, p. 379.

49 Ibid., Vol. I, 11 August 1811, p. 264.

50 Ibid., Vol. II, 21 July 1812, p. 443.

51 Ibid., Vol. I, 16 September 1811, p. 316.

52 Derek Attridge, *The Singularity of Literature*, London: Routledge, 2004, pp. 88–9.

53 Holmes, *Age of Wonder*, p. 78.

54 Ibid., p. 449.

55 Bernard V. Lightman, *Victorian Science in Context*, Chicago, Ill.: University of Chicago Press, 1997), p. 187.

56 Hedley Twidle, '"The Bushmen's Letters": |Xam narratives of the Bleek and Lloyd Collection and their afterlives', in David Attwell and Derek Attridge (eds), *The Cambridge History of South African Literature*, Cambridge: Cambridge University Press, 2012, p.20.

CHAPTER 1: FULHAM

1 Marion Arnold, *South African Botanical Art: Peeling Back the Petals*, Vlaeberg, South Africa: Fernwood Press in association with Art Link, 2001, p. 20.

2 Helen Millar McKay, 'William John Burchell, Botanist: Part I: Introduction and Burchell in St. Helena', *The Journal of South African Botany* 7, 1941, p. 2.

3 McKay, 'William John Burchell, Botanist: Part I', p. 3.

4 Helen Millar McKay, 'William John Burchell, Scientist', *South African Journal of Science* XXXII, 1935, p. 689.

5 Poulton, 'Lecture, 1905', pp. 4–5.

6 Richard Grove, *Green Imperialism: Colonial Expansion, Tropical Island Edens and the Origins of Environmentalism, 1600-1860*, Cambridge: Cambridge University Press, 1995, pp. 348–352.

7 McKay, *Drawings of William J. Burchell: Landscape Sketches*, Vol. 2, p. xv.

8 Wolff de Carvalho, 'The Landscape Art of William John Burchell'.

9 Burchell, *Travels*, Vol. II, 22 July 1812, pp. 448–9.

10 McKay, *Drawings of William J. Burchell: Landscape Sketches*, Vol. 2, p. xv.

11 These can be viewed on http://www.annexgalleries.com/inventory/detail/18380/James-A-Merigot/Bridge-of-Varus-from-A-Select-Collection-of-Views-and-Ruins-in-Rome-and-Its-Vicinity. Accessed 22 December 2014.

12 Kennedy, *Catalogue of Pictures in the Africana Museum*, p. 43.

13 McKay, 'William John Burchell, Botanist: Part I', p. 3.
14 Ibid., p. 4.
15 Ibid., p. 17.
16 Burchell, Letter to his father, 23 June 1807, in Castell, p. 304.
17 Burchell, 'St. Helena Journal', in Castell, 5 September 1807, p. 54.

CHAPTER 2: ST HELENA

1 Burchell, 'St. Helena Journal', in Castell, 9 October 1810, p. 179.
2 Charles Darwin, *The Voyage of the Beagle*, Ware, Hertfordshire: Wordsworth Editions, 1997, p. 461.
3 Frederick Burkhardt (ed), *Charles Darwin: The 'Beagle' Letters*, Cambridge: Cambridge University Press, 2008, p. 393.
4 Darwin, *Voyage of the Beagle*, p. 464.
5 Ibid., p. 463.
6 McKay, 'William John Burchell, Botanist: Part I', p. 6.
7 Burchell, 'St. Helena Journal', 8 October 1807, p. 60.
8 Castell, *William John Burchell*, p. 14.
9 Ibid.
10 Burchell, 'St. Helena Journal', 23 December 1807, p. 79.
11 Ibid.
12 Castell, *William John Burchell*, p. 15.
13 Burchell, 'St. Helena Journal', 24 December 1806, p. 30.
14 Ibid., 24 December 1807, p. 80.
15 Ibid., 10 June 1809, p. 147.
16 Ibid., 11 January 1808, p. 90.
17 Ibid., 18 November 1809, p. 158.
18 McKay, 'William John Burchell, Botanist: Part I', p. 5.
19 Burchell, 'St. Helena Journal', 22 November 1808, p. 125.
20 Ibid., 6 April 1809, p. 141.
21 Ibid., 8 December 1807, p. 71.
22 Ibid., p. 72.
23 Ibid., 2 April 1810, p. 165.
24 Ibid., 3 September 1807, p. 54.
25 Ibid., 9 July 1810, p. 173.
26 Ibid., 22 May 1809, pp. 145–6.
27 Ibid., 27 February 1809, p. 135.
28 Ibid., 29 November 1807, pp. 68–9.
29 Ibid., 9 October 1810, p. 179.
30 Holmes, *Age of Wonder*, p. 450.
31 Burchell, *Travels*, Vol. I, 30 December 1811, p. 504.
32 Burchell, 'St. Helena Journal', 16 December 1807, p. 76.
33 Ibid., 19 March 1809, p.137.
34 Ibid., 21 March 1809, p. 138.
35 Janet Browne, *Charles Darwin: Voyaging*, Vol. 1, London: Pimlico, 2003, p.111.
36 Burchell, 'St. Helena Journal', 17 June 1807, p. 45.
37 Easton, 'Coetzee, the Cape and the question of history', p. 7.
38 Burchell, *Travels*, Vol. II, Chapter XVIII, p. 535.
39 Burchell, 'St. Helena Journal', 12 June 1809, p. 148.
40 Ibid., 8 December 1807, p. 73.
41 Ibid., 27 July 1807, p. 49.
42 Ibid., 21 August 1810, p. 177.
43 Ibid., 1 June 1807, p. 44.
44 Ibid., 20 November 1806, p. 26.
45 Ibid., 10 October 1807, p. 60.
46 Ibid., 11 October 1807, p. 61.
47 Ibid.
48 Thomas Gray, 'Elegy Written in a Country Churchyard', line 55.
49 Burchell, 'St. Helena Journal', 11 October 1807, p. 62.
50 Ibid., 31 December 1807, p. 85.
51 Burchell, *Travels*, Vol. I, 28 October 1811, p. 396.
52 J.M. Coetzee, *White Writing: On the Culture of Letters in South Africa*, Braamfontein, South Africa: Pentz Publishers, 2007, pp. 25-6.
53 Burchell, 'St. Helena Journal', 30 July 1807, p. 49.
54 Ibid., 13 March 1808, p. 101.
55 Ibid., 18 January 1809, p. 128.
56 Ibid., 8 December 1807, p. 70.
57 Ibid., 15 October 1808, p. 121.

58 Ibid., 31 July 1809, p. 153.

59 Ibid., 6 July 1810, p. 172.

60 Burchell, Letter written from St Helena, 23 June 1807, in Castell, pp. 303-4.

61 Burchell, 'St. Helena Journal', 12 May 1808, p. 104.

62 Ibid.

63 Ibid.

64 Burchell, Letter written from St. Helena, 5 May 1808, in Castell, p. 307.

65 Burchell, Letter written from St. Helena, 8 March 1809, in Castell, p. 308.

66 Browne, *Charles Darwin: Voyaging*, p. 113.

67 Poulton, 'Lecture, 1905', p. 6.

68 Burchell, 'St. Helena Journal', 1 August 1807, p. 50.

69 Ibid., 12 August 1807, p. 51.

70 Ibid., 28 August 1807, p. 53.

71 Ibid., 4 July 1808, p. 108.

72 Ibid., 26 October 1808, p. 122.

73 Ibid., 5 January 1810, p. 160.

74 Ibid., 25 January 1810, p. 161.

75 Ibid., 27 January 1810, p. 161.

76 Ibid., 11 July 1810, p. 173.

77 Ibid., 9 October 1810, p. 179.

78 Ibid., 11 October 1810, p. 179.

79 Ibid., 16 October 1810, p. 184.

CHAPTER 3: CAPE TOWN AND VICINITY

1 Carli Coetzee, 'In the archive: records of the Dutch settlement and the contemporary novel' in David Attwell and Derek Attridge (eds), *The Cambridge History of South African Literature*, Cambridge: Cambridge University Press, 2012, p. 148.

2 Nigel Worden, Elizabeth van Heyningen and Vivian Bickford-Smith, *Cape Town: The Making of a City: An Illustrated Social History*, Cape Town: David Philip, 2004, p. 87.

3 Ibid.

4 Burchell, *Travels*, Vol. I, 28 November 1810, p. 13.

5 Ibid., Chapter III, p. 70.

6 Ibid., p. 82.

7 Ibid., Preface, p. v.

8 Ibid., p. vii.

9 Poulton, 'Lecture, 1905', p. 40.

10 Burchell, *Travels*, Vol. II, 3 August 1812, p. 510.

11 Ibid., Vol. I, 11 April 1811, p. 100.

12 Ibid., Vol. II, 12 March 1812, pp. 84–5.

13 Worden et al., *Cape Town*, p. 89.

14 Burchell, *Travels*, Vol. I, 14 November 1810, pp. 3–4.

15 Ibid., p. 3.

16 Ibid.

17 Ibid., 16–17 November 1810, pp. 6–7.

18 Ibid., 26 November 1810, p. 10.

19 Ibid., p. 9.

20 Ibid., p. 10.

21 Ibid., 16–17 November 1810, p. 6.

22 Ibid., 26 November 1810, p. 12.

23 Ibid., 29 November 1810, p. 14.

24 Keith Hamilton Dietrich, 'Of salvation and civilization; the image of indigenous southern Africans in European travel illustration from the sixteenth to the nineteenth centuries', D. Litt. et Phil. thesis, University of South Africa, 1993, p. 202.

25 Burchell, *Travels*, Vol. I, 14 March 1811, p. 68.

26 J.M. Coetzee, 'The Picturesque, the Sublime, and the South African Landscape' in *White Writing*, pp. 38–9.

27 Burchell, *Travels*, Vol. I, p. 71.

28 Dietrich, 'Of salvation and civilization', p. 205.

29 Burchell, *Travels*, Vol. I, 26 November 1810, p. 12.

30 Kennedy, *Catalogue of Pictures in the Africana Museum*, p. 62.

31 Tim Ingold, *Lines: a brief history*, London: Routledge, 2007, pp. 2–3.

32 Burchell, *Travels*, Vol. I, 12 December 1810, pp. 25–26.

33 Ibid., 31 January 1811, p. 51.

34 Ibid., 8 December 1810, pp. 20–2.

35 Ibid., p. 21.

36 Ibid., 12 December 1810, p. 24.

37 Ibid.

38 Ibid., 14 February 1811, p. 62.

39 Ibid., 27 December 1810, pp. 27–8.

40 Ibid., 18 January 1811, p. 38.
41 Burchell, *Travels*, Vol. II, 17 July 1812, p. 413.
42 Janet Browne, *Charles Darwin: The Power of Place*, Vol. 2, Princeton and Oxford: Princeton University Press, 2002, p. 173.
43 Burchell, *Travels*, Vol. I, 3 January 1811, p. 34.
44 Ibid., 5 December 1810, p. 18.
45 Ibid., 17 June 1811, p. 166.
46 Ibid., 23 January 1811, p. 38.
47 Ibid., p. 39.
48 Ibid., 24 January 1811, p. 45.
49 Ibid., p. 40.
50 Ibid., p. 41.
51 Ibid.
52 Ibid., pp. 42–3.
53 Ibid., 43.
54 Ibid.
55 Ibid., p. 47.
56 Ibid., pp. 47–8.
57 Ibid., p. 48.
58 Ibid., Chapter IV, p. 83.
59 Ibid., 18 April 1811, pp. 134–5.
60 Ibid., 10 April, 1811, p. 96.
61 Ibid.
62 Ibid., 26 December 1810, p.27.
63 Ibid., 2 June 1811, p. 157.
64 Ibid., pp. 159–60.
65 Ibid., 10 April 1811, p. 97.
66 Ibid., 29 January 1811, p. 50.
67 Ibid., pp. 50–1.
68 Ibid., 28 November 1810, p. 13.
69 Ibid.
70 Ibid., 29 January 1811, p. 50.
71 Poulton, 'Lecture, 1905', p. 36.
72 Burchell, *Travels*, Vol. I, 29 January 1811, p. 50.
73 Ibid., p. 49.
74 Ibid., 18 February 1811, p. 64.
75 Ibid., p. 582.
76 Ibid., p. 65.
77 Ibid., 30 April 1811, pp.151–2.
78 Ibid., 17 June 1811, pp. 164–5.
79 Ibid., p. 166.
80 Ibid., 8 June 1811, p. 160.
81 Ibid., 17 June 1811, p. 166.
82 Ibid., 18 June 1811, pp. 166–7.
83 Ibid., p. 168.
84 Ibid., p. 169.
85 Ibid.
86 Ibid.
87 Ibid., 19 June 1811, pp. 170–1.

CHAPTER 4: CAPE TOWN
TO KLAARWATER

1 Burchell, *Travels*, Vol. I, 30 July 1811, p. 244.
2 Ibid., Preface, p. viii.
3 Ibid., 7 July 1811, p. 199.
4 Ibid., 19 July 1811, p. 226.
5 Ibid., 7 September 1811, p. 290.
6 Ibid., 30 September 1811, p. 348.
7 Ibid., Contents page.
8 Mary Gunn and L.E Codd, *Botanical Exploration of Southern Africa*, Cape Town: Published for the Botanical Research Institute by A.A. Balkema, 1981, p. 109.
9 Based on the Southern African Biomes Map in Brett M. Bennett, 'Reading the Land: Changing Landscapes and the Environmental History of South Africa', in Michael Godby (ed) *The Lie of the Land: Representations of the South African Landscape*, South Africa: Iziko, 2010, p. 47.
10 Burchell, *Travels*, Vol. I, 19 June 1811, p. 173.
11 Ibid., 16 July 1811, p. 217.
12 Ibid., 19 June 1811, p. 173.
13 Ibid., 21 June 1811, p. 175.
14 Ibid., 23 June 1811, pp. 177–8.
15 Ibid., 1 July 1811, p. 185.
16 Ibid., 9 August 1811, pp. 261–2.
17 Ibid., 12 September 1811, p. 305.
18 Ibid., Vol. II, 24 July 1812, pp. 466–7.
19 Ibid., Vol. I, 25 August 1811, pp.272–3.
20 Ibid., 27 August 1811, pp. 275–6.
21 Ibid., 30 December 1811, p. 504.
22 Ibid., 23 June 1811, p. 178.
23 Ibid., 16 September 1811, p. 316.
24 Ibid., p. 317.
25 Ibid., 17 September 1811, p. 325.
26 Dietrich, 'Of salvation and civilization', p. 205.
27 Ibid.
28 Burchell, *Travels*, Vol. I, 4 July 1811, p. 189.

29 Ibid., 9 July 1811, p. 203.

30 Ibid., 30 September 1811, p. 349.

31 Ibid., 31 August 1811, p. 280.

32 Ibid., 24 June 1811, p. 180.

33 Ibid., 4 July 1811, p. 188.

34 Ibid., 19 April 1811, p. 137.

35 Ibid., 13 July 1811, p. 207.

36 Ibid., 14 July 1811, p. 209.

37 Ibid., 13 July 1811, p. 207.

38 Ibid., 14 July 1811, p. 210.

39 Ibid., 19 July 1811, p. 229.

40 Ibid., p. 228.

41 Ibid., p. 227.

42 Ibid., 20 July 1811, p.230.

43 Ibid., 24 July 1811, p. 237.

44 Ibid., 6 August 1811, p. 253.

45 Ibid., 19–23 August 1811, p. 270.

46 Schapera, Introduction to the Batchworth Press edition of *Travels*, p. xii.

47 Burchell, *Travels*, Vol. I, 19–23 August 1811, p. 270.

48 Ibid., 1 September 1811, pp. 281–2.

49 Nicolas Barker, *Lady Anne Barnard's Watercolours and Sketches: Glimpses of the Cape of Good Hope*, Simon's Town, South Africa: Fernwood Press, 2009, p. 20.

50 Burchell, *Travels*, Vol. I, 4 September 1811, p. 285.

51 Ibid., 13 September 1811, p. 306.

52 Ibid., 8 September 1811, p. 292.

53 Ibid., 6 September 1811, p. 288.

54 Ibid., 4 September 1811, p.285.

55 Ibid., 11 September 1811, p. 299.

56 Ibid., 8 September 1811, p. 291.

57 Ibid.

58 Ibid.

59 Ibid., pp. 291–2.

60 Ibid., p. 292.

61 Ibid., 9 September 1811, p. 294.

62 Ibid., p. 295.

63 Ibid.

64 Ibid., 11 September 1811, p. 302.

65 Ibid., 12 September 1811, p. 303.

66 J.M. Coetzee, *Elizabeth Costello*, London: Vintage, 2004, p.79.

67 Cullinan, *Robert Jacob Gordon*, pp. 44–5.

68 Burchell, *Travels*, Vol. I, 15 September 1811, p. 315.

69 Ibid., 16 September 1811, p. 315.

70 Ibid., p. 316.

71 Ibid., pp. 316–7.

72 Ibid., p. 316.

73 Ibid., p. 317.

74 Ibid., 17 September 1811, p. 320.

75 Ibid., p. 322.

76 Ibid., p. 323.

77 Ibid., p. 324.

78 Ibid., p. 325.

79 Ibid., pp. 325–6.

80 Ibid., p. 325.

81 Mary Louise Pratt, *Imperial Eyes: Travel Writing and Transculturation*, London; New York: Routledge, 2008, p. 40.

82 Burchell, *Travels*, Vol. I, 18 September 1811, p. 326.

83 Ibid., 19 September 1811, p. 328.

84 Ibid., p. 329.

85 Ibid., 20 September 1811, pp. 331–2.

86 Ibid., 19 September 1811, p. 329.

87 Ibid., 21 September 1811, p. 334.

88 Ibid., 30 September 1811, p. 349.

89 Ibid., p. 344.

90 Ibid.

91 Ibid., p. 345.

92 Ibid.

93 Ibid., p. 345–6.

94 Bennett, 'Reading the Land', p. 49.

95 Burchell, *Travels*, Vol. I, 30 September 1811, p. 347.

96 Ibid., pp. 348–9.

97 Ibid., p. 347

98 Ibid., 30 July 1811, p. 244.

99 Ibid., 12 November 1811, p. 444–5.

CHAPTER 5: KLAARWATER AND THE KY-GARIEP

1 Burchell, *Travels*, Vol. I, 1 October 1811, p. 353.

2 Ibid., p. 352.

3 Ibid., 6 October 1811, p. 360.

4 Ibid., p. 361.

5 Ibid., p. 364.

6 Ibid., p. 367.

7   Ibid., pp. 368–70.
8   Ibid., pp. 370–1.
9   Ibid., 1 October 1811, p.352.
10 Ibid., p. 351.
11 Ibid., p. 352.
12 Kennedy, *Catalogue of Pictures in the Africana Museum*, p. 70.
13 Burchell, *Travels*, Vol. I, 1 October 1811, p. 353.
14 Ibid., 20 November 1811, p. 477.
15 Ibid., 20 October 1811, p. 378.
16 Ibid., 21 November 1811, p. 477.
17 Roger Stewart, 'William Burchell's medical challenges: A 19th-century natural philosopher in the field', *South African Medical Journal* 102, no. 4, 2012, p. 254.
18 Burchell, *Travels*, Vol. I, 22 November 1811, p. 481.
19 Ibid., p. 479.
20 Ibid., 6 October 1811, pp. 357–8.
21 Ibid., p. 358–9.
22 Ibid., 20 October 1811, p. 378.
23 Helen Millar McKay, 'William John Burchell, Botanist: Part II: Burchell in South Africa', *The Journal of South African Botany* 7, 1941, p. 62.
24 Burchell, *Travels*, Vol. I, 11 November 1811, pp. 442–3.
25 Ibid., 24 October 1811, p. 381.
26 Ibid., 30 October 1811, p. 410.
27 Ibid., pp. 412–3.
28 Ibid., p. 411.
29 Ibid., 2 November 1811, p. 420.
30 Ibid., p. 424.
31 Ibid., 30 October 1811, p. 413.
32 Ibid., p. 415.
33 Elana Bregin, 'Representing the Bushmen: Through the Colonial Lens', *English in Africa* 27, no. 1, 2000, p. 40.
34 Burchell, *Travels*, Vol. I, 30 October 1811, p. 415.
35 Ibid., 2 November 1811, p. 422.
36 Ibid.
37 Ibid., 26 November 1810, p. 12.
38 Ibid., Vol. II, 15 June 1812, p. 245.
39 Ibid., Vol. I, 24 October 1811, pp. 381–2.
40 Ibid., 29 October 1811, p. 401.
41 Ibid., 24 October 1811, pp. 382–3.
42 Burchell, *Travels*, Vol. I, 13 November 1811, p. 447.
43 Ibid.
44 Ibid.
45 Ibid., p. 448.
46 Ibid., 12 November 1811, p. 443.
47 Ibid., 16 November 1811, p. 456.
48 Ibid., 19 November 1811, p. 468.
49 Ibid., p. 472.
50 Ibid., 16 November 1811, p. 456.
51 A.J.B. Humphreys, 'Burchell's Shelter: The History and Archaeology of a Northern Cape Rock Shelter', *South African Archaeological Bulletin* 30, no. 117/118, 1975, p.3.
52 Ibid.
53 Burchell, *Travels*, Vol. I, 16 November 1811, pp. 456–7.
54 Ibid., p. 457.
55 Ibid., p. 457–8.
56 Ibid., p. 458.
57 Ibid., 17 November, 1811, pp. 458–9.
58 Ibid., p. 459.
59 Ibid., p. 460.
60 Ibid., pp. 460–1.
61 Ibid., 16 November 1811, p. 457.
62 John Keats, 'Lamia' in John Barnard (ed), *John Keats: The Complete Poems*, Harmondsworth, England: Penguin Books, 1976, p. 431, line 230.
63 Burchell, *Travels*, Vol. I, 20 November 1811, p.476.
64 Ibid., 15 January 1812, p. 515.
65 Ibid., 19 January 1812, p. 516–7.

CHAPTER 6: KLAARWATER AND GRAAFF-REINET

1   Burchell, *Travels*, Vol. I, 14 January 1812, p. 512.
2   Ibid., 30 December 1811, p. 503.
3   Ibid., 14 January 1812, p.513.
4   Ibid., 30 December 1811, p. 504.
5   Ibid., 19 January 1812, p. 517.
6   Ibid., 4 February 1812, p. 527.
7   Ibid., 26 January 1812, pp. 522–3.

8 Ibid., 1, 5 February 1812, p. 530.
9 Ibid., 16 February 1812, p. 542.
10 Ibid., 17 December 1811, p. 493.
11 Ibid., 15 January 1812, p. 515.
12 Ibid., 30 December 1811, p. 504.
13 Ibid., p. 505.
14 Geoffrey N. Leech, *A Linguistic Guide to English Poetry*, London: Longmans, 1969, p. 220.
15 Burchell, *Travels*, Vol. I, 20 November 1811, p. 476.
16 Ibid., 5 February 1812, p. 529.
17 Ibid., 30 December 1811, p. 505.
18 Ibid., 1 January 1812, p. 506.
19 Michel Foucault, *The Order of Things: An Archaeology of the Human Sciences*, London and New York: Routledge Classics, 2009, p. 144.
20 Burchell, *Travels*, Vol. I, 30 December 1811, p. 505.
21 Ibid., 15 February 1812, p. 540.
22 Ibid.
23 Ibid., 27 November 1811, pp. 483–4.
24 Ibid., 25 December 1811, pp. 496-7.
25 Isabelle Stengers, 'The Challenge of Complexity: Unfolding the Ethics of Science. In Memoriam Ilya Prigogine', E: Co 6, no. 1–2, 2004, p. 99.
26 Burchell, *Travels*, Vol. I, 29 December 1811, p. 501.
27 Ibid., p. 502.
28 Ibid., 14 January 1812, p. 511.
29 Ibid., Vol. II, 2 March 1812, p. 32.
30 Ibid., Vol. I, 8 January 1812, p. 509.
31 Ibid., 26 January 1812, p. 523.
32 Ibid., 23 February 1812, p. 553.
33 Ibid.
34 McKay, 'William John Burchell, Botanist: Part II', p. 63.
35 Burchell, *Travels*, Vol. I, 22 February 1812, p. 551.
36 Ibid., Vol. II, 24 February 1812, p. 2.
37 Ibid., p. 3.
38 Ibid., Vol. I, 22 February 1812, p. 551.
39 Ibid., Vol. II, 27 February 1812, p. 11.
40 Ibid., p. 14.
41 Ibid., pp. 12–3.
42 Ibid., 26 February 1812, p. 8–9.
43 Ibid., p. 9.
44 Ibid., Vol. I, 5 February 1812, p. 530.
45 Ibid., Vol. II, 3 March 1812, p. 36.
46 Poulton, 'Lecture, 1905', p. 26.
47 Ibid., pp. 23–4.
48 Burchell, *Travels*, Vol. II, 28 February 1812, p. 16.
49 Ibid., 1 March 1812, p. 22.
50 Ibid., p. 23.
51 Ibid., 3 March 1812, pp. 36–7.
52 Ibid., p. 37
53 Ibid., p. 38.
54 Ibid., p. 40.
55 Ibid., 5 March 1812, p. 44.
56 Ibid., 6 March 1812, p. 47.
57 Ibid.
58 Ibid., p. 62.
59 Ibid., 17 July 1812, p. 413.
60 Ibid., 6 March 1812, p. 63.
61 Ibid., p.64.
62 Ibid., p. 66.
63 Ibid., pp. 66–7.
64 Ibid.
65 Ibid., 7 March 1812, p. 72.
66 Ibid., p. 68.
67 Ibid., 8 March 1812, pp. 74–5.
68 Ibid., 9 March 1812, p. 79.
69 Ibid., 12 March 1812, p. 85.
70 Ibid., p. 87.
71 Ibid., 13 March 1812, p. 89.
72 Ibid., p. 90.
73 Ibid.
74 Ibid., 14 March 1812, p. 91.
75 Ibid., p. 92.
76 Ibid., p. 93.
77 Ibid., p. 94.
78 Ibid., 18 March 1812, p. 106.
79 Ibid., p. 108.
80 Elana Bregin, 'Representing the Bushmen', p. 53.
81 Burchell, *Travels*, Vol. II, 18 March 1812, p. 108.
82 Ibid., 21 March 1812, p. 125.
83 Ibid., 18 March 1812, p. 108.

84 Ibid., 21 March 1812, p. 124.
85 Ibid., p. 125.
86 Ibid., 22 March 1812, p. 127.
87 Ibid.
88 Ibid., pp. 128–9.
89 Ibid., p. 129.
90 Ibid., p. 130.
91 Ibid., 23 March 1812, p. 131.
92 Ibid., p. 133.
93 Ibid., p. 134.
94 Ibid., 24 March 1812, p. 134.
95 Ibid., p. 135.
96 Ibid., pp. 135–6.
97 Ibid.
98 Ibid., p. 137.
99 Ibid., 25 March 1812, p. 140.
100 Ibid., 23 April 1812, p. 154.
101 Ibid., 25 April 1812, p. 164.
102 Ibid., 7 April 1812, p. 149.
103 Ibid., 15 March 1812, p. 96.
104 Ibid., 19 March 1812, p. 112.
105 Ibid., 15 March 1812, p.95.
106 Ibid., pp. 95–6.
107 Ibid., 25 April 1812, p. 161.
108 Ibid.
109 Ibid., Vol. I, 14–16 November 1810, p. 5.
110 Ibid.
111 Ibid., pp. 5–6.
112 Ibid., Vol. II, 15 May 1812, p. 203.
113 Ibid., 28 April 1812, p. 171.
114 Ibid., 7 May 1812, p. 188.
115 Ibid., 2 May 1812, p. 182.
116 Ibid., 6 May 1812, p. 185.
117 Nigel Penn, '"Civilizing" the San: The First Mission to the Cape San, 1791 -1806', in Pippa Skotnes, *Claim to the Country: The Archive of Wilhelm Bleek and Lucy Lloyd*, Johannesburg: Jacana; Athens: Ohio University Press, 2007, p. 92.
118 Burchell, *Travels*, Vol. II, 6 May 1812, p. 185.
119 Ibid., 24 May 1812, p. 221.
120 Ibid., 23 May 1812, p. 219.
121 Ibid., 24 May 1812, p. 222.
122 Ibid., p. 223.
123 Ibid.
124 Ibid., 3 June 1812, p. 225.

CHAPTER 7: JOURNEY TO LITAKUN

1 Burchell, *Travels*, Vol. II, 26 June 1812, p. 286.
2 Ibid., 3 June 1812, p. 226.
3 Ibid., 6 June 1812, p. 231.
4 Ibid., pp. 228–9.
5 Ibid., p. 231.
6 Ibid., p. 232.
7 Ibid., 28 June 1812, p. 292.
8 Ibid., 9 June 1812, p. 238.
9 Ibid., p. 237.
10 Elizabeth Green Musselman, 'Plant Knowledge at the Cape: A Study in African and European Collaboration', *The International Journal of African Historical Studies*, Vol. 36, no. 2, 2003, p. 379.
11 Ibid., p. 383.
12 Ibid., p. 384.
13 Burchell, *Travels*, Vol. II, 13 June 1812, p. 243.
14 Ibid., Vol. I, 28 November 1811, pp. 484–5.
15 Ibid., Vol. II, 15 June 1812, p. 244.
16 Ibid.
17 Ibid., p. 245.
18 Ibid., 12 June 1812, p. 240.
19 Ibid., 11 June 1812, p. 240.
20 Ibid., 16 June 1812, p.248.
21 Ibid., 17 June 1812, p. 249.
22 Ibid., 16 June 1812, p. 248.
23 Ibid., 17 June 1812, pp. 250–1.
24 Ibid., 18 June 1812, p. 254.
25 Ibid., 6 June 1812, p. 233.
26 Ibid., 18 June 1812, p. 256.
27 Ibid., pp. 256–7.
28 Ibid., 19 June 1812, p. 260.
29 Stewart and Warner, 'The multi-skilled polymath', p. 4.
30 Burchell, *Travels*, Vol. II, 19 June 1812, pp. 260–3.
31 Ibid., 21 June 1812, p. 271.
32 Ibid., 19 June 1812, p. 265.
33 Ibid., 265–6.
34 Ibid., 21 June 1812, p. 270.
35 Ibid., p. 272.
36 Coetzee, *White Writing*, p. 40.
37 Ibid., p. 42.
38 Burchell, *Travels*, Vol. II, 21 June 1812, p. 272.
39 Ibid., 22 June 1812, p.274.

40 Ibid., 24 May 1812, p. 224.
41 Ibid., 22 June 1812, p. 275.
42 Ibid., 27 June 1812, p. 288.
43 Ibid.
44 Ibid., 26 June 1812, p. 285.
45 Ibid., 24 April 1812, p. 155.
46 Ibid., 26 June 1812, p. 286.
47 Ibid., 28 June 1812, p. 294.
48 Ibid., p. 295.
49 Ibid.
50 Ibid.
51 Ibid.
52 Ibid., 30 June 1812, p. 303.
53 Ibid., 28 June 1812, p. 290.
54 Ibid.
55 Ibid., p. 292.
56 Ibid., p. 293.
57 Ibid., 29 June 1812, p. 299.
58 Ibid., p. 300.
59 Ibid., 30 June 1812, p. 304.
60 Ibid.
61 Ibid., 1 July 1812, p. 306.
62 Ibid., Vol. I, 'Geographical Remarks', p. 581.
63 Ibid., Vol. II, 2 July 1812, p. 312.
64 Ibid.
65 Ibid.
66 Helen Millar McKay, 'William John Burchell, Botanist: Part IV: Botanical interests from 1830–1863', *The Journal of South African Botany*, 7, 1941, p. 183.
67 Burchell, *Travels*, Vol. II, 6 July 1812, pp. 323–4.
68 Ibid., p. 324.
69 Ibid.
70 Ibid., pp. 325–6.
71 Ibid., p. 328.
72 Ibid.
73 Ibid., p. 329.
74 Ibid., 9 July 1812, pp. 333–4.
75 Ibid., 6 July 1812, p. 331.
76 Ibid., 30 July 1812, pp. 490–1.
77 Ibid., p. 491.
78 Ibid., 9 July 1812, p.338.
79 Ibid.
80 Ibid., p. 339.
81 Ibid.
82 Ibid.
83 Ibid., 12 July 1812, pp. 351–2.
84 Ibid., 13 July 1812, p. 353.
85 Ibid., p. 354.
86 Ibid., p. 359.

CHAPTER 8: LITAKUN

1 Burchell, *Travels*, Vol. II, 21 July 1812, p. 443.
2 Poulton, 'Lecture, 1905', p. 33.
3 Burchell, *Travels*, Vol. II, 3 August 1812, p. 510.
4 Ibid., 17 July 1812, p. 415.
5 Stephen Watson (ed), *A City Imagined*, Johannesburg: Penguin Books, 2006, p. 3.
6 Ibid., p. 10.
7 Burchell, *Travels*, Vol. II, 13 July 1812, p. 362.
8 Ibid., pp. 362–3.
9 Ibid., p. 360.
10 Ibid., p. 357.
11 Ibid., p. 358.
12 Ibid., p. 364.
13 Ibid., p. 366.
14 Ibid., pp. 378–9.
15 Ibid., p. 376.
16 Ibid., p. 377.
17 Ibid.
18 Ibid.
19 Ibid., p. 378.
20 Ibid., 14 July 1812, p. 388.
21 Ibid., p. 389.
22 Ibid., p. 390.
23 Ibid., 16 July 1812, p. 403.
24 Ibid., pp. 403–4.
25 Poulton, 'Lecture, 1905', p. 33.
26 Burchell, *Travels*, Vol. II, 16 July 1812, p. 404.
27 Ibid., p. 405.
28 Ibid., 17 July 1812, p. 413.
29 Ibid., pp. 411–2.
30 Ibid., p. 413.
31 Ibid., 13 July 1812, p. 379.
32 Ibid., pp. 379–80.
33 Ibid.
34 Ibid.
35 Ibid., 14 July 1812, p. 383.
36 Ibid., p. 385.
37 Ibid., 22 July 1812, p. 457.

38 Ibid., 23 July 1812, p. 459.
39 Ibid., p. 460.
40 Ibid.
41 Ibid., p. 461.
42 Ibid.
43 Ibid., pp. 461–2.
44 Ibid., p. 462.
45 Ibid., 24 July 1812, p. 465.
46 Ibid., p. 467.
47 Ibid., 25 July 1812, p. 468.
48 Ibid., pp. 468–9.
49 Ibid., p. 469.
50 Ibid., p. 470.
51 Ibid., p. 471.
52 Ibid.
53 Ibid., p. 472.
54 Ibid.
55 Ibid., 26 July 1812, p. 473.
56 Ibid., pp. 472–3.
57 Ibid., p. 473.
58 Ibid.
59 Ibid., Chapter XVII, p. 524.
60 Ibid., 26 July 1812, p. 474.
61 Ibid., 21 July 1812, p. 444.
62 Ibid., 28 July 1812, p. 481.
63 Ibid., 29 July 1812, p. 484.
64 Ibid., 31 July 1812, p. 493.
65 Ibid., 24 July 1812, p. 464.
66 Ibid., 21 July 1812, p. 443.
67 Ibid., pp. 443–4.
68 Ibid., 14 July 1812, p. 395.
69 Ibid., 18 July 1812, p. 425.
70 Ibid., 21 July 1812, pp. 446–7.
71 Ibid., p. 446.
72 Ibid., 22 July 1812, p. 453.
73 Ibid., p. 454.
74 Ibid., p. 455.
75 Ibid., 2 August 1812, pp. 500–1.
76 Ibid., p. 502.
77 Ibid., 2 and 3 August 1812, pp. 502–3.
78 Ibid., 3 August 1812, p. 505.
79 Ibid., p. 506.
80 Ibid.
81 Ibid., p. 507.
82 Ibid., p. 509.
83 Ibid., p. 509–10.

CHAPTER 9: LITAKUN
TO CAPE TOWN

1 Samuel Taylor Coleridge, 'The Delinquent
   Travellers' in Richard Holmes, *Coleridge:
   Darker Reflections*, London: Flamingo,
   1999, p. 553.
2 Ibid., ll. 16–21.
3 Holmes, *Coleridge: Darker Reflections*, p. 553.
4 Roger Stewart, 'Burchell horticulturalist', in
   press (unpublished as of 2015), pp. 5–6.
5 http://trailriderreports.blogspot.com/2010/
   05/burchell-travels.html. Accessed November
   2014.
6 Kennedy, *Catalogue of Pictures in the
   Africana Museum*, p. 87.
7 Jane Pickering, 'William J. Burchell's South
   African mammal collection, 1810–1815',
   Archives of Natural History 24, (3), 1997,
   p. 316.
8 Arnold, *South African Botanical Art*, p.19.
9 Pickering, 'South African mammal collection,
   1810–1815', p.315.
10 Kennedy, *Catalogue of Pictures in the
    Africana Museum*, p. 86.
11 Arnold, *South African Botanical Art*, p. 20.
12 Ibid., p. 23.
13 Roger Stewart, 'Burchell's Garden Route',
    presented at the William John Burchell
    Bicentenary Commemoration, George,
    19 September 2014, p. 17.
14 Ibid.
15 Ibid., p. 1.
16 Ibid., pp. 2 and 30.
17 Jane Carruthers and M. Arnold, *The Life
    and Work of Thomas Baines*, Vlaeberg:
    Fernwood Press, 1995, p. 110.
18 Stewart, 'Burchell's Garden Route', p. 3.
19 Ibid., p. 19.
20 Kennedy, *Catalogue of Pictures in the
    Africana Museum*, p. 98.
21 Stewart, 'Burchell's Garden Route', p. 21.
22 Burchell, *Travels*, Vol. I, Preface, p. vii.

CHAPTER 10: ENGLAND AND BRAZIL

1 Poulton, 'Lecture, 1905', p. 3.
2 Ibid., p. 40.

3 Mike and Liz Fraser, *The Smallest Kingdom: Plants and Plant Collectors at the Cape of Good Hope*, Richmond, Surrey: Kew Publishing, Royal Botanic Gardens, Kew, 2011, p. 81.

4 Stewart, 'Burchell horticulturalist', in press, p. 7.

5 McKay, 'William John Burchell, Botanist: Part II', p. 68.

6 McKay, 'William John Burchell, Botanist: Part III', p. 117.

7 Ibid., p. 116.

8 Poulton, 'Lecture, 1905', p. 40.

9 'The Botanical Register', v. 2, 1816, illustration number 139.

10 Kennedy, *Catalogue of Pictures in the Africana Museum*, p. 99.

11 McKay, 'William John Burchell, Botanist: Part III', pp. 116–7.

12 Andrew Marvell, 'The Garden', *The Norton Anthology of Poetry*, 3rd edition, New York: W.W. Norton, 1983, p. 344, ll. 65–6.

13 'The Botanical Register', illustration number 159.

14 Burchell, *Travels*, Vol. I, 31 January 1811, p. 55.

15 Helen Millar McKay, 'A Scientist's Wagon', *South African Journal of Science* XXXII, 1935, p. 682.

16 Poulton, 'Lecture, 1905', p. 40.

17 Ibid.

18 Burchell's reply to criticism in John Barrow, 'Review of Burchell's "Hints on Emigration to the Cape of Good Hope"', in additional material in *Travels*, pp. 42–45.

19 Helen Millar McKay, 'William John Burchell, Botanist: Part III: Burchell in England and Brazil', *The Journal of South African Botany* 7, 1941, p. 119.

20 Poulton, 'Lecture, 1905', p. 40.

21 McKay, 'William John Burchell, Botanist: Part III', p.119.

22 Burchell, *Travels*, Vol. II, 9 July 1812, p.337.

23 Ibid., Vol. I, 24 October 1811, pp. 383–4.

24 Ibid., Vol. II, 9 July 1812, p. 337.

25 Ian Glenn, 'Eighteenth-century natural history, travel writing and South African literary historiography' in David Attwell and Derek Attridge (eds), *The Cambridge History of South African Literature*, Cambridge: Cambridge University Press, 2012, p. 158.

26 McKay, 'William John Burchell, Scientist', p. 691.

27 Burchell, *Travels*, Vol. I, 24 October 1811, p. 384.

28 Poulton, 'Lecture, 1905', p. 20.

29 Burchell, *Travels*, Vol. I, Preface, p. vii.

30 William J. Burchell, 'Hints on Emigration to the Cape of Good Hope', London: Hatchard, 1819, in additional material in *Travels*, pp. 24–40.

31 John Barrow, 'Review of Burchell's "Hints on Emigration to the Cape of Good Hope"', *Quarterly Review*, Nov. 1819, in additional material in *Travels*, p. 41.

32 Burchell, *Travels*, pp. 577–8.

33 Randolph Vigne, 'Mapping and promoting South Africa: Barrow and Burchell's rivalry', *Historia* 58, 1, May/Mei 2013, p. 19.

34 Ibid., p. 22.

35 Burchell, *Travels*, Vol. I, 'Remarks on the Map; and Geographical Observations', pp. 575–6.

36 Stewart, 'A meticulous cartographer', p.14.

37 Burchell, *Travels*, Vol. I, Legend on Map.

38 Carruthers and Arnold, *Thomas Baines*, p. 132.

39 Burchell, *Travels*, Vol. I, p. 577.

40 Ibid., p. 578.

41 Vigne, 'Mapping', p. 24.

42 McKay, 'William John Burchell, Botanist: Part IV', p. 184.

43 McKay, 'William John Burchell, Botanist: Part III', p. 120.

44 Burchell, 'St. Helena Journal', in Castell, 12 July 1810, p. 173.

45 Pickering, 'Burchell's travels in Brazil', p. 237.

46 Ibid.

47 Letter to Swainson, 15 February 1825, Swainson Correspondence, Linnean Society.

48 Letter to Swainson, 22 February 1825, Swainson Correspondence, Linnean Society.

49 McKay, 'William John Burchell, Botanist: Part III', p. 121.
50 Pickering, 'Burchell's travels in Brazil', p. 239.
51 Ibid.
52 Letter to Swainson, 31 August 1825, Swainson Correspondence, Linnean Society.
53 Ibid.
54 Pickering, 'Burchell's travels in Brazil', p. 239.
55 Ibid., p. 240.
56 Ibid.
57 Kennedy, *Catalogue of Pictures in the Africana Museum*, p. 129.
58 Burchell, *Travels*, Vol. II, 22 July 1812, pp. 448–9.
59 Kennedy, *Catalogue of Pictures in the Africana Museum*, p. 111.
60 Pickering, 'Burchell's travels in Brazil', p. 240.
61 Ibid., p. 244.
62 Ibid., p. 240.
63 Ibid., p. 243.
64 Ibid.
65 W.J. Hooker, 'Mr Burchell's Brazilian Journey', *Botanical Miscellany* 2, 1831, p. 130.
66 Ibid., pp. 128–133.
67 Ibid., p. 128.
68 McKay, 'William John Burchell, Botanist: Part III', p. 126.
69 Pickering, 'Burchell's travels in Brazil' p. 240.
70 Ibid., p. 241.
71 Poulton, 'Lecture, 1905', p. 43.
72 McKay, 'William John Burchell, Botanist: Part III', p. 121.
73 Ibid., p. 126.
74 Ibid., p.127.
75 Ibid.
76 Ibid., pp. 127–8
77 Colin Tudge, *The Secret Life of Trees: How They Live and Why They Matter*, London: Penguin Books, 2006, p. 145.
78 Darwin, *Voyage*, p. 27.
79 McKay, 'William John Burchell, Botanist: Part III', p. 128.
80 Pickering, 'Burchell's travels in Brazil', p. 240.
81 Ibid.
82 Ibid.
83 Poulton, 'Lecture, 1905', p. 44.
84 Pickering, 'Burchell's travels in Brazil', p.240.
85 Ibid., p. 241.
86 McKay, 'William John Burchell, Botanist: Part III', p. 124.
87 Letter to W.J. Hooker, cited in McKay, 'William John Burchell, Botanist: Part III', pp. 124–5.
88 Pickering, 'Burchell's travels in Brazil', pp. 243–4.
89 Poulton, 'Lecture, 1905', p. 43.
90 McKay, 'William John Burchell, Botanist: Part III' p.125.
91 Pickering, 'Burchell's travels in Brazil', p. 243.
92 McKay, 'William John Burchell, Botanist: Part III' p. 125.
93 Letter to W.J. Hooker, 1 November 1830, cited in McKay, 'William John Burchell, Botanist: Part III', p. 126.
94 Pickering, 'Burchell's travels in Brazil', p. 247.
95 Letter to Swainson, 3 October 1839, Swainson Correspondence, Linnean Society.

CHAPTER 11: ENGLAND AND THE CONTINENT

1 Letter to Swainson, 11 December 1824, Swainson Correspondence, Linnean Society.
2 Letter to Swainson, 15 September 1830, Swainson Correspondence, Linnean Society.
3 Letter to Swainson, 28 February 1831, Swainson Correspondence, Linnean Society.
4 Letter to Swainson, 24 January 1831, Swainson Correspondence, Linnean Society.
5 McKay, 'William John Burchell, Botanist: Part IV', p. 176.
6 Ibid., p. 177.
7 Ibid.
8 Poulton, 'Lecture, 1905', p. 45.
9 Ibid., pp. 45–6
10 William Swainson, *Zoological Illustrations*, vol. iii, second series, 1832–33.
11 Poulton, 'Lecture, 1905', p. 45.
12 Letter to Swainson, 28 February 1831, Swainson Correspondence, Linnean Society.

13 Burchell, *Travels*, Vol. I, Preface, p. viii.

14 Ibid., 17 June 1811, p. 165.

15 Ibid., Vol. II, 13 July 1812, p. 366.

16 McKay had a handwritten copy of Burchell's itinerary, now housed in the Historical Papers Archive at the University of the Witwatersrand.

17 McKay, 'William John Burchell, Botanist: Part IV', p. 178.

18 Ibid.

19 Ibid., p. 179.

20 Letter to Swainson, 29 January 1839, Swainson Correspondence, Linnean Society.

21 Letter to Swainson, 3 October 1839, Swainson Correspondence, Linnean Society.

22 Ibid.

23 McKay, 'William John Burchell, Botanist: Part IV', p. 180.

24 Browne, *Charles Darwin: The Power of Place*, p. 115.

25 Poulton, 'Lecture, 1905', p. 51.

26 McKay, 'William John Burchell, Botanist: Part IV', p. 183.

27 Poulton, 'Lecture, 1905', p. 51.

28 Burkhardt, *Charles Darwin: The 'Beagle' Letters*, p. 205.

29 Poulton, 'Lecture, 1905', p. 55.

30 McKay, 'William John Burchell, Botanist: Part IV', p. 175.

31 Poulton, 'Lecture, 1905', p. 55.

32 Ibid., pp. 55–6.

33 Ibid., p. 56.

34 Ibid.

35 Ibid.

36 Burchell, 'St. Helena Journal', in Castell, 16 October 1810, p. 184.

37 Castell, *William John Burchell*, p. 327.

38 Holmes, *Age of Wonder*, p. xx.

39 Coetzee and Attwell, *Doubling the Point*, p. 17.

40 Ibid., p. 391.

41 Burchell, *Travels*, Vol. II, 19 July 1812, pp. 425–6.

42 Ibid., Vol. I, 10 April 1811, p. 96.

43 Milan Kundera, *The Unbearable Lightness of Being*, translated from Czech by Michael Henry Helm, London: Faber and Faber, 1985.

44 William Wordsworth, quoted by Richard Holmes in *The Age of Wonder*, p. xvii: *The Prelude*, 1850, Book 3, ll. 58–64.

45 William Wordsworth, *The Prelude*, 1850, Twelfth Book, ll. 209–218, in Harold Bloom and Lionel Trilling (eds), *Romantic Poetry and Prose*, London and New York: Oxford University Press, 1973, p. 223.

Bibliography

Attridge, Derek. *The Singularity of Literature*. London: Routledge, 2004.

Attwell, David and Derek Attridge (eds). *The Cambridge History of South African Literature*. Cambridge: Cambridge University Press, 2012.

Arnold, Marion. *South African Botanical Art: Peeling Back the Petals*. Vlaeberg, South Africa: Fernwood Press in association with Art Link, 2001.

Barber, Mary Elizabeth. 'Wanderings in South Africa by Sea and Land, 1879', *Quarterly Bulletin of the South African Library* XVII, 1962–1963, pp. 40–53.

Barker, Nicolas. *Lady Anne Barnard's Watercolours and Sketches: Glimpses of the Cape of Good Hope*. Simon's Town, South Africa: Fernwood Press, 2009.

Bennett, Brett M. 'Reading the Land: Changing Landscapes and the Environmental History of South Africa' in Godby, *The Lie of the Land: Representations of the South African Landscape*, pp. 46–59.

Bloom, Harold and Lionel Trilling (eds). *Romantic Poetry and Prose*. London and New York: Oxford University Press, 1973.

Bregin, Elana. 'Representing the Bushmen: Through the Colonial Lens', *English in Africa* 27, no. 1, 2000, pp. 37–54.

Browne, Janet. *Charles Darwin: Voyaging*. Vol. I. London: Pimlico, 2003`.

———. *Charles Darwin: The Power of Place*. Vol. II. Princeton and Oxford: Princeton University Press, 2002.

Burchell, William John. 'Hints on Emigration to the Cape of Good Hope'. London: Hatchard, 1819. Reprinted in *Travels in the Interior of Southern Africa*, edited by A. Gordon-Brown. Cape Town: Struik, 1967.

———. 'St. Helena Journal', in Castell, *William John Burchell (1781–1863) St. Helena (1805–1810)*.

———. *Travels in the Interior of Southern Africa*, edited by Isaac Schapera. London: Batchworth Press, 1953.

———. *Travels in the Interior of Southern Africa*, edited by A. Gordon-Brown. Cape Town: Struik, 1967.

Carruthers, Jane and M. Arnold. *The Life and Work of Thomas Baines*. Vlaeberg: Fernwood Press, 1995.

Castell, Robin. *William John Burchell (1781–1863) St. Helena (1805–1810)*. St Helena: Castell Collection, 2011.

Coetzee, Carli. 'In the archive: records of the Dutch settlement and the contemporary novel' in Attwell and Attridge, *The Cambridge History of South African Literature*, pp. 138–157.

Coetzee, J. M. *White Writing: On the Culture of Letters in South Africa*. Braamfontein, South Africa: Pentz Publishers, 2007.

———. *Elizabeth Costello*. London: Vintage, 2004.

———. *Youth*. London: Secker & Warburg, 2002.

———. and David Attwell (ed). *Doubling the Point: Essays and Interviews*. Cambridge Mass.: Harvard University Press, 1992.

Coleridge, Samuel Taylor. 'The Delinquent Travellers' in Holmes, *Coleridge: Darker Reflections*.

Colvin, Ian D. and Frank Rosslyn Bradlow. *Introduction to Africana*. Cape Town: A. A. Balkema for the Friends of the South African Library, 1979.

Cullinan, Patrick. *Robert Jacob Gordon, 1743–1795: The Man and his Travels at the Cape*. Cape Town: Struik Winchester, 1992.

Darwin, Charles. *The Voyage of the Beagle*. Ware, Hertfordshire: Wordsworth Editions, 1997.

———. Frederick Burkhardt (ed). *Charles Darwin: The 'Beagle' Letters*. Cambridge: Cambridge University Press, 2008.

Dietrich, Keith Hamilton. 'Of salvation and civilization: The image of indigenous southern Africans in European travel illustration from the sixteenth to the nineteenth centuries', D. Litt. et Phil. thesis, University of South Africa, 1993, University of South Africa, 1993.

Easton, Kai. 'Coetzee, the Cape and the question of history', *Scrutiny2: Issues in English Studies in Southern Africa* 11, no. 1, 2006, pp. 5–21.

Eliot, T. S. *Collected Poems 1909–1962*. London: Faber, 1963.

Foucault, Michel. *The Order of Things: An Archaeology of the Human Sciences*. London and New York: Routledge Classics, 2009.

Fraser, Mike and Liz Fraser. *The Smallest Kingdom: Plants and Plant Collectors at the Cape of Good Hope*. Richmond, Surrey: Kew Publishing, Royal Botanic Gardens, Kew, 2011.

Glenn, Ian. 'Eighteenth-century natural history, travel writing and South African literary historiography' in *The Cambridge History of South African Literature*, pp. 158–179.

Godby, Michael (ed). *The Lie of the Land: Representations of the South African Land*. South Africa: Iziko, 2010.

Grove, Richard. *Green Imperialism: Colonial Expansion, Tropical Island Edens and the Origins of Environmentalism, 1600–1860*. Cambridge: Cambridge University Press, 1995.

Gunn, Mary and L. E. Codd. *Botanical Exploration of Southern Africa*. Cape Town: Published for the Botanical Research Institute by A.A. Balkema, 1981.

Holmes, Richard. *Coleridge: Darker Reflections*. London: Flamingo, 1999.

———. *The Age of Wonder: How the Romantic Generation Discovered the Beauty and Terror of Science*. London: Harper Press, 2009.

Hooker, W. J. 'Mr. Burchell's Brazilian Journey', *Botanical Miscellany* 2, 1831, pp. 128–133.

Humphreys, A. J. B. 'Burchell's Shelter: The History and Archaeology of a Northern Cape Rock Shelter', *South African Archaeological Bulletin* 30, no. 117/118, 1975, pp. 3–18.

Ingold, Tim. *Lines: a brief history*. London: Routledge, 2007.

John Keats. 'Lamia' in John Barnard (ed), *John Keats: The Complete Poems*, Harmondsworth, England: Penguin Books, 1976.

Kennedy, R. F. *Catalogue of Pictures in the Africana Museum*. Vol. Six. Johannesburg: Africana Museum, 1966–.

Kundera, Milan. *The Unbearable Lightness of Being*, translated from Czech by Michael Henry Helm. London: Faber and Faber, 1985.

Leech, Geoffrey N. *A Linguistic Guide to English Poetry*. London: Longmans, 1969.

Lightman, Bernard V. *Victorian Science in Context*. Chicago, Ill.: University of Chicago Press, 1997.

Marvell, Andrew. 'The Garden' in *The Norton Anthology of Poetry*. New York: W.W. Norton, 1983.

McKay, Helen Millar. 'A Scientist's Wagon', *South African Journal of Science* XXXII, 1935, 680–683.

———. 'William John Burchell, Scientist', *South African Journal of Science* XXXII, 1935, 689–695.

———. 'William John Burchell, Botanist: Part I: Introduction and Burchell in St. Helena', *The Journal of South African Botany* 7, 1941, 1–18.

———. William John Burchell, Botanist: Part II: Burchell in South Africa', *The Journal of South African Botany* 7, 1941, 61–76.

———. 'William John Burchell, Botanist: Part III: Burchell in England and Brazil', *The Journal of South African Botany* 7, 1941, 115–130.

———. 'William John Burchell, Botanist: Part IV: Botanical interests from 1830-1863', *The Journal of South African Botany* 7, 1941, 173–186.

———. *The South African Drawings of William J. Burchell: The Bachapins of Litakun*. Vol. 1. Johannesburg: Witwatersrand University Press, 1938.

———. *The South African Drawings of William J. Burchell: Landscape Sketches*. Vol. 2. Johannesburg: Witwatersrand University Press, 1952.

Musselman, Elizabeth Green. 'Plant Knowledge at the Cape: A Study in African and European Collaboration', *The International Journal of African Historical Studies*, Vol. 36, no. 2, 2003, pp. 367-392.

Penn, Nigel. '"Civilizing" the San: The First Mission to the Cape San, 1791–1806'. In Pippa Skotnes, *Claim to the Country: The Archive of Wilhelm Bleek and Lucy Lloyd*. Johannesburg: Jacana; Athens: Ohio University Press, 2007, pp. 90–115.

Pickering, Jane. 'William J. Burchell's South African mammal collection, 1810–1815', *Archives of Natural History* 24, (3), 1997, 311–326.

———. 'William John Burchell's travels in Brazil, 1825–1830, with details of surviving mammal and bird collections', *Archives of Natural History* 25, (2),1998, 237–266.

Poulton, E. B. 'William John Burchell: The materials of a lecture delivered before the British Association on August 17, 1905', *Report of the British and South African Associations 1905* III, 1905, pp. 1–56.

Pratt, Mary Louise. *Imperial Eyes: Travel Writing and Transculturation*. London; New York: Routledge, 2008.

Rourke, John. 'Beauty in Truth: Botanical Art in Southern Africa – A Brief Historical Perspective' in Marion Arnold, *South African Botanical Art: Peeling Back the Petals*, pp. 27–65.

Stengers, Isabelle. 'The Challenge of Complexity: Unfolding the Ethics of Science. In Memoriam Ilya Prigogine', *E: Co* 6, no. 1–2, 2004, 92–99.

Stewart, Roger. 'Burchell's Garden Route' presented at the William John Burchell Bicentenary Commemoration, George, 19 September 2014.

———. 'A meticulous cartographer: William Burchell's map of South Africa', *IMCoS Journal* 125, 2011, pp. 12–15.

———. 'William Burchell's medical challenges: A 19th-century natural philosopher in the field', *South African Medical Journal* 102, no. 4, 2012, pp. 252–255.

Stewart, Roger and Brian Warner. 'William John Burchell: The multi-skilled polymath', *South African Journal of Science* 108, no. 11/12, 2012, pp. 1–9.

Twidle, Hedley. '"The Bushmen's Letters": |Xam narratives of the Bleek and Lloyd Collection and their afterlives' in Attwell and Attridge, *The Cambridge History of South African Literature*, pp. 19–41.

Tudge, Colin. *The Secret Life of Trees: How They Live and Why They Matter.* London: Penguin Books, 2006.

Vigne, Randolph. 'Mapping and promoting South Africa: Barrow and Burchell's rivalry', *Historia* 58, 1, May/Mei 2013, pp. 18-32.

Watson, Stephen (ed). *A City Imagined.* Johannesburg: Penguin Books, 2006.

Wolff de Carvalho, Maria Cristina. 'The Landscape Art of William John Burchell (1781–1863)', *Arquitetourismo*, 2013. Accessed May 2015 at http://www.vitruvius.com.br/revistas/read/arquiteturismo/07.073/4700/en_US.

Worden, Nigel, Elizabeth van Heyningen and Vivian Bickford-Smith. *Cape Town: The Making of a City: An Illustrated Social History.* Cape Town: David Philip, 2004.

Wordsworth, William. The Prelude, 1850, Twelfth Book, ll. 209–218, in Harold Bloom and Lionel Trilling (eds), *Romantic Poetry and Prose.*

Index

Numbers in **bold** type refer to illustrations